JN055471

石川県の教員採用試験過去問シリーズ❺

2025年度版

石川県の英語科

過去問

協同教育研究会 編

協同出版

本書には，石川県の教員採用試験の過去問題を収録しています。各問題ごとに，以下のように5段階表記で，難易度，頻出度を示しています。

難 易 度

非常に難しい	☆☆☆☆☆
やや難しい	☆☆☆☆
普通の難易度	☆☆☆
やや易しい	☆☆
非常に易しい	☆

頻 出 度

◎	ほとんど出題されない
◎◎	あまり出題されない
◎◎◎	普通の頻出度
◎◎◎◎	よく出題される
◎◎◎◎◎	非常によく出題される

※本書の過去問題における資料，法令文等の取り扱いについて

本書の過去問題で使用されている資料や法令文の表記や基準は，出題された当時の内容に準拠しているため，解答・解説も当時のものを使用しています。ご了承ください。

はじめに～「過去問」シリーズ利用に際して～

教育を取り巻く環境は変化しつつあり，日本の公教育そのものも，教員免許更新制の廃止やGIGAスクール構想の実現などの改革が進められています。また，現行の学習指導要領では「主体的・対話的で深い学び」を実現するため，指導方法や指導体制の工夫改善により，「個に応じた指導」の充実を図るとともに，コンピュータや情報通信ネットワーク等の情報手段を活用するために必要な環境を整えることが示されています。

一方で，いじめや体罰，不登校，暴力行為など，教育現場の問題もあいかわらず取り沙汰されており，教員に求められるスキルは，今後さらに高いものになっていくことが予想されます。

本書の基本構成としては，出題傾向と対策，過去5年間の出題傾向分析表，過去問題，解答および解説を掲載しています。各自治体や教科によって掲載年数をはじめ，「チェックテスト」や「問題演習」を掲載するなど，内容が異なります。

また原則的には一般受験を対象としております。特別選考等については対応していない場合があります。なお，実際に配布された問題の順番や構成を，編集の都合上，変更している場合があります。あらかじめご了承ください。

最後に，この「過去問」シリーズは，「参考書」シリーズとの併用を前提に編集されております。参考書で要点整理を行い，過去問で実力試しを行う，セットでの活用をおすすめいたします。

みなさまが，この書籍を徹底的に活用し，教員採用試験の合格を勝ち取って，教壇に立っていただければ，それはわたくしたちにとって最上の喜びです。

協同教育研究会

CONTENTS

第1部 石川県の英語科
出題傾向分析 ……………3

第2部 石川県の
教員採用試験実施問題 ……………9

▼2024年度教員採用試験実施問題 ……………10
▼2023年度教員採用試験実施問題 ……………29
▼2022年度教員採用試験実施問題 ……………46
▼2021年度教員採用試験実施問題 ……………64
▼2020年度教員採用試験実施問題 ……………82
▼2019年度教員採用試験実施問題 ……………100
▼2018年度教員採用試験実施問題 ……………116
▼2017年度教員採用試験実施問題 ……………132
▼2016年度教員採用試験実施問題 ……………149
▼2015年度教員採用試験実施問題 ……………162
▼2014年度教員採用試験実施問題 ……………179
▼2013年度教員採用試験実施問題 ……………193
▼2012年度教員採用試験実施問題 ……………206
▼2011年度教員採用試験実施問題 ……………219
▼2010年度教員採用試験実施問題 ……………230
▼2009年度教員採用試験実施問題 ……………242
▼2008年度教員採用試験実施問題 ……………256
▼2007年度教員採用試験実施問題 ……………271
▼2006年度教員採用試験実施問題 ……………284
▼2005年度教員採用試験実施問題 ……………297
▼2004年度教員採用試験実施問題 ……………310
▼2003年度教員採用試験実施問題 ……………323

第１部

石川県の
英語科
出題傾向分析

石川県の英語科　傾向と対策

近年出題されているのは，リスニング問題，文法・語法問題，読解問題，英作文問題などである。問題形式は，ほとんどが記号選択式であるが，記述式の英作文問題もある。問題の指示文がすべて英語なので，過去問題を解くなど，形式に慣れておくことが望ましい。なお，解答時間は90分である。

リスニング問題は，ここ数年，放送された内容に関して選択肢から解答を選ぶ問題と，主に教室で使われる表現を書き取る問題が出題されている。2024年度も両者が出題され，前者は1回，後者は2回の放送であった。問題形式は今後も年度によって多少変更される可能性はあるが，内容としては特に難しくない。聞き取りが苦手な人は，テキストも参照できる教材を繰り返し聞き，音と同時に意味が頭に浮かぶよう学習をして，知っている単語は必ず聞き取れるようにしておく必要がある。現行の学習指導要領において，中学校および高校の英語の授業は英語で行うことが原則になっているため，教室英語の表現は一通り頭に入れておくべきである。また過去には，石川県にゆかりのある人物について出題されたこともあり，県についての知識も知っておくとよいだろう。

文法・語法問題は空所補充形式で，ここ数年は6題が出題されている。出題内容は，品詞の理解を中心とした文法，語彙，語の言い換えなどであった。全体的な難易度はあまり高くはないが，語彙問題についてはやや難解な問題も含まれているため，過去問題を解いてみて正解できない問題があるようなら，標準レベルの文法問題集を1冊仕上げておく必要がある。

読解問題は，長文総合読解問題の形式で3題出題されている。2024年度も2023年度と同じ形式で3題出題され，長文が2題のほか中文の空所補充問題が1題出題された。長文は，英字新聞や書籍などの一部から出されることが多い。2024年度は2021年度と同じように学習指導要領(平成29年告示)の英訳が出題されたが，教育に関する文章が出題される傾向がある。2022年度にはOECDの学習到達度調査の報告，そして2023年度は子供への教育方法が出題されており，今後も同じような傾向が続く可能性もあるため，教育関連の文章を英語で読んでおくとよいだろう。設問はすべて選択式で，2024年度も空所補充，段落整序が中心であり，前後の文のつながりや指示語を常に意識して英文を読み進める力が問われている。難易度は大学入試レベルだが，段落整序や語・文の空所補充問題が多いので，英文の概要をつかむのが難しいかもしれない。また，解答には一定量の英文を読まなければならないので，まずは過去問題を解いて分量に慣れることが必要である。大学入試レベルの長文読解問題集を利用すると同時に，軽い英語の読み物を多読して，英文を読むスピードをつけることが重要である。

英作文問題は，英文の一部に空欄を設けた形式の整序英作文問題と，やや短めの自由英作文問題が出題されている。整除英作文問題については，読解力，文法および語法の知識を総動員した総合的な英語力が求められるため，やや難度が高い問題が出題されている。ただし，難問・奇問というような問題ではないため，標準レベルの問題集で学習すれば十分であろう。

自由英作文は，教師とALTの会話における教師の返答を書く問題と，与えられた英文に続く内容を英語で書く問題が出題されている。基本的な問題形式は，2題とも2021年度から同様の傾向であるが，年度によって解答する分量には違いが見られる。2023年度はALTの質問に対する解答が1文であったのに対して，2024年度は30語以上であった。一方で，2024年度は英文の空所に書く問題が5 ～ 10語と非常に短くなった。どちらの問題形式に対しても，一定の分量で答えられるように準備しておくとよいだろう。ALTの質問に対する解答が求められている問題では，英語の授業に関する知識がやや求められるが，前後の会話を踏まえて書けばよいので，あまり細かい内容まで考える必要はないだろう。さほど心配する必要はないと思われるが，苦手な人は英会話表現集などを参考に，場面表現をチェックしておくとよい。英文の空所に書く問題は，外国語における読解スキルに関する英文から出題された。こちらも英語教育に関する知識があった方が有利ではあるが，英文の内容を踏まえて書けばよいので，専門的な知識がなくても本文を理解できれば十分である。不安があれば，読解問題と同じように様々なトピックの英文に目を通しておき，短めの自由英作文の問題集を1冊仕上げておけば安心である。

過去5年間の出題傾向分析

分類	設問形式	2020年度	2021年度	2022年度	2023年度	2024年度
リスニング	内容把握	●	●	●	●	●
発音・アクセント	発音					
	アクセント					
	文強勢					
文法・語法	空所補充	●	●	●	●	●
	正誤判断					
	一致語句					
	連立完成					
	その他					
会話文	短文会話	●				
	長文会話					
文章読解	空所補充	●	●	●	●	●
	内容一致文					
	内容一致語句	●		●		
	内容記述					
	英文和訳					
	英問英答					
	その他	●	●	●	●	●
英作文	整序	●	●	●	●	●
	和文英訳					
	自由英作	●	●	●	●	●
	その他					
学習指導要領			●			●

第2部

石川県の
教員採用試験
実施問題

2024年度　実施問題

【中高共通】

【１】(Listening Test)

Part A　Listen to the passage. Answer the two questions below by choosing the correct answer from options ① through ④ which will be read later. The passage and the options will be read once.

(1)　According to the passage, what did the number of names of Ancient Romans indicate?

(2)　According to the passage, what is the origin of the way we use middle names today?

Part B　Listen to the passages and the questions. Choose the correct answer from options ① through ④ below. The passages and the questions will be read once.

(1)　Answer：

①　Confidence.　②　Leadership.　③　Prestige.

④　Training and education.

(2)　Answer：

①　The speaker rehearsed the scenario of the school play again and again to act well.

②　The speaker wanted to play the lead role in the fifth-grade school play.

③　When she was in elementary school, the speaker was shy and happy not to get the lead role.

④　When the teacher chose a different girl for the lead role, the speaker cheered her on.

Part C　You will hear expressions teachers often use in English class. Write down the whole expression. Each will be read twice.

(☆☆☆◎◎◎◎)

【2】Choose the best item from ① to ④ below each question to fill in the blank.

(1) The placebo effect is the beneficial influence of a treatment that has no medical value. A sick person [　　] with salt water or given a sugar pill often feels better nonetheless.

① infected　② injected　③ insulted　④ interrupted

(2) It wasn't until forty years after he died that the status of Gustav Mahler as a major composer was reestablished. Only after the destructiveness of World War Ⅱ [　　] to matter to the general and critical public.

① did his work seem　② does his work seem

③ his work seemed　④ his work seems

(3) [　　] is the force that opposes a moving object when the surface of the object rubs against another.

① Flame　② Flaw　③ Fragment　④ Friction

(4) We know that learning any complex skill — be it a foreign language, a musical instrument, riding a bicycle, learning how to swim — [　　] an initial period of conscious, deliberate training.

① requires　② requiring　③ required　④ to require

(5) On a walk to the gym a few blocks away, we might be [　　] by what we want to accomplish during our hour there and not even notice the delicious scents wafting from a restaurant nearby.

① preceded　② preoccupied　③ prescribed　④ proposed

(6) White blood cells are a part of the [　　] system that fights infections, killing bacteria, viruses, and parasites. There are many types of white blood cells, but the most common types are neutrophils and lymphocytes.

① fake　② immune　③ metabolic　④ subjective

(☆☆☆◎◎◎◎◎)

【３】Read the following story and answer the questions below.

If you see a Ferrari driving around, you might intuitively assume the owner of the car is rich — even if you're not paying much attention to them. But as I got to know some of these people I realized that wasn't always the case. Many were mediocre successes who spent a huge percentage of their paycheck on a car.

I remember a fellow we'll call Roger. He was about my age. I had no idea what Roger did. But he drove a Porsche, which was enough for people to draw assumptions.

Then one day Roger arrived in an old Honda. Same the next week, and the next.

"What happened to your Porsche?" I asked. It was repossessed after defaulting on his car loan, he said. There was not a morsel of shame. He responded like he was telling the next play in the game. Every assumption you might have had about him was wrong. Los Angeles is full of Rogers.

Someone driving a $100,000 car might be wealthy. But the only data point you have about their wealth is that they have $100,000 [ア] than they did before they bought the car (or $100,000 [イ] in debt). That's *all* you know about them.

We tend to judge wealth by [ウ], because that's the information we have in front of us. We can't see people's bank accounts or brokerage statements. So we rely on outward appearances to gauge financial success, Cars. Homes, Instagram photos.

Modern capitalism makes helping people fake it until they make it a cherished industry.

But the truth is that wealth is [エ].

Wealth is the nice cars not purchased. The diamonds not bought. The watches not worn, the clothes forgone and the first-class upgrade declined. Wealth is financial assets that haven't yet been converted into the stuff you see.

That's not how we think about wealth, because you can't contextualize what you can't see.

Singer Rihanna nearly went bankrupt after overspending and sued her financial advisor. The advisor responded: "Was it really necessary to tell her that if you spend money on things, you will end up with the things and not the money?"

You can laugh, and please do. But the answer is, yes, people do need to be told that. When most people say they want to be a millionaire, what they might actually mean is "[オ]." And that is literally the opposite of being a millionaire.

Investor Bill Mann once wrote: "There is no faster way to feel rich than to spend lots of money on really nice things. But the way to be rich is to spend money you have, and to not spend money you don't have. It's really that simple."

It is excellent advice, but it may not go far enough. The only way to be wealthy is to not spend the money that you do have. It's not just the only way to accumulate wealth; it's the very definition of wealth.

We should be careful to define the difference between *wealthy* and *rich*. It is more than semantics. Not knowing the difference is a source of countless poor money decisions.

Rich is a current income. Someone driving a $100,000 car is almost certainly rich, because even if they purchased the car with debt you need a certain level of income to afford the monthly payment. Same with those who live in big homes. It's not hard to spot rich people. They often go out of their way to make themselves known.

But *wealth* is hidden. It's income not spent. [カ]. Its value lies in offering you options, flexibility, and growth to one day purchase more stuff than you could right now.

Diet and exercise offer a useful analogy. Losing weight is notoriously hard, even among those putting in the work of vigorous exercise. In his book *The Body*, Bill Bryson explains why:

One study in America found that people [キ] the number of calories they burned in a workout by a factor of four.

They also then consumed, on average, about twice as many calories as they had just burned off... the fact is, you can quickly [ク] a lot of exercise by eating a lot of food, and most of us do.

Exercise is like being rich. You think, "I did the work and I now [ケ] to treat myself to a big meal." Wealth is turning down that treat meal and actually burning net calories. It's hard, and requires self-control. But it creates a gap between what you could do and what you choose to do that accrues to you over time.

The problem for many of us is that it is easy to find rich role models. It's harder to find wealthy ones because by definition their success is more hidden.

There are, of course, wealthy people who also spend a lot of money on stuff. But even in those cases what we see is their [A], not their [B]. We see the cars they chose to buy and perhaps the school they choose to send their kids to. We don't see the savings, retirement accounts, or investment portfolios. We see the homes they bought, not the homes they could have bought had they stretched themselves thin.

(SOURCE: "*The Psychology of Money*" by Morgan Housel)

(No.1) Choose the most suitable word for each blank [ア] and [イ] from ① to ③.

① less　② more　③ other

(No.2) Choose the most suitable option for each blank [ウ] and [エ] from ① to ④.

① what you don't see　② what we are　③ what we see

④ what we used to be

(No.3) Choose the most suitable option for the blank [オ] from ① to ④.

① I'd like to build up a million dollars.

② I'd like to put a million dollars aside.

③ I'd like to save a million dollars.

④ I'd like to spend a million dollars.

(No.4) Choose the most suitable option for the blank [カ] from ① to ④.

① Wealth is a debt due to countless poor money decisions.

② Wealth is a financial asset that was converted into the thing you see.

③ Wealth is an option not yet taken to buy something later.

④ Wealth is an option to show off his or her authority.

(No.5) Choose the most suitable word from ① to ④ for each blank [キ], [ク] and [ケ].

キ ① lessen ② overestimate ③ reproduce ④ undergo

ク ① avoid ② continue ③ ratify ④ undo

ケ ① cease ② deserve ③ hesitate ④ reject

(No.6) Choose the best combination from ① to ④ in order to fill in the blanks [A] and [B].

① A：abundance B：lack

② A：lack B：abundance

③ A：richness B：wealth

④ A：wealth B：richness

(☆☆☆◎◎◎◎◎)

【４】The following is a part of MEXT's Course of Study released in 2017 and 2018. Choose the most suitable word from ① to ④ for each blank [ア], [イ], [ウ] and [エ].

Junior High School　Section 9 Foreign Languages

Ⅰ. OVERALL OBJECTIVE

To develop students' competencies that [ア] the communication such as understanding, expressing and communicating simple information and thoughts etc. as outlined below through language activities of listening, reading, speaking and writing in a foreign language while activating the approaches in communication in foreign languages.

(1) To understand knowledge of the sounds, vocabulary, expressions, grammar and functions of foreign language, acquire these skills which can be utilized in communication when listening, reading, speaking and writing.

(2) To cultivate the ability to understand simple information and thoughts etc. about everyday and social topics in foreign languages, utilize these to express themselves, and communicate in accordance with the purposes, scenes and [イ] in which the communication is taking place.

(3) To deepen the students' understanding of the underlying cultures of foreign languages and fostering an attitude of attempting to [ウ] communicate in foreign languages while giving consideration to the listeners, readers, speakers and writers.

Senior High School　Section 8 Foreign Language

Article 1. OVERALL OBJECTIVE

To develop students' communicative competencies, such as accurately understanding and appropriately expressing and exchanging information, thoughts, etc., as outlined below through the language activities of listening, reading, speaking and writing in a foreign language and integrated language activities which combine these skills.

(1) To deepen students' understanding of foreign language sounds,

vocabulary, expressions, grammar and functions, and acquire the skill of using this knowledge in actual communication through listening, reading, speaking and writing appropriately in accordance with the purposes, scenes and [イ].

(2) To foster the ability to accurately understand the overview, main points, details of information and ideas, and a speaker's or writer's [エ], etc., about everyday and social topics in the foreign language, and appropriately express and exchange information and ideas about these topics in accordance with the purposes, scenes and [イ] in which communication takes place.

(3) To cultivate a willingness to communicate [ウ] and autonomously, deepening understanding of the culture behind the foreign language and considering the listener, reader, speaker or writer.

ア ① disguise ② divert ③ form
④ skip

イ ① obstacles ② situations ③ suburbs
④ tensions

ウ ① annually ② extremely ③ primarily
④ proactively

エ ① generation ② grade ③ intention
④ reward

(☆☆☆◎◎◎◎)

【5】Read the following passage and answer the questions below.

Children develop at [ア] speeds in their bilingual language development. Just as some children learn to crawl, walk or say their first words earlier than others, so the speed of language development varies between children. This is even more so in the development of two languages.

The speed of language acquisition is only partly due to the child's ability. Indeed, some children who turn out to be very able in academic terms are slow in their language development. There is generally [イ] relationship between how quickly someone learns to speak one or two languages and eventual school success. Early language developers are not necessarily likely to be more successful in adult life - however success is defined.

A child's interest in language is also important and is partly separate from ability and language aptitude for language learning. When a child is encouraged and stimulated in language development, an interest in reading, for example, will be [ウ]. Parents who listen with attention to what the child is saying, answer the child in a child-centred way, and make language fun by rhymes and songs will aid language development. A child's motivation to engage in conversation will affect their speed of development.

[カ]

[キ] For other parents, the journey in later childhood and the teenage years seems troublesome, even like backpedalling.

[ク]

[ケ]

If the analogy will stand, language development is like distance running. Some people complete the course with speed, others go at a [エ] pace but still successfully manage to complete the language distance. Parents as spectators sometimes become [オ] by the slow speed of the bilingual course. Parents want adult-like language performance while the child is in the early and middle stages of development.

(SOURCE: "*A Parents' and Teachers' Guide to Bilingualism*" by Colin Baker)

(No.1) Choose the most suitable word from ① to ⑥ for each blank [ア] through [オ]. Each word can be used once.

① agitated ② different ③ increased ④ little
⑤ same ⑥ slower

(No.2) Place these paragraphs from ① to ④ in their appropriate locations [カ] through [ケ].

① Given adequate encouragement, practice and a stimulating environment for language growth, young children find the acquisition of two languages relatively straightforward, painless and effortless. Many children tend to reflect parents' attitudes, behaviour, expectations and beliefs. A positive parent tends to breed a successful child. Parents who expect failure tend to breed less success. This is particularly true of a child's bilingual development.

② Not all bilingual children will reach the same language destination. Family, community and educational circumstances sometimes mean the journey halts at passive bilingualism (that is, understanding but not speaking a second language). Partial or passive bilingualism is not a finishing line. Given a need to become an active bilingual (e.g. by visiting the country where the hitherto 'passive' language is dominant), the journey can be continued to more complete bilingualism.

③ Such concerns seem usual and prevalent among parents of bilingual children. However, if safety in numbers doesn't satisfy, consider comparing your bilingual child against other bilinguals and not against the fastest moving monolingual who sets the pace. Some bilinguals show similar language performance to monolinguals in one of their languages. Some, but not all, develop considerable competence in a second language. Rarely are bilinguals equally fluent in all situations in both their languages.

④ There are hurdles, but few insurmountable barriers, to children reaching whatever bilingual language destination is possible. However, routes to dual language proficiency are sometimes long. This is one reason for undue concern by destination-seeking parents. Early acquisition of two languages for some parents seems like slow motoring

(☆☆☆☆◎◎◎)

【6】Complete the passage by filling in the blanks with all the items written below. Choose the most suitable item from ① to ⑦ for each blank [ア] through [カ].

Whatever the sacrifice of pleasure, it would be made up for by better health — that, at least, has always been nutritionism's promise. But it's difficult to (1) [ ] [ア] [ ] [ ] [ ] [イ] [ ] our health. As mentioned, the low-fat campaign coincided with a dramatic increase in the incidence of obesity and diabetes in America. You could blame this unfortunate fallout on us eaters (2) [ ] [ウ] [ ] [ ] [ ] [エ] [ ] more low-fat food a little too avidly. This explanation suggests that the problem with the low-fat campaign has been in its execution rather than in the theory behind it, and that a better, clearer public health message might have saved us from ourselves. But it is also possible that the advice itself, to replace fats in the diet with carbohydrates, was misguided. As the Hu paper suggests, there is a growing body of evidence that shifting from fats to carbohydrates may lead to weight gain (as well as a host of other problems). This is counterintuitive, because fats contain more than twice as many calories as carbs (9 per gram for fats as compared to 4 for either carbohydrates or protein). The theory is that refined carbohydrates interfere with insulin metabolism in ways that increase hunger and promote overeating and fat storage in the body. (Call it the carbohydrate hypothesis; it's coming.) If this is true, then (3) [ ] [オ] [ ] [ ] [ ] [カ] [ ] the dietary advice enshrined not only in the McGovern "Goals" but also in the National Academy of Sciences report, the dietary guidelines of the American Heart Association and the

American Cancer Society and the U.S. food pyramid bears direct responsibility for creating the public health crisis that now confronts us.

(SOURCE: "*In Defence of Food*" by Michael Pollan)

(1)	① conclude	② contributed	③ eating	④ has
	⑤ scientific	⑥ that	⑦ to	
(2)	① advice	② eat	③ following	④ for
	⑤ official	⑥ the	⑦ to	
(3)	① conclusion	② escaping	③ is	④ no
	⑤ that	⑥ the	⑦ there	

(☆☆☆☆◎◎◎◎)

【7】Complete the passage by filling the blank with 5 to 10 words.

Reading is a complex skill. In our first languages, we employ a variety of micro-skills to help us read. For example, we might skim a particular passage in order to understand the general idea, or gist. Or we might scan through multiple pages of a train timetable looking for a particular time or place. While these micro-skills are second nature when reading in our first languages, when it comes to reading in a foreign language, research suggests that we often abandon most of these reading skills. In a foreign language, we usually start at the beginning of a text and try to understand every single word. Inevitably, we come across unknown or difficult words and quickly get frustrated with our lack of understanding.

One of the main benefits of reading in a foreign language is that you gain exposure to large amounts of words and expressions used naturally. This kind of reading for pleasure in order to learn a language is generally known as 'extensive reading'. It is very different from reading a textbook in which dialogues or texts are meant to be read in detail with the aim of understanding every word. That kind of reading to reach specific learning aims or do tasks is referred to as 'intensive reading'. To put it another way, the intensive reading in textbooks usually helps [　　　　　　], whereas reading stories extensively helps show you natural language in use.

(SOURCE: "*Short Stories in English for Beginners*" by Olly Richards)

(☆☆☆◎◎◎)

【8】The following is a conversation between an ALT (assistant language teacher) and a JTE (Japanese teacher of English). Fill in the gap to make it flow with 30 or more words in English.

ALT : You often say to our students, "Enjoy making mistakes." But they won't try to use English.

JTE : You're right. Maybe they are not confident.

ALT : Why aren't they confident?

JTB : ____

ALT : Sounds nice! Let's try it from next class.

(☆☆☆☆◎◎◎)

解答・解説

【中高共通】

【1】Part A (1) ① (2) ② Part B (1) ② (2) ②

Part C No.1 Talk in your group. No.2 You did a good job. No.3 When you're finished, raise your hand. No.4 Choose the topic you want to write about. No.5 I'd like you to sit in a circle.

〈解説〉スクリプトは公開されていない。Part Aはパッセージを聞き，問題用紙に印刷された質問文を読んで，音声で流れる選択肢から解答を選ぶ4択問題，Part Bはパッセージと質問文を聞き，問題用紙に印刷された選択肢から解答を選ぶ4択問題。ともに放送は1度のみである。Part Cはクラスルームイングリッシュのディクテーションであり，2回放送される。 Part A 設問(1)にあるAncient Romans，そして設問(2)

にあるmiddle namesから，ミドルネームの歴史や起源に関する話題であることが推測できる。 Part B (1) Leadership，Prestige，そしてTraining and educationといった選択肢から，組織に関する話題であることが推測できる。(2) the school play，lead role，elementary schoolといった語句から，ある人物の小学生時代の演劇に関する話題であることが推測できる。Part C ディクテーションではあるが，使用頻度の高いクラスルームイングリッシュであり，語数も多くはない。2回放送されるので，あまり焦らずに丁寧に取り組めばよい。難しい語彙などもないが，スペルミスには注意したい。

【2】(1) ② (2) ① (3) ④ (4) ① (5) ② (6) ②

〈解説〉(1) 空欄を含む英文は「塩水を注射されたり，砂糖の錠剤を与えられたりしたとしても，病人は気分がよくなることが多い」の意である。injectedは「注射された」の意味である。 (2) 空欄を含む英文は「第2次世界大戦の破壊の後になってようやく，彼の作品は一般大衆や批評家にとって重要になったと思われる」の意である。Only afterのようにOnlyで始まる文では倒置が生じることがあることに留意する。 (3) 空欄を含む英文は「動いている物体の表面が他の物体とこすり合った時に対抗する力が摩擦である」の意である。frictionは「摩擦」の意味である。 (4) 空欄を含む英文のダッシュ内を除いた箇所は「いかなる複雑なスキルでも，習得するためには意識的で意図的なトレーニングの期間が必要である」の意である。ダッシュ部を除いて考えると，ダッシュ直前はthat節の主語があることを踏まえると，ダッシュ直後は動詞が必要となることに留意する。 (5) 英文は「数ブロック先のジムに歩いていく途中では，ジムで1時間に達成したいことで頭がいっぱいになり，私たちは近くのレストランから漂うおいしそうなにおいにさえ気づかないかもしれない」の意である。通常be preoccupied withで「～に気をとられて」となる。preoccupiedは「頭がいっぱい，気をとられている」の意味。 (6) 空欄を含む英文は「白血球は，バクテリア，ウイルスそして寄生虫を殺して感染症と戦う免疫システムの一部である」の意である。immuneは「免疫」の意味である。

【3】(No.1)　ア　①　　イ　②　　(No.2)　ウ　③　　エ　①
(No.3)　オ　④　　(No.4)　カ　③　　(No.5)　キ　②　　ク　④
ケ　②　　(No.6)　③

〈解説〉(No.1)　ア　空欄を含む文とその直前の文に着目すると，10万ドルの車を運転している人は裕福かもしれないが，そのことからわかるのは，その人が車を買う前よりも10万ドル持っているお金が少ないということに過ぎない，ということであり①が正解。　イ　空欄アを含んだ箇所の言い換えになっていることを踏まえると，10万ドル借金が多くなった，の意味になる②が正解。　(No.2)　ウ　空欄直後に着目すると，「その情報が私たちの前にあるから」と述べられており，空欄部はその言いかえとなる「目に見えるもの」を意味する③が正解。
エ　空欄の後にある第9パラグラフの4文目に着目すると，富とはまだ目に見えるものには変換されていない金融資産のことであると述べられており，「目に見えないもの」を意味する①が正解。または，空欄エの直前まで，目に見える情報だけで富を判断していることが述べられており，その後Butで逆接になっていることに着目してもよい。
(No.3)　空欄の直後の文に着目すると，そのことは文字通り億万長者とは反対のことであると述べられている。従って，「100万ドルを使いたい」を意味する④が正解。　(No.4)　空欄の直前の2文に着目すると，富は隠されていて，使われていない収入であると述べられている。従って，「富とは，後で何かを買うためにまだ選ばれていない選択肢である」を意味する③が正解。　(No.5)　3つの空欄がある箇所は，裕福さがダイエットにたとえられている箇所であることを踏まえる。
キ　空欄の次の文に着目すると，アメリカ人は平均して運動で消費したカロリーの2倍のカロリーを摂取していると述べられており，運動で消費するカロリーを過剰に見積もっていることがわかる。従って，「過大評価する」を意味する②が正解。　ク　空欄キと同じ箇所に着目する。運動で消費したカロリーよりも多くカロリーを摂取してしまうことから，食べることによって運動した分を取り戻してしまうことがわかる。従って，「取り消す，元に戻す，取り戻す」を意味する④が正解。　ケ　空欄の次の文に着目すると，富とはごちそうを断わって実際にカロリーを消費することであると述べられており，「仕事をしたのだからご馳走を食べるのに値するのだ」の意味になる，②が正解。　(No.6)　空欄を含む文の直前の文に着目すると，モノにたくさんのお金を使う裕福な人もいると述べられており，空欄を含む文はそれと逆接のButでつながっている。この点を踏まえると，私たちが見えることというのは裕福さであって富ではないという意味になる③が正解。なお，Bに入るのがwealthであることがわかれば正解を選ぶことができるため，富が目に見えないものであることを踏まえて解答することもできる。

【4】ア　③　　イ　②　　ウ　④　　エ　③

〈解説〉現行の中学校および高等学校の学習指導要領の英訳版の空欄を補充する問題である。外国語の目標に関する箇所から出題されている。ア　空欄を含む英文の前半は「簡単な情報や考えなどを理解したり表現したり伝え合ったりするコミュニケーションを図る資質・能力を育成することを目指す」の意である。日本語の学習指導要領の内容が浮かばなくても，コミュニケーション能力を高める必要があることを踏まえれば，それ以外の選択肢は不適切であることがわかる。　イ　2つ目の目標であることから，「思考力，判断力，表現力等」に関する目標であることを踏まえる。空欄の直前にあるthe purposes, scenesに着目すると，「目的や場面，状況」の意味になる②が正解。　ウ　3つ目の目標であることから，「学びに向かう力，人間性等」に関する目標であることを踏まえると，「主体的に外国語を用いてコミュニケーションを図ろうとする」の意味になる④が正解。　エ　「思考力，判断力，表現力等」に関する目標であるが，中学校にはなく高等学校の学習指導要領のみに見られる記述であることに留意する。空欄直前にあるspeaker's or writer'sに着目すると，「話し手や書き手の意図」の意味になる③が正解。

【5】(No.1)　ア　②　　イ　④　　ウ　③　　エ　⑥　　オ　①
(No.2)　カ　①　　キ　④　　ク　③　　ケ　②

〈解説〉(No.1)　ア　空欄を含む文の次の文に着目する。言語の発達段階が子どもによって異なると述べられており，空欄を含む文の言い換えになっている。　イ　空欄を含む文の直前の文に着目する。学業では優秀であっても言語の発達が遅い子どももいると述べられており，空欄を含む文の言い換えになっている。　ウ　空欄を含む文の直前の文に着目する。子どもの言葉への興味が重要であることが述べられているので，子どもの言語発達を促すことによって，読書への関心が高まるという意味になる③が正解。　エ　空欄を含む文の直前の文に着目する。例えるとすれば，言語の発達は長距離走のようなものであると述べられており，早く走り終える人もいれば，ゆっくりでもなんとか無事に走り終える人もいるという意味になる⑥が正解。　オ　空欄エを含む文に着目する。言語習得がゆっくりであれば，傍観者であるその両親は動揺してしまうのである。　(No.2)　英文の後半に続くパラグラフを正しく並べる問題である。まず，問題の直前の英文では，会話に関わろうとする子どもの動機づけが，言語発達の速度に影響すると述べられている。すると，十分な励まし，練習，そして刺激的な環境があれば2つの言語も苦もなく楽に習得できるという英文から始まる①が最初である。十分な励ましや刺激的な環境というのが，子どもの動機づけに影響することに着目するとよい。次に，①の後半には失敗を予期する親はあまり成功しない傾向にあり，そしてこのことは特にバイリンガルの発達に当てはまると述べられていることに着目する。このような親の考え方は，④の3文目に，2言語の習得に時間がかかることは，よい成績を求める親が過度な心配をする理由の1つであると述べられていることに対応している。その次は，このバイリンガルの子どもの親の心配に関することが1文目で述べられている③が続く。バイリンガルの子どもの親にとって言語の発達に時間がかかることへの懸念はよくあることだと述べられている。また，③の後半では，あらゆる状況で2言語とも同じように流暢であるバイリンガルはまれであると述べられている。この内容が1文目で言い換えられている②が最後に来ることがわかる。第2言語を理解できても話せないといった受動的な2言語使用で終わるのではなく，能動的なバイリンガルになるには，その言語が話されている国を訪問するなどして完璧なバイリンガルを目指す過程が必要であることが述べられている。

【6】(1) ア ⑥ イ ② (2) ウ ③ エ ⑦ (3) オ ③ カ ①

〈解説〉(1) 空欄を含む英文はBut it's difficult to conclude that scientific eating has contributed to our health.であり，「しかし，科学的な食事が私たちの健康に貢献していると結論づけることは難しい」の意である。空欄の1つ目には動詞の原形が必要であること，そしてcontribute to～が「～に貢献する」の意味であることに着目すればよい。 (2) 空欄を含む英文はYou could blame this unfortunate fallout on us eaters for following the official advice to eat more low-fat food a little too avidly.であり，「このような不幸な結果は，低脂肪の食品をもっと食べた方がよいという公式のアドバイスに熱心に従った私たちのせいかもしれない」の意である。空欄部は食べる側である我々が責められる理由の箇所であり，for followingの形から始めることがわかれば，あとはadviceを修飾する語句などを丁寧に考えていけばよい。 (3) 空欄部はthere is no escaping the conclusion thatであり，空欄部を含む節は，様々な報告書で述べられている食生活のアドバイスには，現在私たちが直面している公衆衛生上の危機を生み出した直接的な責任がある，という結論から逃れることはできないと述べられている。there is no～ingで「～することはできない」の意味になることに着目するとよい。

【７】you with grammar rules and specific vocabulary (7 words)

〈解説〉与えられた英文を読み，空欄部に当てはまる内容を英語で書く問題である。解答は5～10語であり，また空欄直前にhelpがあることを踏まえて書くことに留意したい。空欄部を含む節の主語はthe intensive reading in textbooksであり，その前の2文でintensive reading(精読)は1語1語を理解するなどの特定の目的をもって行われるものであると述べられていることから，その具体例を書けばよい。解答例にあるように文法や単語などの知識の習得に役立つことを書けばよいだろう。

【８】We often point out their mistakes. We should praise them for what they can do. If we can understand what they are trying to tell us, even if it is faltering, they will gradually use English and have more confidence. (40 words)

〈解説〉ALTとJTEの会話を踏まえて，JTEとしてALTの質問に答える内容を30語以上の英語で書くことが求められている。ALTは1つ目の発話で，「間違うことを楽しもう」と言っているけど，生徒たちは英語を使おうとはしないと述べている。それを受けて，JTEは，その原因として生徒たちに自信がないことを挙げ，それを受けてALTがなぜ生徒たちに自信がないかを尋ねている。JTEが「間違うことを楽しもう」と言っている設定を踏まえて，間違いばかりを指摘されていることが原因の1つであることを書きたい。また，JTEの回答を聞いてALTが次の授業でやってみましょう，と言っていることを踏まえて，どうすれば生徒たちの自信を高めるようにできるかについても言及しておく必要があるだろう。

2023年度　実施問題

【中高共通】

【1】(Listening Test)

Part A　Listen to the passage. Answer the two questions below by choosing the correct answer from the options from ① to ④ which will be read later. The passage and the options will be read once.

(1)　According to the passage, which is one example of serendipity?

(2)　According to Dr. Stephann Makri from University College London, what is important to make serendipity happen?

Part B　Listen to the passages and the questions. Choose the correct answer from the options from ① to ④ below. The passages and the questions will be read once.

(1)　Answer:

① Doing exercise has a good impact on academic performance.

② If you work hard to take SAT tests, you will be smarter.

③ People who have better memory can play sports well.

④ Some studies show older people are smarter than younger people.

(2)　Answer:

① Design thinking strategies are helpful only at school.

② Design thinking strategies can help people brainstorm and work together.

③ Many educators think design thinking strategies are a difficult approach for students.

④ Students who do well on their tests can get the biggest benefits of design thinking strategies.

Part C　You will hear expressions teachers often use in English class or when they talk with ALTs. Write down the whole expression. Each will be read twice.

(☆☆☆◎◎◎◎)

【2】Choose the best item from ① to ④ below each question to fill in the blank.

(1) In Germany, we typically use strong words when [　　] or criticizing in order to make sure the message registers clearly and honestly.

① complaining　② interpreting　③ listening
④ neglecting

(2) Even now, in her late 80's, she takes a deep personal interest in every one of her descendants. She writes us love letters. I was reading one the other day on a plane with tears [　　] down my cheeks.

① stream　② streamed　③ streaming　④ to stream

(3) If you live in France or northern Italy, chances are you won't feel the need to make the call, since being six or seven minutes late is within the [　　] of "basically on time."

① barrier　② course　③ layer　④ realm

(4) [　　] more mature, I could have relied on my own intrinsic strength — my understanding of sharing and of growth and my capacity to love and nurture — and allowed my daughter to make a free choice as to whether she wanted to share or not to share.

① If I am　② If I had　③ Had I been　④ Were I

(5) Seeing things through another person's eyes may ease tensions when personal problems become [　　].

① overwhelmed　② overwhelming　③ overwhelmingly
④ to overwhelm

(6) B.F. Skinner, the world-famous psychologist, proved through his experiments that an animal rewarded for good behavior will learn much more rapidly and [　　] what it learns far more effectively than an animal punished for bad behavior.

① resolve　② restrict　③ retain　④ reverse

(☆☆☆☆◎◎◎◎)

【3】Read the following story and answer the questions below.

To sell Pepsodent, then, Hopkins needed a trigger that would justify the toothpaste's daily use. He sat down with a pile of dental textbooks. "It was dry reading," he later wrote. "But in the middle of one book I found a reference to the mucin plaques on teeth, which I afterward called 'the film.' That gave me an appealing idea. I resolved to advertise this toothpaste as a creator of beauty. To deal with that cloudy film."

In focusing on tooth film, Hopkins was ignoring the fact that this same film has always covered people's teeth and hadn't seemed to bother anyone. The film is a naturally [ア] membrane that builds up on teeth regardless of what you eat or how often you brush. People had never paid much attention to it, and there was little reason why they should: You can get rid of the film by eating an apple, running your finger over your teeth, brushing, or vigorously swirling liquid around your mouth. Toothpaste didn't do anything to help remove the film. In fact, one of the leading dental researchers of the time said that all toothpastes — particularly Pepsodent — were worthless.

That didn't stop Hopkins from [イ] his discovery. Here, he decided, was a cue that could trigger a habit. Soon, cities were plastered with Pepsodent ads.

"Just run your tongue across your teeth," read one. "*You'll feel a film* — that's what makes your teeth look 'off color' and invites decay."

"Note how many pretty teeth are seen everywhere," read another ad, featuring smiling beauties. "Millions are using a new method of teeth cleansing. Why would any woman have dingy film on her teeth? Pepsodent removes the film!"

The brilliance of these appeals was that they relied upon a cue — tooth film — [ウ]. Telling someone to run their tongue across their teeth, it turned out, was likely to cause them to run their tongue across their teeth. And when they did, they were likely to feel a film. Hopkins had found a cue that was simple, had existed for ages, and was so easy to trigger [エ].

Moreover, the reward, as Hopkins envisioned it, was even more enticing. Who, after all, doesn't want to be more beautiful? Who doesn't want a prettier smile? Particularly when all it takes is a quick brush with Pepsodent?

After the campaign launched, a quiet week passed. Then two. In the third week, demand exploded. There were so many orders for Pepsodent [オ]. In three years, the product went international, and Hopkins was crafting ads in Spanish, German, and Chinese. Within a decade, Pepsodent was one of the top-selling goods in the world, and remained America's bestselling toothpaste for more than thirty years.

Before Pepsodent appeared, only 7 percent of Americans had a tube of toothpaste in their medicine chests. A decade after Hopkins's ad campaign went nationwide, that number had jumped to 65 percent. By the end of World War Ⅱ, the military downgraded concerns about recruits' teeth because so many soldiers were brushing every day.

"I made for myself a million dollars on Pepsodent," Hopkins wrote a few years after the product appeared on shelves. The key, he said, was that he had "learned the right human psychology." That psychology was grounded in two basic rules:

First, find a simple and obvious cue.

Second, clearly define the rewards.

If you get those elements right, Hopkins promised, it was like magic. Look at Pepsodent: [カ]. Even today, Hopkins's rules are a staple of marketing textbooks and the foundation of millions of ad campaigns.

And those same principles have been used to create thousands of other habits — often without people realizing how closely they are hewing to Hopkins's formula. Studies of people who have successfully started new exercise routines, for instance, show they are more likely to stick with a workout plan if they choose a [キ] cue, such as running as soon as they get home from work, and a [ク] reward, such as a beer or an evening of guilt-free television. Research on dieting says creating new food habits requires a [ケ] cue — such as planning menus in advance — and simple rewards for dieters when they stick to their intentions.

"The time has come when advertising has in some hands reached the status of a science," Hopkins wrote, "Advertising, once a gamble, has thus become, under [A] direction, one of the [B] of business ventures."

(SOURCE: "*THE POWER OF HABIT*" by Charles Duhigg)

(No.1) Choose the most suitable word for each blank [ア] and [イ] from ① to ③.

① censuring ② exploiting ③ occurring

(No.2) Choose the most suitable option for each blank [ウ], [エ] and [オ] from ① to ④.

① that allowed the public hygiene to be spread
② that an advertisement could cause people to comply automatically
③ that the company couldn't keep up
④ that was universal and impossible to ignore

(No.3) Choose the most suitable option for the blank [カ] from ① to ④.

① He had identified a cue — beautiful teeth — and a reward — tooth film — that had persuaded millions to start a daily ritual
② He had identified a cue — beautiful teeth — and a reward — tooth film — that had made millions start a daily ritual
③ He had identified a cue — tooth film — and a reward — beautiful teeth — that had persuaded millions to start a daily ritual
④ He had identified a cue — tooth film — and a reward — beautiful teeth — that had prevented millions from starting a daily ritual

(No.4) Choose the most suitable word from ① to ④ for each blank [キ], [ク] and [ケ].

キ ① secure ② sober ③ specific
④ stingy

ク ① close ② clear ③ collaborative
④ communicative

ケ ① predetermined ② predominated ③ preoccupied
④ prevailed

(No.5) Choose the best combination from ① to ④ in order to fill in the blanks [A] and [B].

① A: able B: most dangerous ② A: able B: safest
③ A: unable B: most dangerous ④ A: unable B: safest

(☆☆☆☆◎◎◎)

【4】The following is a part of Transforming our world: the 2030 Agenda for Sustainable Development. Choose the most suitable word from ① to ④ for each blank [ア], [イ], [ウ] and [エ].

21. The new Goals and targets will come into effect on 1 January 2016 and will guide the decisions we take over the next fifteen years. All of us will work to [ア] the Agenda within our own countries and at the regional and global levels, taking into account different national realities, capacities and levels of development and respecting national policies and priorities. We will respect national policy space for sustained, inclusive and sustainable economic growth, in particular for developing states, while remaining [イ] with relevant international rules and commitments. We acknowledge also the importance of the regional and sub-regional dimensions, regional economic integration and interconnectivity in sustainable development. Regional and sub-regional frameworks can facilitate the effective translation of sustainable development policies into concrete action at national level.

25. We commit to providing inclusive and equitable quality education at all levels − early childhood, primary, secondary, tertiary, technical and

vocational training. All people, irrespective of sex, age, race, ethnicity, and persons with disabilities, migrants, indigenous peoples, children and youth, especially those in [ウ] situations, should have access to life-long learning opportunities that help them acquire the knowledge and skills needed to exploit opportunities and to participate fully in society. We will strive to provide children and youth with a nurturing environment for the full realization of their rights and capabilities, helping our countries to reap the demographic dividend including through safe schools and [エ] communities and families.

ア ① conceive ② implement ③ supplement
④ suspend

イ ① consistent ② miserable ③ strict
④ vital

ウ ① affluent ② arrogant ③ promising
④ vulnerable

エ ① cohesive ② detached ③ monotonous
④ perpetual

(☆☆☆☆◎◎◎)

【5】Read the following passage and answer the questions below.

All children are motivated. Not all children are motivated to behave and work hard. Some children are motivated to do nothing. Think about motivation in two ways. Some motivation comes from inside you — it is internal. Some motivation comes from outside you — it is external. Being overweight is bad for your heart. Losing weight to improve your health requires internal motivation. You have a desire to lose weight. Losing weight to win a bet is an example of external motivation.

Most of us get up and go to work each day for two reasons. We get personal satisfaction from our work — internal. We also get paid — external. We need both. Most of us do not drive at a hundred miles per hour. We know it is unsafe — internal. We do not want to go to jail — external. Internal and external motivation work together to produce a responsible person.

Success creates internal motivation. When your boss [ア] your work, you feel successful and continue to work hard. You can use success to give your child a boost of internal motivation. Point out your child's good behavior and decisions. Your child will feel successful. Success [イ] him to work harder. When you compliment your child for having a clean bedroom, he will feel good inside — he will feel successful. He will be more motivated to keep his room clean.

Many children believe they cannot be successful. This false belief usually comes from repeated failures. Sometimes it is the result of high expectations. Correct this problem by spotlighting the positive. Point out strengths. Show your child where he has made progress. Encourage him to believe in himself. This will help your child feel success. Once success gets started, it continues. Success [ウ] success.

Develop expectations that build on success. This strategy is called ***shaping***. When you are teaching a complex behavior, divide the task into small sequential steps. Expect progress, not perfection. Consider this example.

Liz would like to teach Carlos how to get ready for school. This [エ] getting washed, brushing his teeth, getting dressed, and making his bed. Liz decides that getting washed by himself has first priority. It may take a few days or a few weeks before Carlos becomes proficient at washing. Once this is accomplished, Liz teaches Carlos to brush his teeth and get dressed. Finally, Liz teaches Carlos to make his bed.

[カ]

[キ]

ク

ケ

Parents have a tendency to focus on negative behavior. We tell our children what they are doing wrong. Misbehaviors get our attention. Many parents believe that being critical of mistakes is one way to instill more effort. This is not true. Focus on what your children do well.

Your son [オ] a mediocre job sweeping the garage. Don't say, "You didn't sweep the corners at all. You're so lazy. A six-year-old could do better." This type of criticism is not motivating. This is better: "You got the middle part okay. You missed some dirt in the corners. I'll do one corner to show you how. Then you can do the rest. Do the corners as well as you did the middle, and it will look great."

(SOURCE: "*How to Behave So Your Children Will, Too!*" by Sal Severe)

(No.1) Choose the most suitable word from ① to ④ for each blank [ア] through [オ]. Each word can be used once.

① breeds　② criticises　③ does　④ includes

⑤ motivates　⑥ praises

(No.2) Place these paragraphs from ① to ④ in their appropriate locations [カ] through [ケ].

① A child who misbehaves frequently locks the internal motivation to cooperate. Use praise and encouragement to get success started. Once he experiences good behavior, he will be more motivated to behave in the future. Tell your child when he is doing well. That will motivate him further.

② The small sequence of steps improves the probability of success. Placing all the tasks on Carlos would have been unreasonable. It may have resulted in frustration and failure. Shaping takes time. It is a good method of teaching.

③ Use shaping to improve behavior gradually. Shaping means encouraging better effort. Suppose your child takes forty minutes to do a chore that should take ten minutes. Set a timer and play "Beat the Clock." Reinforce him for completing the job within the limit. Starting with a time limit of ten minutes may cause failure. To improve the chances for success, start with a time limit of thirty minutes. This is still an improvement over forty minutes. After a week, move the limit to twenty-five or twenty minutes. Gradually, you will achieve the ten-minute goal. Shaping improves the chance of successful behavior.

④ When teaching new expectations, reinforce improvements or steps in the right direction. Do not insist on perfect performance on first attempts. Just because you have taught your five-year-old how to make his bed, do not expect him to do the job as well as you. He will be happy with a lumpy bedspread. He will steadily improve with your guidance and encouragement.

(☆☆☆◎◎◎)

【6】Complete the passage by filling in the blanks with all the items written below. Choose the most suitable item from ① to ⑦ for each blank [ア] through [カ].

When an adorable girl in Hawaii approached me and asked if we could be friends, I said yes without hesitation. "But first, (1)[　　] [ア] [　　] [　　] [　　] [イ] [　　] you," I said. "If you could have anything in the world, what would you want most?"

She put her finger to her chin and glanced knowingly at her mom. "To dance," she replied with a confident nod.

I laughed. "No, I meant if you could have absolutely anything in the entire world, what would it be?"

She smiled, now fully understanding my question. "To dance!" she replied again with delight.

"Wow, that's beautiful," I said with a massive grin. Her answer was disarming in its honesty. I thought back to the happiest moments of my life and realized that many of them involved dancing without any inhibition — at my first Michael Jackson concert, at my dad's surprise fortieth birthday party, at our annual Homecoming Dance, and the list went on. The purest joys are available to all of us, and they're unrelated to status, recognition, or material desires. I clearly had a lot to learn from the unsullied perspective of those I would encounter while traveling, so I decided that for the rest of my trip I would spend more time asking questions than trying to provide answers. Listening (2)[　　] [ウ] [　　] [　　] [　　] [エ] [　　] immensely.

In Beijing, I asked a girl near the entrance to the Forbidden Temple what she most wanted in the world, and she said, "A book."

"Really? You can have anything," I urged.

"A book."

Her mother explained that the girl loved school, but didn't have any books of her own. This child's dream was (3)[　　] [オ] [　　] [　　] [　　] [カ] [　　] every single day.

(SOURCE: "*THE PROMISE OF A PENCIL*" by Adam Braun)

(1) ① ask　② have　③ I　④ important
　⑤ something　⑥ to　⑦ very

(2) ① a far　② intensely　③ is　④ more valuable
　⑤ skill　⑥ speaking　⑦ than

(3) ① for　② granted　③ have　④ I
　⑤ something　⑥ to　⑦ took

(☆☆☆☆◎◎◎)

【7】The following is a conversation between an ALT (assistant language teacher) and a JTE (Japanese teacher of English). Fill in the gap to make it flow with one English sentence.

JTE : More and more JTEs use English in English classes. It's a good trend.

ALT : I agree, but what is good for students if JTEs always use English in class?

JTE : ____.

(☆☆☆☆◎◎◎)

【8】Complete the passage by filling in the blank with 30 or more words in English.

Emotional volatility is not the most reliable leadership tool. When you get angry, you are usually out of control. It's hard to lead people when you've lost control. You may think you have a handle on your temper, that you can use your spontaneous rages to manipulate and motivate people. But it's very hard to predict how people will react to anger. They will shut down as often as they will perk up.

Whenever I hear managers justify anger as a management tool, I wonder about all those other leaders who do not need anger to make their subordinates toe the line. Without anger to strike fear in the troops, how do these steady composed leaders ever get anything accomplished?

But the worst thing about anger is how it stifles our ability to change. Once you get a reputation for emotional volatility, you are branded for life. Pretty soon that is all people know about you. For example, basketball coach Bob Knight won three NCAA titles at Indiana University and is only one of two coaches in college history with 800 or more victories. By any measure, he's one of the greatest coaches of all time. But he also has a well-documented history of arguing with referees and tossing chairs across the court.

That reputation overwhelms Knight's record. When people think of Bob Knight, their first thought is his volcanic temper, not his won-lost record.

It's the same in the workplace.

(SOURCE: "*What Got You Here Won't Get You There*" by Marshall Goldsmith)

(☆☆☆☆◎◎◎)

解答・解説

【中高共通】

【1】Part A　(1)　②　(2)　①　Part B　(1)　①　(2)　②

Part C　(No.1)　Keep it up.　(No.2)　Draw a line to the picture.　(No.3)　The class will start in half an hour.　(No.4)　What's the date today?　(No.5)　Do you have any suggestions to make the class better?

〈解説〉スクリプトは非公開である。 Part A　パッセージを聞き，問題用紙に印刷された2つの質問文についてそれぞれ読み上げられる4つの選択肢から正しいものを選ぶ。放送は1回のみ。質問文中にあるserendipity「思いがけない発見や，偶然掘り出し物を見つける幸運や才能」という難解な単語がどのような意味であるのかを推測するのがポイントと考えられる。 Part B　パッセージと2つの質問文を聞き，問題用紙に印刷された4つの選択肢から，それぞれ正しいものを選ぶ。放送は1回のみ。 (1)　academic performance，SAT tests，exercise，sportsといった選択肢中の語句から，勉強と運動の関係に関する話題であることが推測できる。 (2)　全ての選択肢にdesign thinking strategiesという語句があることから，これがキーワードと推測できる。

Part C　授業中の教師の指示や，教師とALTとの対話によく使われる表現のディクテーション問題である。2回放送される。

【2】(1)　①　　(2)　③　　(3)　④　　(4)　③　　(5)　②　　(6)　③

〈解説〉(1)　orの後のcriticizingと同種の意味の語が入ると考えられるので①のcomplainingが適切。　(2)　with＋S＋現在分詞で「Sが～しながら」という付帯状況を表す。with tears streaming down my cheeksで「涙が私の頬を流れながら」という意味となる。　(3)　within the realm of ～で「～な範囲内で」の意。　(4)　Had S 過去分詞という倒置形で仮定法過去完了を表すことができる。　(5)　overwhelmingは主に人以外の物を主語に取り，「(人を)圧倒するような」の意。　(6)　retainは「保持する」の意。

【3】(No.1)　ア　③　　イ　②　　(No.2)　ウ　④　　エ　②　オ　③　　(No.3)　カ　③　　(No.4)　キ　③　　ク　②　　ケ　①　(No.5)　②

〈解説〉(No.1)　ア　a naturally occurring membraneで「自然に発生する薄膜」の意。　イ　That didn't stop Hopkins from exploiting his discovery.で「そのことはホプキンスが自分の発見を活用するのを妨げることはなかった」という意味で，Thatは前文の内容「研究者の一人がすべての歯磨き粉が価値がないと言ったこと」を指す。stop O from～ingで「Oが～するのを妨げる」。　(No.2)　ウ　空所に続く文で「人に舌を歯に這わせるように言うと彼らはその通りにし，膜を感じることがあった」という内容が述べられており，「普遍的で無視することができなかった」の④が適切だと判断できる。　エ　空所の前で「単純な手掛かりを見つけた」とあり，この内容に続くのは，②「広告によって人が自動的に従う」が適切だと判断できる。　オ　空所の前で「多くの注文があった」とあり，この内容に続くのは，③「会社が追い付かないほどの」が適切だと判断できる。　(No.3)　第6段落よりtooth filmがa cueであることがわかるので，③と④に絞られる。a reward「報酬」は

beautiful teethで，人にPepsodentを使って毎日歯を磨くという日常習慣を始めさせるものなので，③が適切と判断できる。 (No.4) キ 後ろのsuch as以下で具体例が述べられていることから，③specific「具体的な」が適切。 ク a clear rewardで「明確な報酬」となる。 ケ 空所後のsuch as planning menus in advanceより，①predetermined「あらかじめ決められた」が適切。 (No.5) Hopkinsが自身の成功例から述べた言葉であり，いずれも肯定的な語である②の組み合わせが適切と判断できる。

【4】ア ② イ ① ウ ④ エ ①

〈解説〉2015年9月に国連サミットで採択された「我々の世界を変革する：持続可能な発展のための 2030 アジェンダ」からの出題である。 ア implement the Agendaで「その議題(アジェンダ)を実施する」の意。 イ consistent with～で「～と一致する，～から逸脱しない」の意。 ウ この項では平等な教育というテーマが述べられており，弱い立場の人でも同様であるというニュアンスの④vulnerable「弱い，脆弱な」が適切。 エ cohesive communities and familiesで「団結力のあるコミュニティや家族」の意。

【5】(No.1) ア ⑥ イ ⑤ ウ ① エ ④ オ ③
(No.2) カ ② キ ③ ク ④ ケ ①

〈解説〉(No.1) ア 褒められればやる気になるという内容なので，⑥のpraisesが適切。 イ 一つの成功でやる気になるという内容なので，⑤のmotivatesが適切。 ウ 成功が次の成功を呼び込むというプラスの循環を示す①のbreedsが適切。 エ 空所の後に具体例が続くので，④のincludesが適切。 オ jobを目的語に取るのは③のdoesとなる。②のcriticisesは前後の文意に合わない。 (No.2) カ 前段落で，Carlosという子に学校へ行くための準備を1つずつ教えるという具体例が述べられている。よってこの内容に続くのはThe small sequence of stepsで始まる②が適切。 キ ②でshapingという語が用いられているが，この語を詳しく説明している③が続くと判断できる。　ク　残りの①と④を比較すると，③の内容を実施する際の注意点を述べている④が続くと判断できる。　ケ　④を踏まえて，子どもに対する接し方を説明している①が続くと判断できる。

【6】(1)　ア　②　　イ　⑥　　(2)　ウ　③　　エ　⑦　　(3)　オ　③　カ　①

〈解説〉(1)　I have something very important to askという語順になる。very importantがsomethingを後ろから修飾することに注意。　(2)　intensely is a far more valuable skill than speakingという語順になる。前文で自分が話すより質問をすることに時間を費やしたという内容が述べられていることから，聞くことが話すことより価値があると筆者は考えていることが判断できる。副詞のfarは比較級moreを強調する用法である。

(3)　to have something I took for grantedという語順になる。take O for grantedで「Oを当然だと思う」。筆者が持っていて当然だと思っていた本を，少女が何よりも欲しがっていたという文意になる。

【7】Students will be motivated by seeing Japanese people speaking English.

〈解説〉日本人の英語教師が授業で英語を使う利点が問われている。解答例では「日本人が英語を話すのを見ることで生徒の動機づけになる」という内容を一文で表現している。

【8】No matter how well you have performed, once you get a reputation for emotional volatility, the reputation may prevail and make your subordinates passive. It is not a true leader who dominates them with anger. (35語)

〈解説〉パッセージに続く内容を書く問題である。テーマはマネージメントにおける感情のコントロールについてであり，空所の前の2つの段落では，感情が不安定だと偉大な業績を成し遂げたとしても，その感情の不安定さの悪い評判が先行してしまうことが述べられている。ボブ・ナイトという800勝を上げたバスケットボールの監督も，その勝利数ではなくその激高しやすい性格が印象付けられているということが，具体例として挙げられている。空所には職場での同様な具体例を入れればよい。解答例では，たとえどんなによい業績を挙げても，感情が不安定であるという評判は部下たちを受動的にし，怒りで支配するのは真のリーダーではないと述べている。

2022年度　実施問題

【中高共通】

【 1 】(Listening Test)

Part A　Listen to the passage. Answer the two questions below by choosing the correct answer from the options from ① to ④ which will be read later. The passage and the options will be read once.

(1)　According to the author, what is the most important need?

(2)　Why do some people have to trust one book?

Part B　Listen to the passages and the questions. Choose the correct answer from the options from ① to ④ below. The passages and the questions will be read once.

(1)　Answer :

①　The distance to the sun

②　The hole in the ozone layer

③　The importance of CFCs

④　The paradox of our times

(2)　Answer :

①　The spread of contagion

②　The spread of false information

③　The study of human construction

④　The study of space

Part C　You will hear expressions teachers often use in English class. Write down the whole expression. Each will be read twice.

(☆☆☆◎◎◎◎)

【 2 】Choose the best item from ① to ④ below each question to fill in the blank.

(1)　Consider baseball's data revolution in the 1990s. Many teams began using increasingly [ ] statistics — rather than relying on old-fashioned human scouts — to make decisions.

① absurd ② antiquated ③ intricate ④ obsolete

(2) Based on experience and knowledge, they try to [ ] fevers, headaches, runny noses, and stomach pains to various diseases.

① connect ② correspond ③ prompt ④ prescribe

(3) There is also some evidence from psychological experiments that subjects [ ] to a violent film will report more anger and hostility, even if they don't precisely imitate one of the scenes.

① accused ② entitled ③ exposed ④ irrefutable

(4) While the desire for more [ ] measures of what happens in classrooms is legitimate, there are many things that go on there that can't readily be captured in numbers.

① common ② objective ③ subjective ④ traditional

(5) Japan is a nation which is [ ] to natural disasters. Over the years, the country has been struck by a series of catastrophes.

① anxious ② equivalent ③ peculiar ④ prone

(6) The appearance of [ ] seems to go against the conventional wisdom that Japan is a more or less culturally or ethnically homogeneous country.

① consensus ② diversity ③ heredity ④ similarity

(☆☆☆◎◎◎◎◎)

【3】Read the following story and answer the questions below.

You have probably heard of "coral bleaching" —that is, coral dying—in which warmer ocean waters strip reefs of the protozoa, called zooxanthellae, that provide, through photosynthesis, up to 90 percent of the energy needs of the coral. Each reef is an ecosystem as complex as a modern city, and the zooxanthellae are its food supply, [ア]; when they die, the whole complex is starved with military efficiency, a city under siege or blockade. Since 2016, as much as half of Australia's landmark Great Barrier

Reef has been stripped in this way. These large-scale die-outs are called "mass bleaching events"; one unfolded, globally, from 2014 to 2017. Already, coral life has declined so much that it has created [　　イ　　], between 30 and 150 meters below the surface, which scientists have taken to calling a "twilight zone." According to the World Resources Institute, by 2030 ocean warming and acidification will threaten 90 percent of all reefs.

This is very bad news, because reefs support as much as a quarter of all marine life and supply food and income for half a billion people. They also [　ウ　] against flooding from storm surges—a function that offers value in the many billions, with reefs presently worth at least $400 million annually to Indonesia, the Philippines, Malaysia, Cuba, and Mexico—$400 million annually to each. Ocean acidification will also [　エ　] fish populations directly. Though scientists aren't yet sure how to [　オ　] the effects on the stuff we haul out of the ocean to eat, they do know that in acid waters, oysters and mussels will struggle to grow their shells, and that rising carbon concentrations will impair fishes' sense of smell—which you may not have known they had, but which often aids in navigation. Off the coasts of Australia, fish populations have declined an estimated 32 percent in just ten years.

It has become quite common to say that we are living through a mass extinction—[　　カ　　]. It is probably also fair to call this an era marked by what is called ocean anoxification. Over the past fifty years, the amount of ocean water with no oxygen at all has [　キ　] globally, giving us a total of more than four hundred "dead zones" ; oxygen-deprived zones have grown by several million square kilometers, roughly the size of all of Europe; and hundreds of coastal cities now sit on fetid, under-oxygenated ocean. This is partly due to the simple warming of the planet, since warmer waters can carry less oxygen. But it is also partly the result of straightforward pollution—a recent Gulf of Mexico dead zone, all 9,000 square miles of it, was [　ク　] by the runoff of fertilizer chemicals washing into the Mississippi from the industrial farms of the Midwest. In 2014, a not-atypical toxic event struck Lake Erie, when fertilizer from corn and soy farms in Ohio spawned an algae bloom that cut off drinking water for Toledo. And in 2018, a dead zone the size of Florida was discovered in the Arabian Sea—so big that researchers believed it might encompass the entire 63,700-square-mile Gulf of Oman, seven times the size of the dead zone in the Gulf of Mexico. "The ocean," said the lead researcher Bastien Queste, "is [ケ]."

Dramatic declines in ocean oxygen have played a role in many of the planet's worst mass extinctions, and this process by which dead zones grow—choking off marine life and wiping out fisheries—is already quite [A] not only in the Gulf of Mexico but just off Namibia, where hydrogen sulfide is bubbling out of the sea along a thousand-mile stretch of land known as the Skeleton Coast. The name originally referred to the detritus of wrecked ships, but today it's [B] apt than ever. Hydrogen sulfide is also one of the things scientists suspect finally capped the end-Permian extinction, once all the feedback loops had been triggered. It is so toxic that evolution has trained us to recognize the tiniest, safest traces, which is why our noses are so exquisitely skilled at registering flatulence.

(SOURCE : "*The Uninhabitable Earth*" by David Wallance-Wells)

(No.1) Choose the most suitable option for each blank [ア] and [イ] from ① to ③.

① an entirely new layer in the ocean

② the basic building block of an energy chain

③ the diversity of life of deep sea animals

(No.2) Choose the most suitable word for each blank [ウ], [エ] and [オ] from ① to ④.

① boost ② damage ③ predict ④ protect

(No.3) Choose the most suitable option for the blank [カ] from ① to ③.

① a period in which a number of dinosaurs have been faced with danger of their lives because of the harsh climate change

② a period in which human activity has multiplied the rate at which species are disappearing from the earth by a factor perhaps as large as a thousand

③ a period in which more and more scientists successfully contribute to environmental conservation and the preservation of endangered species

(No.4) Choose the most suitable word from ① to ④ for each blank [キ], [ク] and [ケ].

キ ① halved ② quadrupled ③ quartered ④ reduced

ク ① delayed ② diminished ③ powered ④ suppressed

ケ ① carbonizing ② hydrating ③ sanitizing ④ suffocating

(No.5) Choose the best combination from ① to ④ in order to fill in the blanks [A] and [B].

①	A: advanced	B: less	②	A: advanced	B: more
③	A: retreated	B: less	④	A: retreated	B: more

(☆☆☆☆◎◎◎◎◎)

【4】The following is a part of Key Features of OECD Programme for International Student Assessment 2018. Choose the most suitable word from ① to ④ for each blank [ア], [イ], [ウ], and [エ].

〈Results in Japan〉

Reading

◆ Reading items which low percentage of Japanese students gave correct answer were, for example, items locating information from a text and items assessing the quality and [ア] of a text.

◆ Students in Japan continue to have problem in explaining their own ideas using evidence so that other people can understand, in open ended-response items in reading.

◆ According to the student questionnaire, students in Japan tend to have a [イ] view towards reading. For example, the percentage of students in Japan who answered "Reading is one of my favourite hobbies" was higher than the OECD average. In addition, such students tend to have higher score in reading.

Questionnaire

◆ In Japan, just as in other OECD member countries, there was a tendency that the percentage of students with low level of [ウ] is higher among students with a lower level of social, economic and cultural status.

◆ Regarding the students' use of ICT, the hours of its use in school lessons is shorter than other countries in Japan. In addition, although students use ICT for various purposes outside of school, their use tends to be [エ] toward chatting and playing video games.

ア ① autonomy ② burden ③ credibility
④ stagnation

イ ① compulsory ② negative ③ positive
④ skeptical

ウ ① hardship ② instance ③ obviousness
④ proficiency

エ ① biased ② confined ③ dedicated
④ tempted

(☆☆☆☆◎◎◎◎)

【5】Read the following passage and answer the questions below.

In 2004, Steve Jobs, CEO, chairman, and co-founder of Apple, was strolling along Madison Avenue in New York City when he noticed something strange, and gratifying. Hip white earphones (remember, back then most earphones came in basic boring black). Looping and snaking out of people's ears, dangling down across their chests, peeking out of pockets and purses and backpacks. They were everywhere. "It was, like, on every block, there was someone with white headphones, and I thought, 'Oh, my God, it's starting to happen,' " Jobs, who'd recently [ア] his company's immensely successful iPod, was quoted as saying.

You could term the popularity of the iPod (and its ubiquitous, iconic white headphones) a fad. Some might even call it a revolution. But from a neuroscientific point of view, what Jobs was seeing was nothing less than the triumph of a region of our brains [イ] with something called the mirror neuron.

In 1992, an Italian scientist named Giacomo Rizzolatti and his research team in Parma, Italy, were studying the brains of a species of monkey — the macaque — In the hopes of finding out how the brain organizes motor behaviors. Specifically, they were looking at a region of the macaque brain [ウ] by neuroscientists as F5, or the premotor area, which registers activity when monkeys carry out certain gestures, like picking up a nut. Interestingly, they observed that the macaques' premotor neurons would light up not just when the monkeys reached for that nut, but also when they saw *other* monkeys reaching for a nut — which [エ] as a surprise to Rizzolatti's team, since neurons in premotor regions of the brain typically don't respond to visual stimulation.

On one particularly hot summer afternoon, Rizzolatti and his team observed the strangest thing of all when one of Dr. Rizzolatti's grad students returned to the lab after lunch holding an ice cream cone, and noticed that the macaque was staring at him, almost longingly. And as the grad student raised the cone to his mouth and took a tentative lick, the electronic monitor hooked up to the macaque's premotor region [オ] — *bripp, bripp, bripp.*

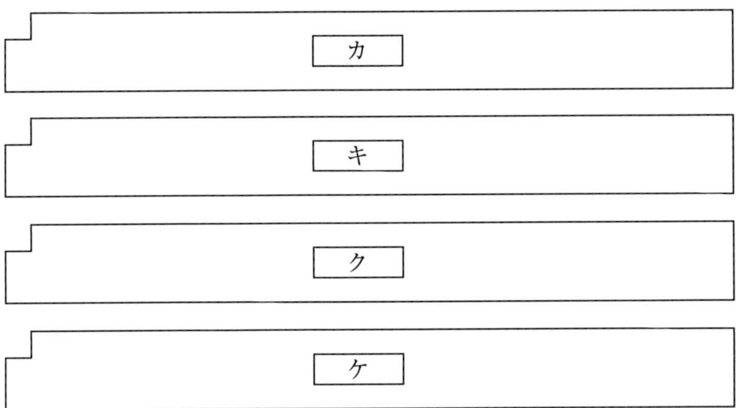

Have you ever wondered why, when you're watching a baseball game and your favorite player strikes out in the top of the ninth inning, you cringe — or alternately, why, when your home team scores a goal or a touchdown, you pump your arm in the air? Or why, when you're at the movies and the heroine starts weeping, tears well up in your own eyes? What about that rush of exhilaration you feel when Clint Eastwood or Vin Diesel dispatches a villain — or that alpha-male stride-in-your-step you still feel an hour after the movie ends? Or the feeling of grace and beauty that floods through you as you observe a ballet dancer or listen to a world-class pianist? Chalk it up to mirror neurons. Just like Rizzolatti's monkeys, when we watch someone do something, whether it's scoring a penalty kick or playing a perfect arpeggio on a Steinway grand piano, our brains react as if we were actually [コ] these activities ourselves. In short, it's as though seeing and doing are one and the same.

(SOURCE: "*buy · ology*" by Martin Lindstrom)

(No.1) Choose the most suitable word from ① to ⑥ for each blank [ア] through [オ]. Each word can be used once.

① associated　② came　③ fired　④ known

⑤ launched　⑥ observed

(No.2) Place these paragraphs from ① to ④ in their appropriate locations [カ] through [ケ].

① But the monkeys' mirror neurons didn't fire up at the sight of just *any* gesture either a grad student or another monkey made. Rizzolatti's team was able to demonstrate that the macaques' mirror neurons were responding to what are known as "targeted gestures" — meaning those activities that involve an object, such as picking up a nut, or bringing an ice cream cone to your mouth, as opposed to random movement, such as crossing the room or simply standing there with your arms crossed.

② Do humans' brains work in the same way? Do we, too, mimic how others interact with objects? Well, for obvious ethical reasons scientists can't place an electrode into a working human brain. However, fMRI and EEG scans of the regions of the human brain thought to contain mirror neurons, the inferior frontal cortex and superior parietal lobule, point to yes, as these regions are activated both when someone is performing an action, as well as when the person observes another person performing an action. The evidence supporting the existence of mirror neurons in the human brain is so compelling, in fact, that one eminent professor of psychology and neuroscience at the University of California has said, "What DNA is for biology, the Mirror Neuron is for psychology."

③ The monkey hadn't done a thing. It hadn't moved its arm or taken a lick of ice cream; it wasn't even holding anything at all. But simply by *observing* the student bringing the ice cream cone to his mouth, the monkey's brain had mentally imitated the very same gesture.

④ This amazing phenomenon was what Rizzolatti would eventually dub "mirror neurons" at work — neurons that fire when an action is being performed and when that same action is being observed. "It took us several years to believe what we were seeing," he later said.

(No.3) Choose the best option for the blank [コ].

① observing ② performing ③ responding to
④ studying

(☆☆☆☆◎◎◎◎)

【6】Complete the passage by filling in the blanks with all the items written below. Choose the most suitable item from ① to ⑧ for each blank [ア] through [カ].

Benjamin Bloom and his team noted the same pattern in their studies of world-class performers. Almost without exception, the supportive and demanding parents in Bloom's study were "models of the work ethic (1) [ ] [ア] [ ] [ ] [ ] [イ] [ ] [ ], they did their best in whatever they tried, they believed that work should come before play, and that one should work toward distant goals." Further, "most of the parents found it natural to encourage their children to participate in their favored activities." Indeed, one of Bloom's summary conclusions was that "parents' own interests somehow get communicated to the child... . We found over and over again that the parents of the pianists would send their child to the tennis lessons but they would take their child to the piano lessons. And we found just the opposite for the tennis homes."

It's indeed remarkable how many paragons of grit have told me, with pride and awe, that their parents are their most admired and influential role models. And it's just as telling that so many paragons have, in one way or another, developed very similar interests to those of their parents. Clearly, these exemplars of grit grew up not just imitating their parents but also emulating them.

This logic leads to the speculative conclusion that (2) [ ] [ ] [ウ] [ ] [ ] [エ] [ ] [ ] be gritty, because not all psychologically wise parents *model* gritliness. Though they may be both supportive and demanding, upper-right-quadrant moms and dads may or may not show passion and perseverance for long-term goals.

If you want to bring forth grit in your child, first ask how much passion and perseverance you have for your own life goals. Then ask yourself (3) [　　] [　オ　] [　　] [　　] [　　] [　カ　] [　　] [　　] your child to emulate you. If the answer to the first question is "a great deal," and your answer to the second is "very likely," you're already parenting for grit.

(SOURCE: "*GRIT*" by Angela Duckworth)

(1) ① as　② hard　③ in
④ regarded　⑤ that　⑥ they
⑦ were　⑧ workers

(2) ① all children　② not　③ parents
④ psychologically wise　⑤ to　⑥ up
⑦ will grow　⑧ with

(3) ① encourages　② how　③ it is
④ likely　⑤ parenting　⑥ that
⑦ to　⑧ your approach

(☆☆☆☆◎◎◎◎)

【7】The following is a conversation between an ALT (assistant language teacher) and a JTE (Japanese teacher of English). Fill in the gap to make it flow with one English sentence.

ALT : Hi, we are going to give our students a speaking test tomorrow, right?
JTE : Yes.
ALT : How are we going to evaluate their performances?
JTE : We will use these rubrics for evaluation. We will show them to the students at the start of each lesson.
ALT : Oh, really? I didn't know that. But why do you show rubrics to the students?
JTE : ＿＿＿＿＿＿＿＿＿＿＿＿＿＿＿＿＿＿＿＿＿＿＿＿＿＿＿＿＿＿

(☆☆☆☆◎◎◎)

【8】Complete the passage by filling in the blank with 30 or more words in English.

Doctors and policymakers in the rich world are increasingly worried about loneliness. Researchers define loneliness as perceived social isolation: a feeling of not having the number of social contacts one would like. To find out how many people feel this way, *The Economist* and the Kaiser Family Foundation (KFF), an American non-profit group focused on health, surveyed nationally representative samples of people in three rich countries. The study found that over 9% of adults in Japan, 22% in America and 23% in Britain always or often feel lonely, or lack companionship, or else feel left out or isolated.

One villain in the contemporary debate is technology. Smartphones and social media are blamed for a rise in loneliness in young people. This is plausible. Data from the OECD, a club of mostly rich countries, suggest that in nearly every member country the share of 15-year-olds saying that they feel lonely at school rose between 2003 and 2015. The smartphone makes an easy scapegoat. A sharp drop in how often American teenagers go out without their parents began in 2009, around the time when mobile phones became ubiquitous. Rather than meet up as often in person, so the story goes, young people are connecting online.

But this need not make them lonelier. [ ]

(SOURCE: "*UNCOMMON KNOWLEDGE*" by Tom Standage)

(☆☆☆☆◎◎◎)

解答・解説

【中高共通】

【1】Part A　(1)　③　(2)　④　Part B　(1)　②　(2)　②

Part C　(No.1)　Take it easy.　(No.2)　Who knows the answer?　(No.3)　Whose turn is it?　(No.4)　Let me know when you're ready.　(No.5)　What would you like to do on Wednesday?

〈解説〉スクリプトは公開されていない。　Part A　質問文だけが問題用紙に印刷されており，パッセージと4つの選択肢が1回だけ放送される。設問文にあるthe authorやtrust one bookから，パッセージは本の読み方に関する話題であることが推測できる。　Part B　4つの選択肢だけが問題用紙に印刷されており，パッセージと質問文が1回だけ放送される。　(1)　太陽，オゾン層そしてフロン類といった選択肢から，地球環境に関する話題であることが推測できる。　(2)　選択肢に統一性はないが，人間の営みについての調査や報告に関する話題であることが推測できる。　Part C　クラスルーム・イングリッシュのディクテーションで，2回放送される。使用頻度の高い表現であり，語数も多くはない。

【2】(1)　③　(2)　①　(3)　③　(4)　②　(5)　④　(6)　②

〈解説〉(1)　intricate「複雑な」。英文は「1990年代における野球のデータ革命を考えよう。多くのチームが意思決定を行うために，昔ながらの人間のスカウトに頼るというよりも，ますます複雑な統計データを使い始めた」の意となる。　(2)　connect A to B「AとBを結びつける」。英文は「経験と知識に基づいて，彼らは熱，頭痛，鼻水そして腹痛を様々な病気に結びつけようとする」の意となる。　(3)　exposed to A「Aにさらされる」。英文は「暴力的な映画を見た被験者は，映画のシーンを正確に模倣しなくても，怒りや敵意を抱きやすいという心理学の研究結果に基づく証拠もある」の意となる。　(4)　objective「客観的な」。英文は「教室での出来事について，より客観的な尺度が欲しいと思うのはもっともだが，教室には容易に数字では捉えることができないことがたくさんある」の意となる。　(5)　be prone to A「Aする傾向にある，Aしがちである」。英文は「日本は自然災害が多い国である。何年にもわたって，一連の大災害に見舞われてきた」の意となる。(6)　diversity「多様性」。英文は「多様性の出現は，日本はおおむね文化的・民族的に同種の国であるという伝統的な社会通念に反するようだ」の意となる。

【3】(No.1)　ア　②　　イ　①　　(No.2)　ウ　④　　エ　②
オ　③　　(No.3)　カ　②　　(No.4)　キ　②　　ク　③　　ケ　④
(No.5)　②

〈解説〉(No.1)　ア　第1段落1文目と2文目の前半で，サンゴ礁は近代都市と同じくらい複雑な生態系であり，褐虫藻が光合成で生産するエネルギーがサンゴの餌であることが述べられている。空所アは直前の部分とコンマでつながっていることから，その言い換えになっていることがわかる。したがって，②「エネルギー連鎖の基本的な構成要素」が適切。　イ　空所前後に着目すると，サンゴが大きく減少したことで，水深30メートルから150メートルの間に作られたものであることがわかる。よって，①「海中の完全に新しい層」が適切。
(No.2)　ウ　直前の文にサンゴ礁が様々な利益をもたらしていることが書かれていることに着目すると，「サンゴ礁は高潮による洪水も防いでくれる」と考え，protect「保護する，守る」が適切。　エ　その空所前後に着目すると，海洋酸性化が魚類の集団に対して行う内容であることがわかる。よって，damage「損害を与える」が適切。
オ　空所を含む節は「科学者たちは，人類が海から引き上げている食べ物に与える影響に対して(　　　)する方法がわかっていない」。predict「予測する」が適切。　(No.3)　直前にあるダッシュの前には，私たちは大量絶滅の時代に生きていると一般にいわれるようになったことが述べられている。よって，②「人類の活動が，種が地球上から滅亡する割合をおそらく千倍にも大きくした時代である」が適切。
(No. 4)　キ　空所前後では，「過去50年にわたって無酸素の海水量が地球規模で(　　　)し，400以上ものデッドゾーンがある」と述べられている。よって，quadrupled「4倍になった」が適切。残りの選択肢はいずれも減少の意味合いを持つ。　ク　空所を含む節では，「酸素の少ない海水が増えたのは直接的な汚染も原因の1つであり，近年のメキシコ湾の9,000平方マイルものデッドゾーンの全ては，化学肥料の放出によって(　　　)された」と述べられている。よって，powered「(動力源が)動力を与えた，動かした」が適切。　ケ　直前の文では，アラビア海にフロリダ州ほどの巨大なデッドゾーンが見つかったと述べられているので，suffocating「息苦しい，呼吸ができない」が適切。
(No. 5)　A　選択肢はadvanced「進んだ」とretreated「後退した」。よって，「海水中の酸素減少に伴うデッドゾーンの拡大によって生じる種の絶滅は，メキシコ湾だけでなくナミビアでも既に進んでいる」とするのが適切。　B　選択肢はmoreとless。more apt than everで「これまで以上に適切」の意。「スケルトン(骸骨)海岸の名前は，もとは難破船の残骸にちなんだものだが，(硫化水素のために大量の海洋生物が死滅している)今日では，かつてよりもさらにふさわしくなった」とするのが適切。

【4】ア　③　　イ　③　　ウ　④　　エ　①
〈解説〉2018年度に実施されたOECDによる生徒の学習到達度評価に関する問題である。　ア　英文は「日本人生徒の正答率が低かった読解問題の例としては，テキストから情報を探す問題や，テキストの質や(　　　)を評価する問題があった」の意なので，credibility「信頼性」が適切。　イ　英文は「生徒へのアンケートによれば，日本人生徒は読書を(　　　)に捉えている」の意。空所の後の文に，読書が趣味の1つであると答えた日本人生徒の割合が高いことが述べられていることに着目すると，positive「前向きな」が適切。　ウ　英文は「他のOECD加盟国と同様に，日本においても，社会的，経済的そして文化

的な水準が低いほど，(　　　)が低い生徒の割合が高くなる傾向があった」の意なので，proficiency「熟達度」が適切。他の選択肢は，hardship「困難，困窮」，instance「実例」，obviousness「明白性」で文脈に合わない。　エ　英文は「さらに，生徒たちは学校外で様々な目的でICTを活用しているが，その使用目的は，チャットやゲームに(　　　)傾向がある」の意。よって，biased「偏っている」が適切。

【5】(No.1)　ア　⑤　　イ　①　　ウ　④　　エ　②　　オ　③
(No.2)　カ　③　　キ　④　　ク　①　　ケ　②　　(No.3)　コ　②

〈解説〉(No.1)　ア　英文は「『どの街角にも白いヘッドホンを着けた人がいて，“ああ，始まったな”と思った』と，大成功したiPodを(　　　)したばかりのジョブズが言ったと伝えられている」の意なので，launched「発売した」が適切。　イ　英文は「しかし，脳科学的にみれば，ジョブズが見ていたものは，いわゆるミラーニューロンと(　　　)する脳の領域の勝利にほかならない」の意なので，associated「関連する」が適切。空所の直後にあるwithに着目するとよい。
ウ　空所の後にあるasに着目したい。known as Aで「Aとして知られている」。英文は「具体的には，研究者たちは，マカク属(猿)の脳の中で，木の実を取るようなある種の動作を行う時に活動する，脳科学者によってF5として知られている運動前野を調べていた」となる。
エ　come as a surprise「意外な結果である，驚きである」。英文は「リゾラッティの研究チームにとっては意外な結果であった。脳の運動前野は，通常，視覚的な刺激には反応しないためである」となる。
オ　英文は「大学院生がアイスクリームコーンを口に運んで舐めてみると，マカク属の脳の運動前野に接続されている電子モニターの機械が(　　　)」の意である。よって，fired「(エンジン・コンピュータなどが)始動した」が適切。　(No.2)　直前にある空所オを含んだ英文の内容を直接的に説明している③が最初の段落であると判断できる。猿自体は動作しなかったが，学生の動作を観察していただけで，猿の脳が同じ動作を模倣したと述べられている。その次は，この猿を対象とした実験の結果をまとめた④が続く。リゾラッティがこの現象をミラーニューロンと名付けたと述べられているが，“ミラーニューロン”にダブルクォーテーションがついていることから，ここで用語として初めて導入されているとわかる。よって，④は，同じくmirror neuronsに言及している①や②より，前に位置すると判断できる。④のあとには，猿のミラーニューロンが活性化しない条件について述べている①が続く。ミラーニューロンは，対象物のある目標動作がないと働かないと述べている。最後は，猿を対象とした実験から得られた結果が，人間の脳にも応用されるかを述べている②である。　(No.3)　英文は「リゾラッティの猿のように，私たちは誰かが，ペナルティキックで得点をあげたり，グランドピアノでアルペジオを弾いたりするのを見ると，脳はまるで自分自身がそれらを実際に(　　　)かのように反応する」の意である。よって，performing「行っている」が適切。

【6】(1)　ア　⑤　　イ　①　　(2)　ウ　⑧　　エ　⑦　　(3)　オ　④　カ　⑦

〈解説〉(1)　整序するとin that they were regarded as hard workers。空所部を含んだ英文は「ほぼ例外なく，ブルームの研究における協力的で厳格な両親は，『勤勉な労働者とみなされ，することは全力で取り組み，遊びは仕事の後にすべきであり，遠い目標に向けて働くべきと信じている，という点で労働倫理の模範』であった」の意である。　(2)　整序するとnot all children with psychologically wise parents will grow up to。空所部を含んだ英文は「心理学的に賢い両親全てが粘り強さの模範になるとは限らないため，このロジックは心理学的に賢い両親を持つ全ての子どもたちが，必ずしも粘り強くなるとは限らないという推論を導く」の意である。　(3)　整序するとhow likely it is that your approach to parenting encourages。空所部を含んだ英文は「そして，自分の子育てが，子どもに自分を見習うよう促す可能性がどれくらいあるか，自分自身に尋ねてみてください」の意である。

【7】By looking at them, students understand how hard they should work in class to achieve the goal and feel motivated.

〈解説〉与えられた会話文におけるJTEの立場になり，ALTの質問に対する回答を英語で書く問題。生徒のスピーキングテストをどうやって評価するのかと聞くALTに対し，JTEは毎回の授業前に生徒たちにルーブリックを提示するつもりだと答えている。そしてALTがその理由を尋ねているという場面である。ルーブリックとは，表を使って学習の達成度を測定する評価方法のことで，ルーブリックを提示することは，教師が生徒に求めるパフォーマンスを共有することにつながるため，生徒に見通しを持たせたり，生徒が目標を具体的に理解するのを助けたりすることができる。これらを1文の英語で書けばよい。

【8】Technology allows them more opportunities to express themselves and enables them to communicate with more people. For example, they can make friends with whom they can share their hobbies easily. In this way, they can feel more connected. (38 words)

〈解説〉英文の後半に続く内容を英語で書く問題である。英文の前半では，富裕国において孤独感を感じる人が増えており，その原因として技術発展が挙げられている。スマートフォンやソーシャルメディアが批判される一方で，アメリカでは携帯電話が普及した2009年ごろから子どもが両親と外出する頻度が激減しており，若者がオンラインでつながるようになったと述べられている。そして，空所を含んだ段落冒頭では「しかし，このことが必ずしも若者をより孤独にするとは限らない」と述べられていることを踏まえると，オンラインにおいても，十分なコミュニケーションが可能であるということを説明すればよいだろう。解答例のように，オンラインにおけるコミュニケーションのメリットとして，同じ趣味を持つ多くの人とつながることができるといったことを書けばよい。

2021年度　実施問題

【中高共通】

【１】(Listening Test)

Part A　Listen to the passage. Answer the two questions below by choosing the correct answer from the options from ① to ④ which will be read later. The passage and the options will be read once.

(1)　What "good news" do we need to concentrate on?

(2)　Why does collective leadership still require individuals to make the first move?

Part B　Listen to the passages and the questions. Choose the correct answer from the options from ① to ④ below. The passages and the qestions will be read once.

(1)　Answer: [　　　]

①　People have access to knowledge through the Internet.

②　There are governments with religious and ideological differences.

③　There are international rules for the quality of products.

④　Political relationships among countries are managed by the International Monetary Fund.

(2)　Answer: [　　　]

①　People depended on horses, steam trains, or sailing ships to trade their goods.

②　Christopher Columbus found the Americas while searching for new trade routes.

③　Competition between countries abolishes improvements in transportation.

④　Increased connections encourage countries to promote friendly relations.

Part C　You will hear expressions teachers often use in English class. Write down the whole expression. Each will be read twice.

(☆☆☆◎◎◎◎)

【2】Choose the best item from ① to ④ below each question to fill in the blank.

(1) I was worried that I wouldn't [ ] the speech without crying.

① get through　② go off　③ incorporate with

④ stand up for

(2) Even in the wake of the Second World War, Western liberals still had a very hard time [ ] their supposedly universal values to non-Western people.

① applied　② applying　③ applying for　④ applying to

(3) Zuckerberg says that Facebook is [ ] to continue improving our tools to give you the power to share your experience with others.

① committed　② compiled　③ conveyed　④ convinced

(4) [ ] is literally the suffering that we feel when we yearn for the past to come back to us, yet psychologists find that it is mostly a pleasant state.

① Fantasy　② Illusion　③ Nostalgia　④ Stereotype

(5) We rely on our genes to [ ] the smooth running of our body's normal growth processes.

① aspire　② disrupt　③ endure　④ ensure

(6) Switching to [ ] vehicles is likely to save the lives of a million people every year.

① ambiguous　② ample　③ anonymous　④ autonomous

(☆☆☆☆◎◎◎)

【3】Read the following essay and answer the questions below.

Should we allow the buying and selling of human organs — the hearts, kidneys and livers needed for transplants that can save the lives of seriously ill patients? Many of us would say no. We'd be horrified at the thought of poor people dying because they couldn't [ア]. That's why the sale of organs is illegal. Doctors decide which patients will [イ], but patients often have to wait a long time. In the United States in 2006, 70,000 patients were waiting for kidneys but fewer than 11,000 transplants were carried out and 5,000 people died or became too sick to have one. The American economist Alvin Roth (b.1951) used economic principles to [ウ] without people buying and selling them.

Roth's solution is based on the fact that humans have two kidneys but can survive on a single one, so if your brother needed a kidney you might decide to give him one of yours. The problem is that when the doctors do tests on you and your brother, they might find that your kidney isn't compatible — that it isn't a 'match' for him. Your brother has to go on waiting for a compatible kidney to turn up. Suppose there was another patient and another donor, completely unknown to you, who were in a similar position. What if your kidney was a match for the other patient and the other donor's was a match for your brother? Surely it would be a good idea to do a swap? This is the essence of Roth's solution. It's a version of a basic economic situation: [エ] then we can exchange our goods and both gain. The thing is, it's hard to find each other, which is why we use money: [オ].

Roth designed a system that allowed advantageous exchanges of kidneys without any money changing hands. The first thing is to keep a database of kidney donors and kidney patients. The database is used to find matching kidneys and to exchange them. With advanced mathematics and computer programming Roth was able to calculate complex sequences of exchanges between patients and donors which found matching kidneys for many more patients than before. His method was used to create the New England Program for Kidney Exchange, which worked across fourteen kidney transplant centres in New England in the United States. Thousands of patients received kidneys who wouldn't [A] have done.

Roth's system shows what a huge difference economics can make to people's lives. It's also an example of a different type of economics. So far we've thought about economics as describing how the economy works and judging how well it works. Economists like Roth go further: they use economic theories to create new parts of the economy out there in the real world. Even though it doesn't involve buying and selling, kidney exchange is like a market in the sense that it allows people to [B] things with each other. When Roth set up his database and computer programmes he created something similar to a market where none existed before. It's an example of a new field of economics known as 'market design'.

Most of us will never need to get hold of a kidney, of course, A really famous example of market design — one to do with the mobile phones in our pockets — affects many more of us, and in contrast to kidney exchange it involved buyers paying huge sums of money to sellers. In the 1990s and 2000s, governments hired economists to help sell licences to companies who wanted to use the radio spectrum to set up mobile phone networks. [カ]. But governments couldn't do that for spectrum licences: these kinds of licences had never been sold before and no one knew how much they were worth. Governments decided to auction them. In an auction one seller tries to get the best price from a group of competing buyers. Auctions have been used for centuries to sell artworks and crops. In ancient times there were slave auctions, and once the entire Roman Empire was put up for auction. What's different in today's auctions is that many of them were designed by economists using an important new field of economics called 'auction theory'.

In auctions, some people know more than others. In an art auction, bidders know how much they value a painting, but the seller doesn't, Bidders want the painting for as [C] a price as possible. They'd like to pretend that they value the painting less than they really do. Sellers, on the other hand, want to make sure that winning bidders pay their true valuations. Here, sellers and bidders are playing a game with each other in which some people have more information than others, so auction theory draws on the tools of game theory and information economics that we came across in earlier chapters. Designing auctions is about solving problems of strategy and information to make sure that the bidder with the [　D　] valuation wins, and that the seller [　E　] profit.

(SOURCE: "*A LITTLE HISTORY of ECONOMICS*" by NIALL KISHTAINY)

(No. 1) Choose the most suitable option for each blank [ア], [イ] and [ウ] from ① to ③.

① afford the kidneys that rich people could easily buy

② benefit from transplants and then try to find them suitable donors

③ come up with a way of incrensing the number of organs available for transplant

(No. 2) Choose the most suitable sentence for each blank [エ] and [オ] from ① to ③.

① I sell my fish for £ 3 and then go and buy some cheese

② if I have some fish and want some cheese and you have some cheese and want some fish

③ if you feel hungry and go into a supermarket to get some cheese, then you will find a huge variety to choose from

(No. 3) Choose the most suitable sentence for the blank [カ] from ① to ③.

① The economists insisted that people refrain from using the radio spectrum because of the health problem

② The radio spectrum was so expensive that the government asked other companies to find another way

③ When you're selling apples it's easy: you look at how much apples sell for and sell yours for that amount

(No. 4) Choose the most suitable word from ① to ④ for each blank [A], [B] and [C].

A ① however ② nevertheless ③ otherwise
④ whereas

B ① buy ② create ③ sell
④ swap

C ① competitive ② fair ③ high
④ low

(No. 5) Choose the best combination from ① to ④ in order to fill in the blanks [D] and [E].

① D: highest E: maximises
② D: highest E: minimises
③ D: lowest E: maximises
④ D: lowest E: minimises

(☆☆☆◎◎◎)

【4】The following is a part of General Provisions of MEXT's New Course of Study Guidelines (2017-2018 Revision). Choose the most suitable word from ① to ④ for each blank [ア], [イ], [ウ] and [エ].

Each school should implement class improvements for realization of the proactive, [ア] and authentic learning of the students while anticipating the integration of contents such as units and subject matter, and the hours, so that the matters specified in Ⅰ. 3 from (1) to (3)※ are realized without bias.

In particular, each school should pay attention to the fact that the [イ] and ways of thinking pertinent to each subject (discipline-based epistemological approaches, hereinafter referred to as "Approaches") can be forged in students with their experiences to apply the knowledge and skills they have acquired through subject learning and other educational activities, to exert their abilities to think, make judgement and express themselves, and to [ウ] their motivation to learn, and humanity so that they will grasp and consider targeted subject matter appropriately and deeply and should also promote learning with a focus on the process where students can deepen their understanding by integrating sporadically acquired fragments of knowledge, [エ] closely examined information into thoughts, work out the solutions to the problems they have detected, and come up with new creations based on their desires and ideas, while utilizing Approaches they have acquired through learning, pertinent to each subject.

※ (1) Ensure that knowledge and skills are acquired.

(2) Develop the students' abilities to think, make judgements and express themselves.

(3) Cultivate the motivation to learn and humanity.

ア ① interactive ② interceptive ③ interchangeable
④ intercultural

イ ① consent ② intuition ③ perspectives
④ wit

ウ ① confine ② demonstrate ③ distract
④ revise

エ ① comply ② evoke ③ transport
④ weave

(☆☆☆◎◎◎)

【5】Read the following essay consisting of six paragraphs and answer the questions below.

The communication industry is arguably the one where computers have had the greatest [ア] of all so far. After the introduction of computerized telephone switchboards in the fifties, the internet in the sixties, and the World Wide Web in 1989, billions of people now go online to communicate, shop, read news, watch movies or play games, accustomed to having the world's information just a [イ] away — and often for free. The emerging *internet of things* promises improved efficiency, accuracy, [ウ] and economic benefit from bringing online everything from lamps, thermostats and freezers to biochip transponders on farm animals.

These spectacular successes in connecting the world have brought computer scientists a fourth challenge: they need to improve not only verification, validation and control, but also ***security*** against malicious software ("malware") and hacks. Whereas the aforementioned problems all resulted from unintentional mistakes, security is directed at ***deliberate malfeasance***. The first malware to draw significant media [エ] was the so-called Morris worm, unleashed on November 2, 1988, which exploited bugs in the UNIX operating system. It was allegedly a misguided [オ] to count how many computers were online, and although it infected and crashed about 10% of the 60,000 computers that made up the internet back then, this didn't stop its creator, Robert Morris, from eventually getting a tenured professorship in computer science at MIT.

[カ]

[キ]

[ク]

[ケ]

(SOURCE: "*Life 3.0*" by Max Tegmark)

(No. 1) Choose the most suitable word from ① to ⑥ for each blank [ア] through [オ]. Each word can be used once.

① attempt ② attention ③ click ④ convenience

⑤ identification ⑥ impact

(No. 2) Place these paragraphs from ① to ④ in their appropriate locations [カ] through [ケ].

① As a result, I roll my eyes whenever I read about some new system being allegedly 100% secure and unhackable, Yet "unhackable" is clearly what we need future AI systems to be before we put them in charge of, say, critical infrastructure or weapons systems, so the growing role of AI in society keeps raising the stakes for computer security. While some hacks exploit human gullibility or complex vulnerabilities in newly released software, others enable unauthorized login to remote computers by taking advantage of simple bugs that lingered unnoticed for an embarrassingly long time. The "Heartbleed" bug lasted from 2012 to 2014 in one of the most popular software libraries for secure communication between computers, and the "Bashdoor" bug was built into the very operating system of Unix computers from 1989 until 2014. This means that AI tools for improved verification and validation will improve security as well.

② Other malware exploits vulnerabilities not in software but in people. On May 5, 2000, as if to celebrate my birthday, people got emails with the subject line "ILOVEYOU" from acquaintances and colleagues, and those Microsoft Windows users who clicked on the attachment "LOVE-LETTER-FOR-YOU.txt. vbs" unwittingly launched a script that damaged their computer and re-sent the email to everyone in their address book. Created by two young programmers in the Philippines, this worm infected about 10% of the internet, just as the Morris worm had done, but because the internet was a lot bigger by then, it became one of the greatest infections of all time, afflicting over 50 million computers and causing over $5 billion in damages. As you're probably painfully aware, the internet remains infested with countless kinds of infectious malware, which security experts classify into worms, Trojans, viruses and other intimidating-sounding categories, and the damage they cause ranges from displaying harmless prank messages to deleting your files, stealing your personal information, spying on you and hijacking your computer to send out spam.

③ Unfortunately, better AI systems can also be used to find new vulnerabilities and perform more sophisticated hacks. Imagine, for example, that you one day get an unusually personalized "phishing" email attempting to persuade you to divulge personal information. It's sent from your friend's account by an AI who's hacked it and is impersonating her, imitating her writing style based on an analysis of her other sent emails, and including lots of personal information about you from other sources. Might you fall for this? What if the phishing email appears to come from your credit card company and is followed up by a phone call from a friendly human voice that you can't tell is AI-generated? In the ongoing computer-security arms race between offense and defense, there's so far little indication that defense is winning.

④ Whereas malware targets whatever computer it can, *hackers* attack specific targets of interest — recent high-profile examples including Target, TJ Maxx, Sony Pictures, Ashley Madison, the Saudi oil company Aramco and the U.S. Democratic National Committee. Moreover, the loots appear to be getting ever more spectacular. Hackers stole 130 million credit card numbers and other account information from Heartland Payment Systems in 2008, and breached over a billion(!) Yahoo! email accounts in 2013. A 2014 hack of the U.S. Government's Office of Personnel Management breached personnel records and job application information for over 21 million people, allegedly including employees with top security clearances and the fingerprints of undercover agents.

(☆☆☆☆◎◎◎)

【６】Complete the passage by filling in the blanks with all the items written below. Choose the most suitable item from ① to ⑧ for each blank [ア] through [カ].

Asking questions not only makes an order more palatable; (1) [ア] [　] [　] [　] [イ] [　] [　]. People are more likely to accept an order if they have had a part in the decision that caused the order to be issued.

When Ian Macdonald of Johannesburg, South Africa, the general manager of a small manufacturing plant specializing in precision machine parts, had the opportunity to accept a very large order, he was convinced that he would not meet the promised delivery date. The work already scheduled in the shop and the short completion time needed for this order made it seem impossible for him to accept the order.

Instead (2) [　] [　] [ウ] [　] [　] [　] [エ] [　] through, he called everybody together, explained the situation to them, and told them how much it would mean to the company and to them if they could make it possible to produce the order on time. Then he started asking questions: "Is there anything we can do to handle this order?" "Can anyone think of different ways to process it through the shop that will make it possible to take the order?" "Is (3) [　] [オ] [　] [　] [　] [カ] [　] [　] help?"

The employees came up with many ideas and insisted that he take the order. They approached it with a "We can do it" attitude, and the order was accepted, produced and delivered on time.

(SOURCE: "*How to Win Friends & Influence People*" by DALE CARNEGLE)

(1)
① ask　　② it
③ of　　④ often stimulates
⑤ the creativity　　⑥ the persons
⑦ you　　⑧ whom

(2) ① accelerate ② and rush
③ his people ④ of
⑤ pushing ⑥ the order
⑦ their work ⑧ to

(3) ① any ② our hours or
③ personnel assignments ④ that
⑤ there ⑥ to adjust
⑦ way ⑧ would

(☆☆☆☆◎◎◎)

【7】The following is a conversation between an ALT (assistant language teacher) and a JTE (Japanese teacher of English). Fill in the gap to make it flow with one English sentence.

ALT : Ms. Ishikawa, have you heard of "PDCA" ?

JTE : Yes. This process is said to be effective for education. You have to think about how to do "PDCA" ?

ALT : I see. How do you implement this process to improve students' English proficiency in English education?

JTE : ____.

(☆☆☆◎◎◎)

【8】Complete the passage by filling in the blank with 30 or more words in English starting with the given word.

Technology exaggerates both the vices and the virtues of humanity. Our vices are made worse because now they are downloadable, portable, and socially transmissible. The ability to distract or delude yourself has never been greater, and as a result we are facing crises of both privacy and politics. Though those dangers are real, there is also opportunity created in their wake. For those who know how to use technology wisely, it is the easiest time in history to teach yourself something new. An amount of information vaster than was held by the Library of Alexandria is freely accessible to anyone with a device and an internet connection. Top universities such as Harvard, MIT, and Yale are publishing their best courses for free online. Forums and discussion platforms mean that you can learn in groups without ever leaving your home.

Added to these new advantages is software that accelerates the act of learning itself. Consider learning a new language, such as Chinese. A half century ago, learners needed to consult cumbersome paper dictionaries, which made learning to read a nightmare.

Today's learner

(SOURCE: "*ULTRALEARNING*" by Scott H. Young)

(☆☆☆☆◎◎◎)

解答・解説

【中高共通】

【1】Part A　(1)　③　　(2)　④　　Part B　(1)　①　　(2)　④

Part C　(No.1)　Any volunteers?　　(No.2)　You're getting better.　(No.3)　How do you pronounce it?　　(No.4)　Would you turn off the light?　　(No.5)　Put your eraser between you and your partner.

〈解説〉スクリプトは非公開である。Part Aはパッセージを聞き，問題用紙に印刷された質問文を読んで，音声で流れる選択肢から解答を選ぶ4択問題，Part Bはパッセージと質問文を聞き，問題用紙に印刷された選択肢から解答を選ぶ4択問題。ともに放送は1度のみである。Part Cはディクテーションで2回放送される。 Part A (1) 私たちはどんな『良いニュース』に意識を向けるべきかが問われている。(2)の質問文中のleadership still require individuals to make the first moveから，パッセージのトピックは，人を動かすためのリーダーシップに関する話題だと推測できる。 Part B (1) 選択肢に統一性はないが，国際的な政治もしくは経済などの話題だと考えられる。 (2) コロンブスの名前や交易，移動手段に関する単語が見られることから，国際関係についての話題だと推測できる。 Part C 教師がよく教室で使う指示文が放送される。いずれも基本的な表現であるが，スペルミスには注意すること。

【2】(1) ① (2) ② (3) ① (4) ③ (5) ④ (6) ④

〈解説〉(1) 英文は「私はそのスピーチを泣かずに終えられないだろうと心配だった」の意である。get throughは「～をやり終える，切り抜ける」。 (2)「第2次世界大戦直後でさえ，西洋の自由主義者は，普遍的価値観と考えられていたものを非西洋人に適用することに非常に苦労していた」。have a hard time ～ingは「～するのにとても苦労する」，apply A to B「AをBに適用する」。 (3)「フェイスブックは，経験を他者と分かち合う力を与える私たちの道具を改良し続けることに，全力を尽くしているとザッカーバーグは述べている」。be committed to ～ingは「～することに全力を尽くす，専心する」。 (4)「懐古は過去が戻ってきてほしいと懐かしく思う時に感じる苦しみであるが，心理学者はこれが大抵は心地よい状態であることを発見している」。nostalgiaは「懐古，ノスタルジア」。 (5)「私たちは，遺伝子に頼って，身体の正常な成長過程のスムーズな進行を確保している」。rely on A to do「Aが～するのを当てにする，頼る」，ensureは「確かにする」。
(6)「自律走行車に切り替えることは年間百万人の命を救う可能性がある」。autonomousは「自律的な，自動の」。

【3】(No.1)　ア　①　　イ　②　　ウ　③　　(No.2)　エ　②
オ　①　　(No.3)　カ　③　　(No.4)　A　③　　B　④　　C　④
(No.5)　①

〈解説〉(No.1)　ア　poor peopleが主語なので①「裕福な人が容易に買える腎臓を買う余裕がなかった」が適切。can affordは「～を買う余裕がある」。　イ　doctorsが主語なので②「どの患者が臓器移植から恩恵を得られるかを決定し，彼らに適切なドナーを探そうとする」が適切。ウ　直前のeconomic principles「経済的指針」を説明する内容が空所ウなので③「臓器移植に利用できる臓器の数を増やす方法を思いつく」が適切。　(No.2)　エ　直後のwe can exchange our goods and both gainから，お互いに交換できる物を持っているという内容が入ると考えられるため②が適切。　オ　物を交換する人を探すのが困難であるため私たちはお金を使うのであると直前に述べられている。よって空所に入るのは物々交換ではなく売買をするという内容であるため①が適切。
(No.3)　空所直前では1990年代や2000年代では携帯電話のネットワークを構築するために電波スペクトルを用いたいという企業にライセンスを売るのを手助けする経済学者を政府が雇用したことが述べられている。空所直後には電波スペクトルのライセンスにおいてはそうすることができなかったと述べられている。ここから，空所には容易に行うことができた内容もしくは具体例が入ると考えられる。よって，③「りんごを売るならとても簡単だ。りんごがいくらで売れるのかを見てその値段で売ればよい」が適切だと判断できる。
(No.4)　A　otherwise「もしそうでなければ」はよく仮定法と共に用いられる。　B　exchangeと同様の意味を持つswap「交換する」が適切。C　オークションでは入札者はできるだけ安い値段で入札したいものであるためlowが適切。　(No.5)　最終パラグラフではオークションの性質が述べられている。最も高い評価額の入札者が勝ち，売り手は利益を最大化するのがその性質と考えられるので，①が適切と判断できる。

【4】ア ①　イ ③　ウ ②　エ ④

〈解説〉中学校学習指導要領(平成29年告示)の英訳からの出題である。抜粋箇所は，日本語版の「第1章　総則　第3　教育課程の実施と学習評価　1　主体的・対話的で深い学びの実現に向けた授業改善」に該当する。　ア　空所前後の日本語は「単元や題材など内容や時間のまとまりを見通しながら，生徒の主体的・対話的で深い学びの実現に向けた授業改善を行うこと」である。「対話的」はinteractiveが適切。　イ　空所前後の日本語は「各教科等の特質に応じた物事を捉える視点や考え方」である。「視点」はperspectiveが適切。　ウ　空所前後の日本語は「学びに向かう力，人間性等を発揮させたり」である。「発揮する」はdemonstrateが適切。　エ　空所前後の日本語は「情報を精査して考えを形成したり」である。weave A into Bは「AからBをまとめ上げる，作り上げる」の意味。

【5】(No.1)　ア ⑥　イ ③　ウ ④　エ ②　オ ①
(No.2)　カ ②　キ ④　ク ①　ケ ③

〈解説〉(No.1)　ア　have a great impactで「大きな影響を持つ」。ここでは形容詞greatの最上級greatestが用いられている。　イ　空所直前ではインターネットの発達によって手軽に様々なことができるようになったことが述べられている。それを端的に表現しているのがjust a click away「マウスでクリックするだけ」となる。　ウ　空所を含む文ではあらゆる物におけるインターネットの様々な利点について述べられているためconvenienceが適切。　エ　drawと結びつくのはattentionで，「注意を引く」の意。　オ　直後にto不定詞を続けられるのはattemptのみで「～する試み」の意。　(No.2)　カ　前パラグラフでは最初のマルウェアについて述べられている。その後に，Other malwareという書き出しでさらに大きな被害をもたらした別のマルウェアの説明が続くと考えられるため，②が適切。　キ　①と③の冒頭では，冒頭のAs a resultやUnfortunatelyという語句や，その後の文が②のパラグラフと結びつかないことから，②に続くのは④と判断する。④のパラグラフでは，マルウェアと対比して，ハッカーの実例とその大きな被害が紹介されている。　ク　④のパラグラフでのハッカーの実例に続くのは，冒頭で「筆者は，100%ハッキングされないとされている新しいシステムについて書かれているものを読むと，あきれて目をむいてしまう」と疑念を表している①と判断できる。roll one's eyesは「目をむく，あきれた表情をする」の意味。　ケ　①のパラグラフの最後でAIシステムの安全性が求められていることが述べられている。よって，①に続くのは，AIシステムまでも利用した，友人を装うメールなどのさらに進化したハッキングの脅威があり，まだ安全は確保されていないという現状が述べられている③であると判断できる。

【6】(1)　ア　④　　イ　⑧　　(2)　ウ　③　　エ　②　　(3)　オ　①　カ　③

〈解説〉(1)　空所部分を整序するとit often stimulates the creativity of the persons whom you askとなる。whomの先行詞はpersonsと確定できるため，the persons whom you askまでをまずひとかたまりとする。stimulatesに3単現のsがあることから主語はitかthe creativityのどちらかだが，the creativityを主語にしてしまうとitが目的語となるが，何を指すのか不明である。itが主語とすると前文のasking questionsを指すことになり，the creativityを目的語に取ることになり，全体がうまくつながる。　(2)　空所部分を整序するとof pushing his people to accelerate their work and rush the orderとなる。instead of「～の代わりに，～ではなく」。he called以下は会社の従業員に丁寧に状況の説明を行っているという記述であるため，逆接の意味のinstead of以下では，それとは逆の不親切で雑な対応が来ることがわかる。ofの後は名詞か動名詞となるので，動名詞のpushingをofの後につなげ，push his people to do「従業員に～するようせかす」の形を作る。to以下はaccelerate their workとrush the orderをandで結びつける。　(3)　空所部分を整序するとthere any way to adjust our hours or personnel assignments that would helpとなる。Is there anything～?の疑問文が2文前にあるため，ここでも同様の形式が用いられると予測できる。wayの後はto不定詞を取ることができるのでadjustを置き，our hours or personnel assignmentsを目的語として，「勤務時間や人員配置を調整する」となる。その後は関係代名詞thatでwould helpとつなげる。

【7】An important part of this process is that after the plan has been executed, success or failure will always be evaluated and lead to improvement.

〈解説〉PDCAとはビジネス用語でよく用いられるPlan(計画)，Do(実行)，Check(評価)，Action(改善)を繰り返し行うことで，継続的な業務の改善を促すサイクルである。解答例のように「計画と実行の後に，評価を行い改善に結びつける」と簡潔にまとめればよい。

【8】(Today's learner) has spaced-repetition systems to memorize vocabulary, document readers that translate with the tap of a button, voluminous podcast libraries offering endless opportunities for practice, and translation apps that smooth the transition to immersion. (33words)

〈解説〉最初のパラグラフではインターネットなどの技術の進化による長所と短所について述べられている。空所部分のある第2パラグラフでは，新たな利点として言語学習のためのソフトウェアが加わったことが冒頭に書かれ，次の文では便利な機器がなかった過去の時代の苦労は大変なものであったと述べられている。それを受けての空所部分で，主語がToday's learnerとなっていることから，解答例のような繰り返し練習するポッドキャストや語彙を覚えるためのシステム，翻訳のアプリケーションを活用することができるという，現代に実在する具体的な活用例を述べればよいだろう。

2020年度　実施問題

【中高共通】

【１】(Listening Test)

Part A　Listen to the passage. Answer the two questions below by choosing the correct answer from the options from ① to ④ which will be read later. The passage and the options will be read once.

(1)　What didn't Issac Newton know?

(2)　How can geologists build up gravitational maps of the Earth beneath?

Part B　Listen to the passages and the questions. Choose the correct answer from the options from ① to ④ below. The passages and the questions will be read once.

(1)　Answer : [ ]

①　You actually need friends to have good relationships with others.

②　Having friends is good because they celebrate good things with us.

③　If you have good friends, you are 50 percent more likely to live longer.

④　Being lonely can be more dangerous for our health than smoking 15 cigarettes a day.

(2)　Answer : [ ]

①　It's easy to bring up two or more kids under the same roof.

②　More than 31 percent of children were happy because their brother or sister was a good friend.

③　An argument between siblings is a good opportunity to face problems in an emotionally safe environment.

④　It's good for our physical health to communicate in the family.

Part C　You will hear expressions teachers often use in English class. Write down the whole expression. Each will be read twice.

(☆☆☆◎◎◎)

【2】Choose the best item from ① to ④ below each question to fill in the blank.

(1) Humanity has very little time [   ] wean itself from fossil fuels.

① leaving ② left to ③ to leave ④ to leave to

(2) Those who are [   ] clothes end up confused about how to dress themselves in mufti.

① indifference at ② indifference with ③ indifferent from
④ indifferent to

(3) It is true that the more often you get what you demand, the [   ] that you will start to believe it's because you deserve it — an unattractive attitude at any age.

① better is likely ② better likely it is ③ more is likely
④ more likely it is

(4) Historians often argue that globalisation [   ] a first peak in 1913, then went into a long decline during the era of the world wars and the Cold War.

① reached ② regulated ③ resisted ④ revised

(5) To compete successfully in an [   ] global market, a company has to know the costs of its entire economic chain and has to work with other members of the chain to manage costs and maximize yield.

① increase competing ② increased competition
③ increasing competitor ④ increasingly competitive

(6) We cannot yet tell with certainly what the next society and the next economy will look [   ].

① alike ② back ③ forward ④ like

(☆☆☆◎◎◎◎◎)

【3】Read the following story and answer the questions below.

It was 1989 and I was in a remote and extremely poor village named Makanga in the Bandundu region of what was then Zaire and is now the

Democratic Republic of Congo. I was part of a team investigating an epidemic of the incurable paralytic disease called konzo that I had first discovered in Mozambique years earlier.

The research project had been two years in the planning and everything — all the approvals, drivers, translators, and lab equipment — had been meticulously prepared. But I had made one serious mistake. [ア] I wanted to interview all the villagers and take samples of their food, and their blood and urine, and I should have been with the head of the village when he explained that to them.

That morning, as I had been quietly and methodically setting up in the hut, I heard villagers starting to gather outside. They somehow seemed uneasy but I was [A] with getting the blood sample machine to work. Eventually I managed to start the diesel generator and do a test run with the centrifuge. The machines were noisy and it was only when I switched them off that I heard the raised voices. Things had changed in seconds. I bent forward and stepped out of the low door. It had been dark in the hut and when I straightened up at first I couldn't see a thing. Then I saw: a crowd of maybe 50 people, all upset and angry. Some of them were pointing their fingers at me. Two men raised muscled arms and waved big machete knives.

That was when the teacher, my translator, suggested we run. I looked right and left and saw [B] to go. If the villagers really wanted to hurt me there were enough of them to hold me back and let the machete men cut me down.

"What's the problem?" I asked the teacher.

"They are saying that you are selling the blood. You are cheating us. You are giving money only to the chief, and then you are going to make something with the blood that will hurt us. They say you shouldn't steal their blood."

This was very bad. [イ] "Can I explain?" I asked the villagers. "I can either leave your village right away, if you want, or I can explain why we have come."

"Tell us first," the people said. (Life is boring in these remote villages, so they probably thought, We can let him talk first, and we can kill him afterward.) The crowd held back the men with the machetes: "Let him talk."

This was the talk we should have had before. If you want to go into a village to do research, you have to take small steps, take your time, and be respectful. You have to let people ask all their questions, and you have to answer them.

[ウ] I had photos from Mozambique and Tanzania, where I had studied konzo before, which I showed them. They were very interested in the photos. "We think it's linked to how you prepare the cassava," I said.

"No, no, no," they said.

"Well, we want to do this research, to test whether we are right. If we can find out, maybe you won't get the disease anymore."

Many of the children in the village had konzo. We had noticed them when we first arrived, lagging behind while the other children ran alongside our jeep with charming curiosity. I had spotted some children in this crowd with the classic spastic walking style too.

People began to mumble. One of the machete men, the more dangerous-looking one, with bloodshot eyes and a big scar down his forearm, started screaming again.

And then a barefoot woman, perhaps 50 years old, stepped out of the crowd. She strode toward me and then turned, threw out her arms, and in a loud voice said, "Can't you hear that it makes sense, what he is saying? Shut up! It makes sense. This blood test is necessary. Don't you remember everyone who died from measles? [カ] OK?"

The crowd shouted back, unmollified. "Yes, measles vaccine was good. But now they want to come take our blood, blah, blah, blah."

The woman paused, then took a step toward the crowd. "How do you think they discovered the measles vaccine? [キ] No, they do what this doctor calls" — and she looked at me — "RE-SEAR-CHE." As she repeated the word the translator had used for research, she turned round and pointed at me. "That is how they find out how to cure diseases. Don't you see?"

We were in the most remote part of Bandundu, and here this woman had stepped up like the secretary of the Academy of Science and defended scientific research.

"I have a grandchild crippled for life by this *konzo*. The doctor says he can't cure it. [ク] This makes sense to me. We, the people of Makanga, need this 'research.'" Her dramatic talent was amazing. But she didn't use it to distort the facts. She used it to explain them. Forcefully, in a manner I had seen confident African women act in villages many times before, she rolled up her left sleeve. She turned her back on the crowd, pointed with her other hand to the crook of her arm, and looked me in the eyes. "Here, Doctor. Take my [ケ]."

(SOURCE： "FACTFULNESS" by Hans Rosling)

(No.1) Choose the most suitable sentence for each blank [ア], [イ] and [ウ] from ① to ④.

① I asked him if he would translate for me and then I turned to the crowd.

② I had not explained properly to the villagers what I wanted to do and why.

③ I started to explain that we were working on a disease named konzo.

④ I tried to buy the blood of the agitated crowd in front of me.

(No.2) Choose the most suitable word from ① to ④ for each blank [A] and [B].

A ① accompanied ② occupied ③ satisfied ④ treated

B ① anywhere ② nowhere ③ somewhere ④ wherever

(No.3) Complete the story by filling in each blank [カ] [キ] and [ク] with the most suitable item from ① to ③.

① But if we let him study us, perhaps he will find a way to stop it, like they stopped measles, so that we don't have to see our children and our grandchildren crippled anymore.

② Do you think it grows on trees in their countries? Do you think they pulled it out of the ground?

③ So many of our children died. Then they came and gave the children the vaccine, remember, and now no child ever dies of that disease.

(No.4) Choose the most suitable word from ① to ④ for the blank [ケ].

① blood ② food ③ grandchild ④ machete

(No.5) Choose the sentence from ① to ⑤ which does not match the content of the story.

① The writer didn't hear the villagers' raised voices until he switched off the blood sample machine.

② The writer's translator suggested to him that they should run away when they were surrounded by the angry villagers.

③ It was not easy for the writer to convince the villagers of the safety of the research.

④ The writer noticed that some children were suffering from measles when he arrived at the village.

⑤ The woman's grandchild became disabled because of the incurable paralytic disease called konzo.

(☆☆☆◎◎◎◎◎)

【4】The following is a part of the official translations of the CEFR Global Scale. Choose the most suitable word from ① to ④ for each blank [ア], [イ], [ウ], and [エ]. (CEFR: Common European Framework of Reference for Languages)

Independent User	B2	Can understand the main ideas of complex text on both concrete and abstract topics, including technical discussions in his/her field of specialisation. Can interact with a degree of fluency and spontaneity that makes regular interaction with native speakers quite possible without [ア] for either party. Can produce clear, detailed text on a wide range of subjects and explain a viewpoint on a topical issue giving the advantages and disadvantages of various options.
	B1	Can understand the main points of clear standard input on familiar matters regularly [イ] in work, school, leisure, etc. Can deal with most situations likely to arise whilst travelling in an area where the language is spoken. Can produce simple connected text on topics which are familiar or of personal interest. Can describe experiences and events, dreams, hopes & ambitions and briefly give reasons and explanations for opinions and plans.
Basic User	A2	Can understand sentences and frequently used expressions related to areas of most immediate [ウ] (e.g. very basic personal and family information, shopping, local geography, employment). Can communicate in simple and routine tasks requiring a simple and direct exchange of information on familiar and routine matters. Can describe in simple terms aspects of his/her background, immediate environment and matters in areas of immediate need.
	A1	Can understand and use familiar everyday expressions and very basic phrases aimed at the [エ] of needs of a concrete type. Can introduce him/herself and others and can ask and answer questions about personal details such as where he/she lives, people he/she knows and things he/she has. Can interact in a simple way provided the other person talks slowly and clearly and is prepared to help.

ア　① intuition　② melancholy　③ strain
　　④ translation

イ　① decreased　② encountered　③ illuminated
　　④ quoted

ウ　① doctrine　② relevance　③ segment
　　④ transaction

エ　① dismay　② intervention　③ phase
　　④ satisfaction

(☆☆☆◎◎◎)

【５】Read the following essay consisting of seven paragraphs and answer the questions below.

The modern economy grows thanks to our trust in the future and to the willingness of capitalists to reinvest their profits in production. Yet that does not suffice. Economic growth also requires energy and raw materials, and these are finite. When and if they run out, the entire system will collapse.

But the evidence provided by the past is that they are finite only in theory. Counter-intuitively, while humankind's use of energy and raw materials has [ア] in the last few centuries, the amounts available for our exploitation have actually *increased*. Whenever a shortage of either has threatened to slow economic growth, investments have [イ] into scientific and technological research. These have invariably produced not only more efficient ways of exploiting existing resources, but also completely new types of energy and materials.

Consider the vehicle industry. Over the last 300 years, humankind has [ウ] billions of vehicles — from carts and wheelbarrows, to trains, cars, supersonic jets and space shuttles. One might have expected that such a prodigious effort would have [エ] the energy sources and raw materials available for vehicle production, and that today we would be scraping the bottom of the barrel. Yet the opposite is the case. Whereas in 1700 the global vehicle industry relied overwhelmingly on wood and iron, today it has at its disposal a cornucopia of new-found materials such as plastic, rubber, aluminium and titanium, none of which our ancestors even knew about. Whereas in 1700 carts were built mainly by the muscle power of carpenters and smiths, today the machines in Toyota and Boeing factories are powered by petroleum combustion engines and nuclear power stations. A similar revolution has [オ] almost all other fields of industry. We call it the Industrial Revolution.

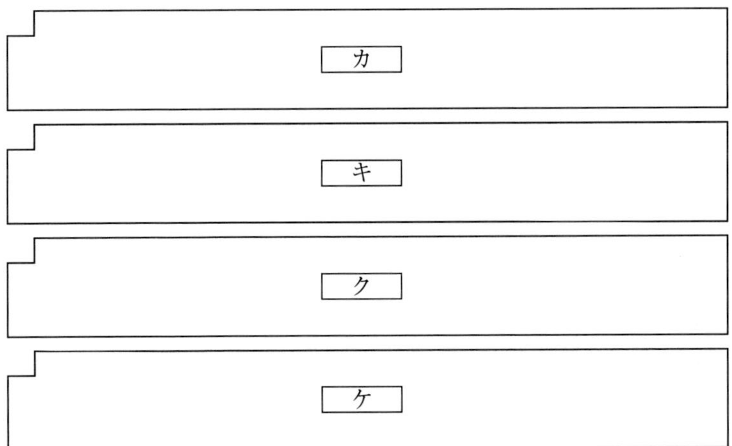

(SOURCE：“*Sapiens -A Brief History of Humankind-*” by Yuval Noah Harari)

(No.1)　Choose the most suitable word from ① to ⑥ for each blank [ア] through [オ]. Each word can be used once.

① exhausted　② flowed　③ manufactured

④ mistaken　⑤ mushroomed　⑥ swept

(No.2)　Place these paragraphs from ① to ④ in their appropriate locations [カ] through [ケ].

① An even bigger problem was that people didn't know how to convert one type of energy into another. They could harness the movement of wind and water to sail ships and push millstones, but not to heat water or smelt iron. Conversely, they could not use the heat energy produced by burning wood to make a millstone move. Humans had only one machine capable of performing such energy conversion tricks: the body. In the natural process of metabolism, the bodies of humans and other animals burn organic fuels known as food and convert the released energy into the movement of muscles. Men, woman and beasts could consume grain and meat, burn up their carbohydrates and fats, and use the energy to haul a rickshaw or pull a plough.

② For millennia prior to the industrial Revolution, humans already knew how to make use of a large variety of energy sources. They burned wood in order to smelt iron, heat houses and bake cakes. Sailing strips harnessed wind power to move around, and watermills captured the flow of rivers to grind grain. Yet all these had clear limits and problems. Trees were not available everywhere, the wind didn't always blow when you needed it, and water power was only useful if you lived near a river.

③ Human history was consequently dominated by two main cycles: the growth cycles of plants and the changing cycles of solar energy (day and night, summer and winter). When sunlight was scarce and when wheat fields were still green, humans had little energy. Granaries were empty, tax collectors were idle, soldiers found it difficult to move and fight, and kings tended to keep the peace. When the sun shone brightly and the wheat ripened, peasants harvested the crops and filled the granaries. Tax collectors hurried to take their share. Soldiers flexed their muscles and sharpened their swords. Kings convened councils and planned their next campaigns. Everyone was fuelled by solar energy — captured and packaged in wheat, rice and potatoes.

④ Since human and animal bodies were the only energy conversion device available, muscle power was the key to almost all human activities. Human muscles built carts and houses, ox muscles ploughed fields, and horse muscles transported goods. The energy that fuelled these organic muscle-machines came ultimately from a single source — plants. Plants in their turn obtained their energy from the sun. By the process of photosynthesis, they captured solar energy and packed it into organic compounds. Almost everything people did throughout history was fuelled by solar energy that was captured by plants and converted into muscle power.

(☆☆☆☆◎◎◎)

【6】Complete the passage by filling in the blanks with all the items written below. Choose the most suitable item from ① to ⑧ for each blank [ア] through [カ].

The foundation of effective leadership is thinking through the organization's mission, defining it, and establishing it, clearly and visibly. The leader sets the goals, sets the priorities, and sets and maintains the standards. He makes compromises, of course; indeed, effective leaders are painfully aware that they are not in control of the universe. (Only misleaders — the Stalins, Hitlers, Maos — suffer from that delusion.) But before accepting a compromise, (1) [ ] [ ] [ ] [ア] [ ] [ ] [イ] [ ]. The leader's first task is to be the trumpet that sounds a clear sound.

What distinguishes the leader from the misleader are his goals. Whether the compromise he makes with the constraints of reality — which may involve political, economic, financial, or interpersonal problems — are (2) [　　] [　　] [ウ] [　　] [　　] [エ] [　　] [　　] determines whether he is an effective leader. And whether he holds fast to a few basic standards (exemplifying them in his own conduct), or whether "standards" for him are what he can get away with, determines whether the leader has followers or only hypocritical time-servers.

The second requirement (3) [　　] [オ] [　　] [　　] [　　] [カ] [　　] [　　] as rank and privilege. Effective leaders are rarely "permissive." But when things go wrong — and they always do — they do not blame others. If Winston Churchill is an example of leadership through clearly defining mission and goals, General George Marshall, America's chief of staff in World War Ⅱ, is an example of leadership through responsibility. Harry Truman's folksy "The buck stops here" is still as good a definition as any.

(SOURCE： "*THE ESSENTIAL DRUCKER*" by Peter F. Drucker)

(1) ① has　② is　③ leader
④ right and desirable　⑤ the effective　⑥ thought
⑦ through　⑧ what

(2) ① compatible　② from　③ his
④ lead away　⑤ mission and goals　⑥ or
⑦ them　⑧ with

(3) ① as　② is　③ leadership
④ rather than　⑤ responsibility　⑥ see
⑦ that　⑧ the leader

(☆☆☆☆◎◎◎◎)

【７】The following is a conversation between an ALT (assistant language teacher) and a JTE (Japanese teacher of English). Fill in the gap to make it flow with one English sentence.

ALT : Ms. Ishikawa, will you give some comments on my lesson plan?

JTE : Fun games are good to entertain students, but I'm afraid they won't learn much in this lesson.

ALT : I see. Do you have any suggestions to make the lesson better?

JTE : ____.

(☆☆☆◎◎◎)

【8】Complete the passage by filling in the blank with 30 or more words in English starting with the given word.

In the twenty-first century we are flooded by enormous amounts of information, and even the censors don't try to block it. Instead, they are busy spreading misinformation or distracting us with irrelevancies. If you live in some provincial Mexican town and you have a smartphone, you can spend many lifetimes just reading Wikipedia, watching TED talks, and taking free online courses. No government can hope to conceal all the information it doesn't like. On the other hand, it is alarmingly easy to inundate the public with conflicting reports and red herrings. People all over the world are but a click away from the latest accounts of the bombardment of Aleppo or of melting ice caps in the Arctic, but there are so many contradictory accounts that it is hard to know what to believe. Besides, countless other things are just a click away, making it difficult to focus, and when politics or science look too complicated it is tempting to switch to some funny cat videos, celebrity gossip, or porn.

In such a world, the last thing a teacher needs to give her pupils is more information. They already have far too much of it.

Instead,

(SOURCE： "*21 Lessons for the 21st Century*" by Yuval Noah Harari)

(☆☆☆◎◎◎)

解答・解説

【中高共通】

【1】Part A　(1)　②　　(2)　④　　Part B　(1)　③　　(2)　③

Part C　(No.1)　Three minutes left.　　(No.2)　Your writing is excellent.
(No.3)　One for each group.　　(No.4)　Let's give her a big hand.
(No.5)　Could you introduce yourself to the class?

〈解説〉スクリプトは公開されていない。Part A，Part Bは選択問題(4択)で放送は1回，Part Cは記述式のディクテーションで，2回放送される。Part A　問題用紙には質問文だけが印刷されており，パッセージと選択肢は音声で流れる。質問文中のIssac Newtonやgravitational mapsから，地球の重力についてのトピックであろうと推測できる。　Part B　パッセージと質問文を聞き，印刷された選択肢から正答を選ぶ。
(1)　選択肢は友人がいることのメリット(いないことのデメリット)に関するものであり，各選択肢の違いを事前に確認しておくとよい。
(2)　選択肢は兄弟姉妹や家族に関するものである。①は兄弟姉妹を育てることの容易さ，②と③は兄弟がいることのメリット，そして④は家族でのコミュニケーションのメリットについてである。　Part C　放送されるのは，教師が使う教室英語である。記述式問題ではあるが，ほとんどが頻出表現であり，スペルが難しい単語も少ない。焦らずに丁寧に取り組みたい。

【2】(1)　②　　(2)　④　　(3)　④　　(4)　①　　(5)　④　　(6)　④

〈解説〉(1)　英文は「人類が化石燃料から脱却するまでほとんど時間が残されていない」の意である。time left to～は「～するために残された時間」の意であり，wean以降がto不定詞でtimeを説明する形になっている。　(2)　英文は「服装に無頓着な人は私服の着用に困ることになる」の意である。「～に無頓着である」の意であるbe indifferent to～の形にする。　(3)　英文は「求めるものが手に入る機会が多くなればなるほど，自分がそれに値するからだとより信じやすくなるのは事実である。これは年齢を問わず厄介な考え方なのだが」の意である。「the＋比較級～，the＋比較級...」は「～すればますます...である」の意である。likelyの比較級はmore likelyであることから，①と②は誤り。また，基本的にこの構文は比較級の後に主語＋動詞の形になることから，空欄後のthat節の形式主語であるitを含んだ④が適切。 (4) 英文は「グローバル化は1913年に最初のピークを迎え，その後の世界大戦や冷戦の間は長期間の後退をしていたと歴史家たちがよく議論している」の意である。「ピークを迎える(機運が高まる)」はreach a peakで表現する。 (5) 英文は「ますます競争の激しいグローバル市場で競り合うために，会社は経済連鎖全体のコストを知り，コストの管理と利益の最大化のために協力しなくてはならない」の意である。空欄前に冠詞，空欄後に名詞があることから，副詞＋形容詞の形になっている④が適切。 (6) 英文は「次世代の社会や経済がどのようになるか，まだ確信をもって言えない」の意である。空欄前のlookに着目し，look like～「～のようである」の形にする。

【3】(No.1) ア ② イ ① ウ ③ (No.2) A ② B ②
(No.3) カ ③ キ ② ク ① (No.4) ① (No.5) ④

〈解説〉(No.1) ア 空欄アの前に「致命的な失敗をした」とあり，後に「村の住民に対するインタビューを行い，食事，血液そして尿のサンプルを取りたかった」とある。そのため，失敗の内容を表す②「村の住民に対して，なぜ私がそうしたいのか，ちゃんと説明をしなかった」が適切。 イ 空欄イの後に「『説明させてほしい』と村の住民に頼んだ」とある。よって，①の「通訳をしてもらえるかたずねてから，群衆の方を向いた」が適切。 ウ 空欄ウの前に「村で調査をする場合には時間をかけて丁寧に手順を踏む必要がある」とあり，後に「以前，コンゾの研究を行ったモザンビークやタンザニアの写真を，村の住民に見せた。彼らは，写真に強い関心を持っていた」とある。したがって，③の「コンゾという名前の病気に取り組んでいたことを説明し始めた」が適切。 (No.2) A 空欄Aを含む文は，「血液サンプルの機械を起動させるのにかかりきりだった」の意味となる。be occupied with「～で忙しい，～に専念する」。 B 空欄Bを含む文は，「左右を見たが行き場がなかった」の意味となる。nowhere to go「行き場がない」。この後の話の展開から，著者たちが走って住民たちから逃げられなかったことがわかるだろう。 (No.3) カ 空欄カの前に「この血液検査が必要だ。麻疹で亡くなった人を覚えていないのか」とあるので，外部の医療関係者によって，子どもたちが麻疹で命を落とさなくなったと述べている③が適切。 キ 空欄キの前に「どのようにして彼らが麻疹のワクチンを見つけたと思うのか」とあり，後に「違う。この医者が『リサーチ』と呼んでいるものから見つけたのだ」とある。よって，ワクチンの入手方法として適切でない内容を述べている②「木から生えたり，地面から引っこ抜いたりするとでも思うのか」が適切。 ク 空欄クの前に「私にはコンゾのせいで手足が不自由になった孫がいる」とあり，後に「私たちにはこの研究が必要だ」とある。よって，これ以上同じ病気に苦しむ子どもたちを減らすために，著者たちに研究をさせたいということを述べている①が適切。(No.4) 文脈から，女性の発言は「お医者さん，どうぞ私の血を採ってください」と推測できる。それ以外は話の展開から不適切である。(No.5) 本文に合致しない内容を選ぶ問題である。(No.3)の空欄カの部分にあるように，著者たちが村に来る前から麻疹のワクチンは普及していたことから，④の「麻疹に苦しんでいる子どもがいた」という部分が誤りである。

【4】ア ③ イ ② ウ ② エ ④

〈解説〉CEFR(Common European Framework of Reference for Languages「外国語の学習・教授・評価のためのヨーロッパ言語共通参照枠」)のglobal scale「等級」におけるA1からB2レベルの説明文に関する問題である。 ア 空欄アを含む箇所は「お互いに緊張せずに母語話者とやり取りができるくらい，流暢さと自然さを伴っている」の意となる。

「緊張」を意味する③が適切。　イ　空欄イを含む箇所は「職場，学校そして娯楽などで出会う身近な話題に関して，明瞭で標準的な話し方であれば，主な内容は理解できる」の意となる。「出会う」を意味する②が適切。　ウ　空欄ウを含む箇所は「直接的に関わりのある分野に関する英文や頻出の表現を理解することができる」の意となる。「関わり」を意味する②が適切。　エ　空欄エを含む箇所は「具体的な欲求を充足するための日常的な表現や基本的な言い回しを理解し，使用することができる」の意となる。「充足，満足」を意味する④が適切。

【5】(No.1)　ア　⑤　　イ　②　　ウ　③　　エ　①　　オ　⑥
(No.2)　カ　②　　キ　①　　ク　④　　ケ　③

〈解説〉(No.1)　ア　空欄アを含む文の前に「エネルギーや原料に限りはあるが，それは理論上にすぎない」と述べていることから，空欄アを含む文は「直観には反するが，人類のエネルギーや原料の使用はここ数世紀で急速に増大した一方で，私たちが開発に使用できる量は増えている」の意となる。「急速に増える」を意味する⑤が適切。
イ　空欄イを含む文は「エネルギーまたは原料の不足が経済成長を減速させたときは，科学や技術研究への投資が行われてきた」の意となる。「(投資やお金)が流れる」を意味する②が適切。　ウ　空欄ウを含む文は「ここ300年以上の間，人類は数十億台もの乗り物を製造してきた」の意となる。「製造する」を意味する③が適切。　エ　空欄エを含む文は「そのような膨大な努力によって乗り物の生産に必要なエネルギー源や材料を使い果たしてしまい，その残りを使用しているのではないか，と思う人もいるかもしれない」の意となる。「使い果たす」を意味する①が適切。　オ　空欄オを含む文は「同じような革命がほとんどの分野の産業に広がっている」の意となる。「広がる，風靡する」を意味する⑥が適切。　(No.2)　英文の後半に続くパラグラフを正しく並べる問題である。　カ　問題の前の英文では，産業革命によって使用できるエネルギー源や材料が増えていることが述べられている。そこで，産業革命というキーワードに着目し，産業革命よりもずっと前の先史時代から人類は多様なエネルギー資源を用いていたという内容の②を最初に置く。　キ　②の後半に，先史時代の人類は木，風そして水といった自然の力を利用していたが，それらはいつでも利用できないという問題があったと述べられている。そこで，問題というキーワードに着目し，古代の人類が抱えるエネルギー資源の利用に関する問題を述べている①をつなげる。　ク　①の後半には，古代の人類はエネルギーを変換することに限界があり，ヒトや動物が代謝によって得たエネルギーを人力車や鋤などの運動エネルギーにしか用いることができなかったと述べられている。そこで，ヒトや動物の運動エネルギーというキーワードに着目し，それらが人類の様々な活動で活用されたことが書かれている④を続ける。　ケ　④の後半には，歴史上の人類の活動は全てが太陽エネルギーによって支えられていたことが述べられている。そこで，人類の歴史と太陽エネルギーに着目すると，人類の歴史が植物の成長サイクルと太陽エネルギーの変化に左右されてきたと書かれている③が続くとわかる。

【6】(1)　ア　⑥　　イ　②　　(2)　ウ　③　　エ　④　　(3)　オ　⑦　カ　①

〈解説〉(1)　空欄部を整序すると，the effective leader has thought through what is right and desirableとなる。空欄部を含んだ英文は「しかし，妥協を受け入れる前に，有能なリーダーは何が正しくて望ましいかを熟慮する」の意である。　(2)　空欄部を整序すると，compatible with his mission and goals or lead away from themとなる。空欄部を含んだ英文は「現実の制約—それは政治的，経済的，財政的，または対人関係的な問題である—によって行う妥協が彼の使命や目標に適合しているか，または離れているかどうかが，彼が有能なリーダーであるかを決める」の意である。　(3)　空欄部を整序すると，is that the leader see leadership as responsibility rather thanとなる。空欄部を含んだ英文は「2つ目の条件は，リーダーが指導者の地位を階級や特権ではなく責任と捉えることである」の意である。

【7】Why don’t you make it a review of the previous lesson by having them use the words and phrases they have learned?

〈解説〉与えられた会話文におけるJTEの立場になり，ALTに提案する内容を英語で書く問題である。ALTがゲームを中心とした指導案を考えてきたので，生徒たちがあまり学ぶことができない懸念を伝えたところ，それに対する助言を求めてきたという場面である。解答例のように，ゲームを中心とする方向性は維持しつつ，既有知識を活用させるよう工夫するという提案のほかに，ゲームを中心とする代わりに，現実の使用場面を意識した言語活動を提案することも可能だろう。

【8】(Instead,) people need the ability to make sense of information, to tell the difference between what is important and what is unimportant, and above all to combine many bits of information into a broad picture of the world. (37 words)

〈解説〉英文の後半に続く内容を英語で書く問題である。英文の前半では，21世紀は様々な情報が容易に手に入る情報過多の時代であり，情報リテラシーが求められていること，そして，生徒が既に多くの情報を持っていることから，教師の役割はただ多くの情報を与えることではないと述べられている。この流れを受けて，Insteadにつながるように，この情報過多時代に求められる教師の役割を英語で記述すればよい。解答例のように，生徒の情報リテラシーを高める手立てを論じればよいだろう。

2019年度　実施問題

【中高共通】

【１】(Listening Test)

Part A　Listen to the passages and the questions. Choose the correct answers to the questions. Then mark the number ①, ②, ③, or ④ on your answer sheet. Each passage and question will be read once.

(1)　Answer : [　　]

① No other planet in the universe has so many colors.

② Through a process called evaporation, water flows into the seas.

③ Water can be gentle when it is liquid, and rough when solid.

④ Water goes through a cycle that never ends, playing a vital role for life.

(2)　Answer : [　　]

① Foreigners often praise Japanese politeness.

② He traveled in Europe and America.

③ Japanese people apologize too much.

④ Politeness is a matter of personal opinion.

Part B　Listen to the passage and answer the two questions by choosing the correct answers from the alternatives below. The passage will be read once.

(1)　When was the first plastic made?

① In 1907.　② In 1945.　③ In 1950.　④ In 1998.

(2)　How does the production of plastic in 2015 compare to that in 1998?

① 9.1 billion tons.　② 448 million tons.

③ Twice the amount.　④ Twenty perent more.

Part C　You will hear expressions teachers often use in English class. Write down the whole sentence. Each sentence will be read twice.

(☆☆☆◎◎◎)

【2】Choose the best item from ① to ④ below each question to fill in the blank.

(1) Most important, however, [ ] the first prize in the oratorical contest was a year's scholarship in the college.

① that was the fact ② the fact that ③ the fact was that

④ was the fact that

(2) Scientists tried to find out how long the human brain could labor without reaching 'a diminished capacity for work,' the scientific [ ] of fatigue.

① anticipation ② definition ③ institution

④ medication

(3) My mother wanted me to [ ] religious work, so I thought seriously of becoming a foreign missionary.

① devote my life to ② devote to my life for

③ devoting my life to ④ devoting to my life for

(4) General Motors Research Laboratories have spent [ ] trying to find out how and why a spark in the cylinder sets off an explosion that makes a car run.

① year of time and million of dollar

② year of time and millions of dollars

③ years of time and millions of dollars

④ years of times and millions of dollars

(5) While conducting adult-education classes in New York City, I have discovered that one of the [ ] regrets of many adults is that they never went to college.

① major ② majorities ③ majority ④ majors

(6) If you need to apologize to someone and you can't bring yourself to do so in person, you can hire the Tianjin Apology Company to apologize [ ].

① for your sympathy ② on your behalf ③ up to yourself

④ within yourself

(☆☆☆◎◎◎◎)

【３】Read the following passage and answer the questions below.

How do we even decide whether two animals belong in the same species or in two different species? Where animals reproduce sexually, we can come up with a sort of definition. Animals belong to different species if they don't breed together. There are borderline cases like horses and donkeys, which can breed together but produce offspring (called mules or hinnies) that are infertile — that is, that cannot have offspring themselves. We therefore place a horse and a donkey in different species. More obviously, horses and dogs belong to different species because [ア], and couldn't produce offspring if they did, even infertile ones. But spaniels and poodles belong to the same species because [イ], and the puppies that [ウ].

Every scientific name of an animal or plant [エ] two Latin words, usually printed in *italics*. The first word refers to the 'genus' or group of species and the second to the individual species within the genus. *Homo sapiens* ('wise man') and *Elephas maximus* ('very big elephant') are examples. Every species is a member of a genus. *Homo* is a genus. So is *Elephas*. The lion is *Panthera Leo* and the genus *Panthera* also includes *Panthera tigris* (tiger), *Panthera pardus* (leopard or 'panther') and *Panthera onca* (jaguar). *Homo sapiens* is the only [オ] species of our genus, but fossils have been given names like *Home erectus* and *Homo habilis*. Other human-like fossils are sufficiently different from *Homo* to be placed in a different genus, for example *Australopithecus africanus* and *Australopithecus afarensis* (nothing to [カ] Australia, by the way: australo - just means 'southern', which is where Australia's name also comes from).

Each genus belongs to a *family*, usually printed in ordinary 'roman' type with a capital initial. Cats (including lions, leopards, cheetahs, lynxes and lots of smaller cats) make up the family Felidae. Every [A] belongs to an *order*. Cats, dogs, bears, weasels and hyenas belong to different families within the [B] Carnivora. Monkeys, apes (including us) and lemurs all belong to different families within the [　B　] Primates. And every order belongs to a class. All mammals are in the [　C　] Mammalia.

Can you see the shape of a tree developing in your mind as you read this description of the sequence of groupings? It is a family tree: a tree with many branches, each branch having sub-branches, and each sub-branch having sub-sub-branches. The tips of the twigs are species. The other groupings－class, order, family, genus－are the branches and sub-branches. The whole tree is all of life on Earth.

Think about why trees have so many twigs. Branches branch. When we have enough branches of branches of branches, the total number of twigs can be very large. That's what happens in evolution. Charles Darwin himself drew a branching tree as the only picture in his most famous book, *On the Origin of Species*. He sketched an early version in one of his notebooks some years earlier. At the top of the page he wrote a mysterious little message to himself: 'I think'. What do you think he meant? Maybe he started to write a sentence and one of his children interrupted him so he never finished it. Maybe he found it easier to represent quickly what he was thinking in (ク) this diagram than in words. Perhaps we shall never know. There is other handwriting on the page, but (ケ) it is hard to decipher. It is tantalizing to read the actual notes of a great scientist, written on a particular day and never meant for publication.

(SOURCE : "*THE MAGIC OF REALITY*" by Richard Dawkins)

(No.1) Choose the most suitable item for each blank [ア], [イ] and [ウ] from ① to ④.

① they can produce infertile offspring

② they don't even try to interbreed

③ they happily interbreed

④ they produce are fertile

(No.2) Choose the most suitable word or phrase from ① to ④ for each blank [　エ　], [　オ　] and [　カ　].

[エ] ① agrees with ② belongs to ③ brings about
④ consists of

[オ] ① declining ② including ③ surviving
④ vanishing

[カ] ① do with. ② give with ③ handle with
④ treat with

(No.3) Choose the best combination from ① to ⑥ to fill in the blanks [A], [B] and [C].

① A: class B: family C: order
② A: class B: order C: family
③ A: family B: class C: order
④ A: family B: order C: class
⑤ A: order B: class C: family
⑥ A: order B: family C: class

(No.4) Choose the most suitable phrase from ① to ④ that the underlined words (ク) refer to.

① a branching tree ② a mysterious little message
③ his most famous book ④ one of his notebooks

(No. 5) Choose the most suitable expression from ① to ④ that can replace the underlined part (ケ) without changing the meaning.

① it is difficult to understand the meaning
② it is too complicated to encode
③ putting a message into a code is tough
④ you can't discover his handwriting

(☆☆☆◎◎◎)

【4】The following is a part of the essay "Working Toward Transforming Clansses" by Marcel Van Amelsvoort. Chooese the most suitable words from ① to ③ for each blank [ア], [イ], and [ウ].

Demand more from your students. In my experience, too much of the thinking work in English classes is being done by the teachers. More should be done by students. Make students think more, explain more, produce more. I was surprised to never see any dictation or dictogloss activities done in the dozens of classes I observed, for example, although such activities require [ア] by teachers and can really get students cognitively engaged. And there are many other activities that get students to be more cognitively and socially engaged in English classes: timed-pair conversations, [イ], sentence-combining activities, for example. Teachers need a large set of activity options for classes that are easy to use, effective for getting students to think and use the target language more, and can be assessed. Such activities already exist. Teachers just need to get familiar with them, and comfortable with them. That takes training and coordination time, and it takes courage to break out of our comfort and familiarity zones and experiment with [ウ].

[ア]　① active part　② huge burden　③ minimal preparation

[イ]　① presentation carousels　② proficiency levels　③ school boards

[ウ]　① different approaches　② multi-media materials　③ productive rest

(☆☆◎◎◎)

【5】Read the following Passage consisting of eleven paragraphs and answer the questions below.

From the time I was a small boy, throughout the early stages of young manhood, and during my adult life, I was a professional worrier. My worries were many and varied. Some were real; most of them were [ア]. Upon [イ] occasion I would find myself without anything to worry about—then I would worry for fear I might be overlooking something.

Then, two years ago, I started out on a new way of living. This required making a self-analysis of my faults—and a very few virtues—a 'searching and fearless moral inventory' of myself. This brought out clearly what was causing all this worry.

The fact was that I could not live for today alone. I was [ウ] of yesterday's mistakes and fearful of the future.

I was told over and over that 'today was the tomorrow I had worried about yesterday.' But it wouldn't work for me. I was advised to live on a twenty-four-hour program. I was told that today was the only day over which I had any control and that I should make the most of my opportunities each day. I was told that if I did that, I would be so busy I would have no time to worry about any other day—past or future. That advice was [エ], but somehow I found it hard to put these darned ideas to work for me.

Then like a shot from out of the dark, I found the answer—and where do you suppose I found it? On a Northwestern Railroad platform at seven p.m. on May 31, 1945. It was an important hour for me. That is why I remember it so clearly.

We were taking some friends to the train. They were leaving on *The City of Los Angeles,* a streamliner; to return from a vacation.

War was still on—crowds were heavy that year.

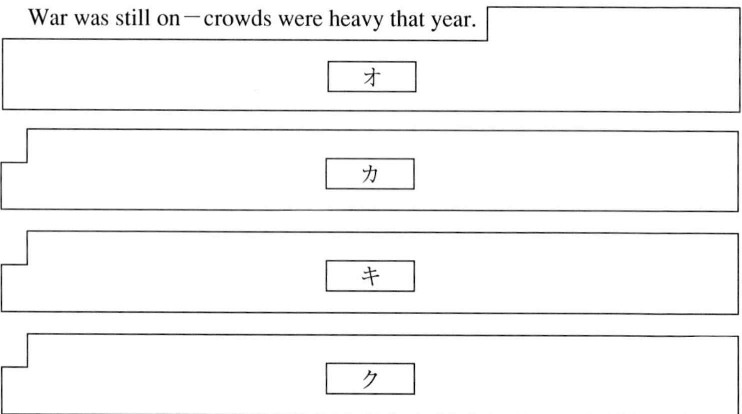

And now by praying each morning, I get my green light for that day. I also occasionally get amber lights that slow me down. Sometimes I get red lights that stop me before I crack up.

No more worrying for me since that day two years ago when I made this discovery. During those two years, over seven hundred green lights have shown for me, and the trip through life is so much easier without the worry of what color the next light will be. No matter what color it may be, I will know what to do.

(SOURCE : "*How to Stop Worrying and Start Living* " by Dale Carnegie)

(No.1) Choose the most suitable word from ① to ⑤ for each blank [ア] through [エ]. Each word can be used once.

① fretful ② imaginary ③ logical ④ prosperous ⑤ rare

(No.2) Place these four passages in their appropriate locations [オ] through [ク].

① I asked myself why I didn't have a good signal system for my life. My answer was－I did have one. God had given it to me. He controls it, so it has to be foolproof. I started looking for a green light. Where could I find it? Well, if God created the green lights, why not ask Him? I did just that.

② Instead of boarding the train with my wife, I wandered down the tracks toward the front of the train. I stood looking at the big shiny engine for a minute. Presently I looked down the track and saw a huge semaphore. An amber light was showing. Immediately this light turned to a bright green. At that moment, the engineer started clanging a bell; I heard the familiar 'All aboard!' and, in a matter of seconds, that huge streamliner began to move out of the station on its 2300-mile trip.

③ My mind started spinning. Something was trying to make sense to me. I was experiencing a miracle. Suddenly it dawned on me. That engineer had given me the answer I had been seeking. He was starting out on that long journey with only one green light to go by. If I had been in his place, I would want to see all the green lights for the entire journey.

Impossible, of course, yet that was exactly what I was trying to do with my life－sitting in the station, going noplace, because I was trying too hard to see what was ahead for me.

④ My thoughts kept coming. That engineer didn't worry about trouble that he might encounter miles ahead. There probably would be some delays, some slowdowns, but wasn't that why they had signal systems? Amber lights－reduce speed and take it easy. Red lights－real danger up ahead－stop. That was what made train travel safe. A good signal system.

(☆☆☆☆◎◎◎)

【６】Complete the passage by filling in the blanks with all the items written below. Choose the most suitable item from ① to ⑧ for each blank [ア] through [カ]

Long lines at airport security checkpoints make air travel an ordeal. But not everyone has to wait in the serpentine queues. Those who buy first-class or business-class tickets can use priority lanes that take them to the front of the line for screening. British Airways calls it Fast Track, (1) [ ] [ア] [ ] [ ] [ ] [ ] [イ] [ ] control.

But most people can't afford to fly fist-class, so (2) [ ] [ ] [ウ] [ ] [ ] [エ] [ ] [ ] privileges as an à la carte perk. For an extra $39, United Airlines will sell you priority boarding for your flight from Denver to Boston, along with the right to cut in line at the security checkpoint. In Britain, London's Luton Airport offers an even more affordable fast-track option: wait in the long security line or pay £3 (about $5) and go to the head of the queue.

Critics complain that a fast track through airport security should not be for sale. Security checks, they argue, are a matter of national defense, not an amenity like extra legroom or early boarding privileges; the burden of keeping terrorists off airplanes should be shared equally by all passengers. The airlines reply that everyone is subjected to the same level of screening; only the wait varies by price. As long as everyone receives the same body scan, they maintain, a shorter wait in (3) [ ] [ ] [オ] [ ] [ ] [ ] [ ] [カ].

(SOURCE : "*What Money Can't Buy*" by Michael Sandel)

(1) ① a service ② also lets ③ at
④ high-paying passengers ⑤ jump
⑥ passport and immigration ⑦ that ⑧ the queue

(2) ① buy ② coach passengers ③ have begun
④ line - cutting ⑤ offering ⑥ the airlines
⑦ the chance ⑧ to

(3) ① a convenience ② be ③ free ④ is
⑤ should ⑥ the security line ⑦ they ⑧ to sell

(☆☆☆☆◎◎◎)

【7】The following is a conversation between a student and a teacher. Fill in the gap to make it flow with one English sentence.

Student : Ms. Tanaka, I finished my internship at the ABC Company yesterday. I'm going to make a phone call to thank them. What should I say?

Teacher : A phone call? ______________________________.

Student : Thank you for your advice. I will do so.

(☆☆◎◎◎)

【8】Complete the passage by filling in the blank with 30 words or more in English.

In my twenties, I went on a two-week backpacking trip in Europe with a close friend from my monastery. When we arrived at the airport in Rome, our spirits were high. We had known each other for a couple of years and got along very well. I liked his sense of humor and warm−hearted nature, and he appreciated my adventurous spirit and optimism. Since he did not speak much English, I felt obliged to stay close to him. After the first seven days of spending every moment together, we'd run out of things to talk about and both became irritable. It was not because of any concrete problem in our friendship; it was just that we longed for some time alone. So the following morning I suggested we take different routes and meet up at the hostel at night. My fiend welcomed my suggestion.

As I left the hostel, I felt free — I knew I could choose to do whatever I liked for the day; I did not have to negotiate with my friend about where to go first and what to see next. But as the morning turned into the afternoon, I was reminded of the advantages of traveling with a friend. [ ] When I arrived at our hostel at the end of the day, I was quite happy to see my friend. Over dinner we found many new things to talk about in recounting our respective days.

(SOURCE : "*The Things You Can See Only When You Slow Down*" by Haemin Sunim)

(☆☆☆◎◎◎)

解答・解説

【中高共通】

【1】Part A (1) ④ (2) ③ Part B (1) ① (2) ③

Part C No.1 Switch roles. No.2 Shuffle your cards. No.3 Who wants to try? No.4 Could you be more specific? No.5 Let's move on to another topic.

〈解説〉スクリプトは公開されていない。Part A，Part Bとも英文を聞いて(Part Aでは英文と質問文)，問題用紙に印刷された選択肢から解答を選ぶ選択形式である。Part Bでは質問文も印刷されている。ともに放送は1回のみなので，あらかじめ質問文や選択肢に目を通しておきたい。Part Cは2回放送される。教室で教師が使う指示文を書き取らせる記述式問題である。 Part A (1) planet, water, liquid, solidなどから地球上の水について述べられていることが推測できる。evaporationは「蒸発」の意味のやや難しい単語。 (2) politeness「礼儀正しさ」, foreigner, travel, apologize「謝罪する」Japanese peopleなどから日本人と外国人の礼儀正しさの違いについての話だと推測できる。

Part B (1) 最初にプラスチックが作られた年が問われている。④はつい最近の年代なので正解ではないと予測できるだろう。リスニングでは数値を問われることも多いので，苦手な人は正確に聞き取れるよう練習しておくこと。 (2) 2015年と1998年の生産量の比較が問われているので定数の解答である①・②は除外できる。 Part C No.2のShuffleは，聞き取れてもスペルが難しいので注意。No.4のCould you be more specific?「もっと詳しく教えていただけませんか？」や，No.5のLet's move on to another topic.「別の話題に移ろう」は日常会話でも用いるので丸ごと覚えておくとよい。

【2】(1) ④ (2) ② (3) ① (4) ③ (5) ① (6) ②

〈解説〉(1) 倒置構造の文で冒頭のMost importantが補語。空欄にbe動詞＋主語が入る。the factが主語でthatはthe factと同格の接続詞である。 (2) a diminished capacity for work「低下する作業能力」の言い換えがその後に続く。空欄にdefinitionを入れて「疲労の科学的定義」が最適。①は「予期」，③は「機関，制度」，④は「医薬」の意味。 (3) want someone to do「人に～してほしいと思う」とdevote A to B「AをBに捧げる」の組み合わせ。 (4) year, million, dollarは可算名詞なので複数形にする。timeは「時間」を表すときは不可算名詞である(「回数や機会」の意味で使うときは可算名詞となる)。 (5) one of 名詞の複数形で「～の一つ」を表す。regret「後悔」が名詞で，名詞を修飾するのは形容詞のmajor「重要な，主要な」。 (6) on one's behalfは「～の代わりに」という意味。謝らなければいけないのに面と向かってすることができないなら，「代わりに」謝ってもらうという文意。

【3】No.1 ア ② イ ③ ウ ④ No.2 エ ④ オ ③ カ ① No.3 ④ No.4 ① No. 5 ①

〈解説〉No.1 ア 第1パラグラフ第3文に「動物は交配しなければ違う種に属する」と述べられている。空欄の前ではその具体例として「犬と馬は異なる種に属する」と記されており，空欄にはその理由が入るので，②「犬と馬は交配しようとさえしない」が適切である。

イ 「スパニエル犬とプードルは同じ種に属する」の理由が空欄に入るため，アと逆の意味の選択肢が入るとわかる。したがって③「それらは適切に交配できる」が適切である。 ウ 空欄の前のthatはthe puppiesを先行詞とする関係代名詞である。よって④「スパニエル犬とプードルが産んだ子犬は繁殖力がある」が適切。 No.2 エ 動物あるいは植物のあらゆる学名は2つのラテン語の単語から「成り立っている」となるため④が適切。①agree withは「～に同意している」，③bring aboutは「～を引き起こす」の意味。 オ 同文のbut以下で，ホモ・エレクトスやホモ・ハビリスの化石のことが述べられているため，ホモ・サピエンスは我々人類の属の唯一の「生き残っている」種であるとなる③が適切である。 カ nothing to do with「～に関係がない」は重要な熟語表現なので覚えておこう。 No. 3 このパラグラフではgenus(属)－family(科)－order(目)－class(綱)という生物分類について述べられており，最も下位のgenusから上位のclassに向かって順に説明されている。よってA，B，Cの空欄は④が入る。 No. 4 第4パラグラフではfamily tree(家系図)，第5パラグラフではbranching tree(枝分かれした木)のことが述べられている。本文の内容を踏まえると枝分かれというのは生物分類の下位を指すことがわかるだろう。第5パラグラフ第5文に「チャールズ・ダーウィンは『種の起源』という彼の最も有名な本に枝分かれした木を描いた」と書かれている。そして下線部のdiagramは「図表」の意味であることからa branching treeを指すことが読み取れるだろう。　No. 6　decipherは「解読する」という意味なのでunderstand the meaningと言い換えられている①が適切。

【4】ア　③　　イ　①　　ウ　①

〈解説〉ア　空欄を含む文の逆接の接続詞althoughの前後の内容を確認する。前では「観察した数十の授業の中でディクテーションやディクトグロス活動を見たことは一度もないことに驚いている」と記されている。そのため逆接の接続詞althoughの後には，それらの活動に利点があるという内容が来ることがわかる。「教師にとって，③『最小限の準備』で済む」という利点が適切。　イ　生徒をもっと英語の授業に認知的，社会的に関与させる活動の具体例が入るので①「順番に行うプレゼンテーション」が適切。carouselは「回転木馬」の意味でここでは順番に行う活動のことを指している。②は「習熟度レベル」，③は「教育委員会」の意味。　ウ「快適で慣れ親しんだ領域から脱して［ウ］を試みることは勇気がいる」という文なので空欄に入るのは①「異なったアプローチ」が適切。

【5】No.1　ア　②　　イ　⑤　　ウ　①　　エ　③　　No.2　オ　②　カ　③　　キ　④　　ク　①

〈解説〉No.1　ア　冒頭の2文で筆者が心配性である自分のことを述べている。Some were real「心配事のいくつかは実際のものだ」の逆の意味が空欄に来ると読み取れるため，②の「想像上のものだ」が適切。イ　そのように心配事ばかりの筆者なのだから，「何も心配事のない自分に気づく」のは，⑤の「めったにない」ケースなのである。
ウ　前文で「私は今日だけを生きることができなかった」と述べられている。そして空欄の文は「昨日の間違いに［ウ］未来を恐れていた」とある。前文との関連から過去にも未来にも後悔・心配ばかりしているという内容であることが読み取れる。よってfretful「イライラして」が適切。　エ　このパラグラフでは筆者が今日1日だけに集中して生きるというプログラムを受けたことが述べられている。毎日精いっぱい生きるようにすれば過去も未来も心配する時間などないというアドバイスはとても「論理的」なものと言えるだろう。　No.2　オ　③・④のthat engineerに着目。オより前にこの人物が出てきていないためこの2つは最初に来ないことがわかる。①は「神から与えられて答えを見つけた」という内容であり，前のパラグラフとつながらないので不可。よって②が入る。　カ　②のパラグラフにthe engineerがあるためそれを受けるthat engineerがある③・④のどちらかが来ることがわかる。③にthat long journeyがあることに着目すると，②の最後に2300-mile tripという語句があり④には該当する語句がないことからこれを指すことがわかり③が入る。　キ　③では列車の機関士が自分の求めていた答えをくれたと述べられている。さらに筆者の思考は続き，機関士と自分との物事に対する姿勢の違いに気づくのが④に書かれておりスムーズに③とつながる。　ク　④の最後にa good signal systemとあり，①でも冒頭で同じ語句が使われている。また①の後に神に祈るという内容が続くので前後がスムーズにつながることが読み取れる。

【6】(1)　ア　⑦　　イ　③　　(2)　ウ　⑤　　エ　⑧　　(3)　オ　①　カ　⑧

〈解説〉(1)　ファーストクラスとビジネスクラスの乗客は優先的にセキュリティチェックを受けられるシステムが直前のFast Trackと呼ばれているものである。カンマがあることからFast Trackを説明する名詞が続くと考えられる。②のalso letsは動詞で主語は3人称単数だとまず読み取れる。目的語はhigh-paying passengers，補語はjump the queueで「高いお金を払っている乗客に，列に割り込むことを許す」となる。残りの選択肢から考えるとa serviceに関係代名詞thatを続ければうまくつながることがわかる。at passport and immigration control「入国審査で」が文末に来る。　(2)　空欄の前に「ほとんどの人はファーストクラスの席を買う余裕はない」と記されているのと選択肢から，「エコノミークラスの人でも列に割り込む権利を買うことができる」といった内容が来ると考えられる。主語はthe airlinesで動詞はhave begun，目的語に動名詞offeringが来る。offerの後には人＋物が続き，coach passengers the chance to buy line-cuttingとなる。　(3)　このパラグラフではFast Trackを買う権利についての批判と，それに対する航空会社の「乗客は同じセキュリティチェックを受けるのだから，列に割り込む権利が取引され，待つ時間だけが値段によって変わるのは問題ない」という反論が書かれている。これに基づくと，a shorter wait in the security line is a convenience they should be free to sell「セキュリティチェックの列により短い時間しか待たないことは自由に売ることができるべき利便性である(セキュリティチェックの待ち時間を短縮できるという利便性を売るのは自由である)」となる。

【7】No, you should write a letter to express your gratitude formally.

〈解説〉インターンシップ先の会社に電話で感謝の意を述べようという生徒に対し，教師が何らかのアドバイスを与えたことがわかる。A phone call? と教師が聞き返していることから，電話ではなくもっと丁寧な対応のほうがよいという教師の意図を読み取る。

【8】Eating alone was no fun; it felt more like a chore than a time for enjoyment and relaxation. Also, I didn't take any pictures of myself that day because I did not want to bother strangers. (36words)

〈解説〉最初のパラグラフでは，友人と旅行すると毎日一緒にいて話すこともなくなりお互いイライラしてくるため，いったん別行動することにしたと述べられている。第2パラグラフの空欄前では，筆者は1人になったことで自由気ままに行動できることを楽しんでいたが，時間が経つにつれ友人と一緒にした冒険について思い出している様子が書かれている。よって空欄には「1人だとやはり楽しくない，寂しい」といった内容が来ると読み取れる。この感情を踏まえた筆者の1人での行動を，指定語数である30語程度で答えればよい。

2018年度　実施問題

【中高共通】

【 1 】(Listening Test)

Part A　Listen to the passage. Choose two sentences that best match the content of the passage from the five sentences written below.

The passage will be read onece.

① The inch is approximately the length of a man's thumb.

② The yard became a standard for measuring lengths of cloth.

③ Eventually more standard units were adopted because human body parts are not all the same size.

④ The cubit is a unit of measure using the upper arm.

⑤ None of these old units are used any more.

Part B　Listen to the passages and the questions. Choose the correct answers to the questions written below. Then mark the number ①, ②, ③, or ④ on your answer sheet. Each passage and question will be read once.

(1)

① Absorbing singnals in the sand.

② Between the bottom and the surface.

③ By sending signals to the ocean floor.

④ Near sandy bottoms.

(2)

① Pouring the drinks into their glasses is a way to poison guests.

② The clinking of glasses before a toast is what remains of this ritual.

③ The host cannot poison his guest's drink because they will share the drink together.

④ The host will be very happy if his guest clinks his glass against his.

Part C　Listen to the sentences and write down the whole sentence. Each sentence will be read <u>twice</u>.

(☆☆☆◎◎◎)

【2】Choose the best item from ① to ④ below each question to fill in the blank.

(1) People all hoped [　　] a peaceful settlement of long-standing territorial dispute between the two countries.

① between　② for　③ on　④ to

(2) A : You've just got over your cold. Are you really going to climb Mt. Haku tomorrow?

B : I'm not sure. [　　] climb or not depends on my health status.

① If I　② My　③ That of my　④ Whether I

(3) Although e-mail is a relatively recent technological tool, different societies have already [　　] radically different patterns for useing it.

① been developed　② being developed　③ developed

④ developing

(4) A : How's the work coming along?

B : Pretty good, though it'll take [　　] days to finish it with complete success.

① another five　② five another　③ more five

④ other five

(5) The company gained international attention as soon as it launched a new laptop characterized by being the world's [　　].

① light　② lighter　③ lightest　④ lightness

(6) A : What should we do to prevent global warming?

B : First of all we have to consider reducing electricity [　　] in our daily lives.

① compassion　② comprehension　③ consumption

④ conviction

(☆☆◎◎◎)

【3】Read the following passage and answer the questions below.

Many of us come to the topic of willpower with ideas about what it is: a personality trait, a virtue, something you either have or you don't, maybe a kind of brute force you muster up in difficult situations. But [ア]. It's an evolved capacity and an instinct that everyone has --- a careful calibration of what's happening in your brain and body. But we've also seen that if you are stressed or depressed, your brain and body may not cooperate. Willpower can be disrupted by sleep deprivation, poor diet, a sedentary lifestyle, and a host of other factors that sap your energy, or keep your brain and body stuck in a chronic stress response. To every doctor, diet guru, or nagging spouse convinced that [イ], this reserch should be a reality check. Yes, your mind is important, but your body also needs to (オ).

Science also points us to a critical insight: Stress is the enemy of willpower. So often we believe that [ウ], and we even look for ways to increase stress --- such as waiting until the last minute, or criticizing ourselves for being lazy or out of control --- to motivate ourselves. Or we use stress to try to motivate others, turning up the heat at work or coming down hard at home. This may seem to work in the short term, but in the long term, nothing drains willpower faster than stress. The biology of stress and the biology of self-control are simply incompatible. Both the fight-or-flight and pause-and plan responses are about energy management, but [エ]. The fight-or-flight response floods the body with energy to act instinctively, and steals it from the areas of the brain needed for wise decision making. The pause-and-plan response sends that energy to the brain --- and not just anywhere in the brain, but specifically to the self-control center, the prefrontal cortex. Stress encourages you to focus on (カ), short-term goals and outcomes, but self-control requires keeping the big picture in mind. Learning how to better manage your stress is one of the most important things you can do to improve your willpower.

In recent year, a number of high-profile pundits have claimed that

Americans have lost their collective willpower. If this is true, it may have [A] to do with the loss of core American values, as the pundits have claimed, and [B] to do with the increased levels of stress and fear in today's society. A 2010 national survey by the American Psychological Association found that 75 percent of people in the United States experience high levels of stress. It's not surprising, giving the events of the last decade, from terrorist attacks and flu epidemics to environmental disasters, natural disasters, unemployment, and near economic collapse. These national stresses (キ) on our physiology and self-control. Researchers at Yale University School of Medicine found that during the week after September 11, 2001, patients' heart rate variability decreased significantly. We were a nation overwhelmed, and it's not surprising that rates of drinking, smoking, and drug use [C] for months following the attacks of 9/11. The same pattern emerged during the height of the economic crisis of 2008 and 2009. Americans reported indulging in [D] foods more often to cope with the stress, and smokers reported smoking more cigarettes and giving up attempts to quit.

(SOURCE : "*THE WILLPOWER INSTINCT*" by Kelly McGonigal)

(No. 1) Choose the most suitable item for each blank [ア] [イ], [ウ] or [エ] from ① to ⑤. Then mark the number ①, ②, ③, ④ or ⑤ on your answer sheet.

① science is painting a very different picture of willpower
② stress is the only way to get things done
③ they redirect your energy and attention in very different ways
④ we need to take more seriously the tasks of managing stress
⑤ willpower is just a matter of making up your mind

(No. 2) Choose the most suitable word or phrase from ① to ④ for each blank (オ), (カ) and (キ).

(オ) ① get along with ② get it out ③ get on board
④ get you down

(カ) ① decision-making ② energy ③ immediate
④ self-control

(キ) ① take a chance ② take a look ③ take a nap
④ take a toll

(No. 3) Choose the best combination from ① to ④ in order to fill in the blank [A] and [B].

① A: little B: little ② A: little B: more
③ A: more B: little ④ A: more B: more

(No. 4) Choose the best combination from ① to ④ in order to fill in the blank [C] and [D].

① C: decreased D: healthy ② C: decreased D: unhealthy
③ C: increased D: healthy ④ C: increased D: unhealthy

(☆☆☆☆◎◎◎)

【4】The following is a description of how to make pair work more effective. Choose the most suitable word from ① to ⑨ for each blank [ア] through [ウ].

One student has an incomplete set of instructions on how to get to a friend's party and is not [ア] what time it starts. The other student has been to the house before and has a map of how to get there. He also has an invitation which states the time. They phone each other to get details.

In the above example, if both students had the same handout the conversation would be [イ] and pointless. Why tell each other details that they both know anyway?

However, the information gap forces them to arrive at a complete set of facts after exchanging the missing parts. Through tables of facts that are [ウ], maps which have places missing, drawings with missing parts, timetables, brochures and many more visual props, you can simulate real communication gaps for controlled practice work.

(SOURCE：“*ALT HANDBOOK*” by British Council)

① accurate	② artificial	③ continuous	④ emotional
⑤ incomplete	⑥ integrated	⑦ natural	⑧ proficient
⑨ sure			

(☆☆◎◎◎)

【5】Read the following article consisting of nine paragraphs and answer the questions below.

One of my childhood memories is listening with my family to the popular American radio show, Garrison Keillor's *A Prairie Home Companion*. Keillor's deep baritone voice is still heard Saturday afternoons on hundreds of National Public Radio stations as he makes gentle fun of Minnesotans (and just about everyone else).

For years, one of the regular skits on Keillor's show was about the French chef, Maurice, the proprietor of the mythical Café Boeuf, who sees any customer as a potential verbal sparring [ア]. My favorite sketch involves Keillor calling to make a reservation at the Café Boeuf, only to be questioned vigorously by Maurice (in a ridiculously fake French accent, of course). What will Keillor be wearing? How can Maurice be sure that Keillor's tie will work with the restaurant's wallpaper? The more Keillor explains his sartorial choices, the more passionately Maurice questions and challenges him. It was through these sketches that I was first introduced to the image of the French as inveterate debaters.

When I moved to France, this [イ] was echoed in the daily news. Strikes and demonstrations seemed to be part of the social fabric, triggered by everything from an increase in college tuition to a proposed change in pension plans. But I really didn't experience the French love of [ウ] on a personal level until one evening when I was invited with my (French) husband Eric to a dinner party at the home of Hélène Durand, a friend from Eric's school days.

Hélène and her husband lived near a golf course west of Paris. There were four couples around the table. All were French, except for me. As the [　エ　] progressed, the group was laughing and getting along beautifully, with Hélène and her best friend Juliette entertaining everyone with funny tales about their mishaps on the golf course that afternoon.

But, then, halfway into the meal, something unfortunate happened -- or so I thought, from my American perspective.

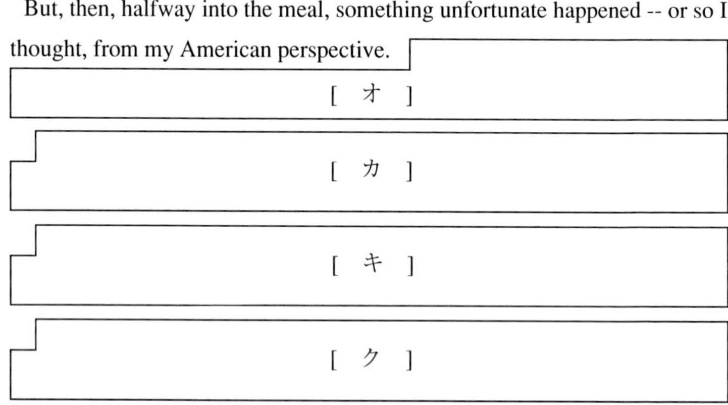

Now think for a moment how a scene like this might play out in a business setting. Imagine the confusion that might arise among a team of people from varying cultures with dramatically different attitudes toward open disagreement. Uncomfortable? Unsettling? To say the least.

(SOURCE：“*THE CULTURE MAP*” by Erin Meyer)

(No. 1)　Choose the most suitable word from ① to ⑤ for each blank [　ア　] through [　エ　]. Each word can be used once.

① debate　② dinner　③ emergency　④ partner
⑤ stereotype

(No. 2)　Place these four passages in their appropriate locations [　オ　] through [　ク　].

① Having absolutely no desire to become embroiled in the debate and offend at least one of my new friends, I found my answer very quickly: “I have no opinion.” And to my utter surprise, within a few minutes, the topic changed to who was going where for the upcoming holidays -- with no hard feelings whatsoever. I watched in bafflement as Juliette and

Hélène went arm in arm to the kitchen to get coffee, their laughter ringing through the apartment, best friends as always.

② Juliette and Hélène got into a big argument over whether the town's annual golf event, which occurs every spring practically in Hélène's backyard, was a good thing or a bad one. Hélène declared fervently that she was "*totalement contre*" (completely against) the golf tournament. Juliette interrupted: "*Hélène, tu dis ça parces que tu es égoïste. Moi, je suis pour*!" ("You say that because you are selfish. I am all for it!"). The other guests began to take sides. Voices were rising and hands were waving.

③ Now, in my own American culture, this type of debate at the dinner table is a very bad sign. It would likely result in someone -- perhaps several someones -- leaving the room in a huff, slamming the door, and not returning. So I was growing increasingly uncomfortable when Juliette looked directly at me and said, "Well, Erin, what do you think?"

④ Of course, a disagreement at the dinner table can happen in just about any culture. But the fact that Hélène and Juliette could engage in such spirited public battle with no apparent impact on their friendship marks the episode as distinctly cultural.

(☆☆◎◎◎)

【6】Complete the passage by filling in the blanks with all the items written below. Choose the most suitable item from ① to ⑧ for each blank [ア] through [カ].

As my search for lunch in New Delhi suggests, the skills (1) [ ] [ア] [ ] [ ] [ ] [ ] [ ] [イ] one culture to another. In the United States and other Anglo-Saxon cultures, people are trained (mostly subconsciously) to communicate as literally and explicitly as possible. Good communication is all about clarity and explicitness, and (2) [ ] [ウ] [ ] [ ] [ ] [ ] [エ] [ ] firmly on the communicator: "If you don't understand, it's my fault."

By contrast, in many Asian cultures, including India, China, Japan, and Indonesia, messages are often (3) [　　] [　オ　], [　　] [　　] [　　] [　　] [　カ　] [　　]. Good communication is subtle, layered, and may depend on copious subtext.

(1) ① an effective　② being　③ communicator
④ dramatically　⑤ from　⑥ in
⑦ involved　⑧ vary

(2) ① accountability　② accurate　③ for
④ is　⑤ of　⑥ placed
⑦ the message　⑧ transmission

(3) ① between　② conveyed　③ implicitly
④ read　⑤ requiring　⑥ the lines
⑦ the listener　⑧ to

(☆☆◎◎◎)

【7】Look at the picture below and complete the sentence to describe the situation. You should describe the situation in one sentence and use the words "bus" and "Kenrokuen" .

(☆◎◎◎)

【8】Read the paragraph and complete the paragraph by filling in the blank with an appropriate example of 30 words or more.

Misunderstanding between Japanese and American speakers are also influenced by different ways of structuring information. The American value of directness is contrasted with the Japanese value of maintaining harmony. Japanese use a variety of conventions to avoid direct disagreement.

For example,

To a Japanese who is expecting similar forms of arguments, the directness of American conversation often appears rude inconsiderate. An American, on the other hand, often becomes annoyed at the confusing rhetoric and unnecessary beating around the bush of Japanese speakers.

(SOURCE： "*Crosscultural Understanding*" by Gail Robinson)

(☆☆◎◎◎)

解答・解説

【中高共通】

【1】Part A ②，③ Part B (1) ③ (2) ② Part C No.1 Turn off the light. No.2 Who's absent today? No.3 Would you say that louder? No.4 Circle the photograph you like. No.5 May I interrupt you for a second?

〈解説〉スクリプトは公開されていない。リスニング問題では，あらかじめ選択肢に目を通して内容を予測しておくことが鉄則。 Part A inch, yardなどから測定単位の由来について述べられていることが推測できる。inch は男性の親指の幅である。 Part B (1) 選択肢から想像できることが少ないが，①と③に出てくる単語signals「信号」，②のsurface「海面」，④のbottom「海底」を頭に入れておく。　(2)　乾杯時にグラスを鳴らし合うことの意味についての話だと想像する。①のpour「注ぐ」，poison「毒殺する，毒を盛る」，②のclink「カチンと鳴らす」，toast「乾杯」，ritual「儀式」を頭に入れておく。　Part C　出題されている英文はそれほど難しくない。音の連結や消滅に注意する。

【2】(1)　②　　(2)　④　　(3)　③　　(4)　①　　(5)　③　　(6)　③

〈解説〉(1)　hope for～は，「～に期待する」という意味。　(2)「私が山に登るかどうかは私の健康状態による」という意味。whetherとifは同義で使えるが，「～かどうかは」のように主語にする場合はwhetherのみ使用可。　(3)「電子メールは比較的最近の科学技術道具であるけれども，様々な社会がそれを使用する全く異なった型をすでに発展させている」となる。現在完了形であるので空所には過去分詞が入る。(4)　あと5日はanother five days。five more daysとも言える。　(5)「その会社は世界最軽量が特徴の新しいノートパソコンに着手すると，すぐに国際的な注目を浴びた」という意味。　(6)　reduce「減少させる」の目的語にあたることからelectricity consumption「電力消費量」が入る。他の選択肢はcompassion「同情」，comprehension「理解」，conviction「確信」という意味。

【3】No.1　ア　①　　イ　⑤　　ウ　②　　エ　③　　No.2　オ　③　カ　③　　キ　④　　No.3　②　　No.4　④

〈解説〉No.1　ア　空所の前では，自制心が「性格的な特徴・美徳・困難な状況で奮い起こす馬鹿力のようなもの」，空所の後では「人間だれしもが持っている進化した能力であり本能である」と記されている。空所の前後では，全く異なる見解であることから，①「科学は自制心を全く異なるものと描いている」がふさわしい。　イ　空所を含む文の意味は「～と確信している医者，食の権威者，口うるさい配偶者にとってこの研究は真実を思い知らされる機会となるはずだ」。この研究の「この」は，1文前の「自制心は睡眠不足や貧相な食事，座ってばかりの生活様式，エネルギーを弱め，脳や体を慢性的なストレス反応にはまり込んだ状態にする他のたくさんの要因によって乱されることがある」を指す。すなわち自制心は心の問題だけではなく，体の問題でもあることを言わんとしている。「医者，食の権威者，口うるさい配偶者は⑤(自制心はただ単に決断するかどうかの問題である)と確信している」と考える。　ウ「自分自身にやる気を起こさせるため，土壇場まで待ち，怠惰や制御不能を理由に自己批判をして，ストレスを増幅させる方法を探しさえする」のは，非常に頻繁に，②「ストレスが物事をなし遂げる唯一の方法である」と信じるから，と考える。エ　fight-or-flight responseとpause-and-plan responseはともにエネルギー管理に関わることであるが，空所直後にそれらの作用がどのように異なるのか具体的な記述がある。したがって③「(それら2つの反応は)エネルギーや注意を全く異なる方向に向けるのである」が適切。fight-or-flight responseは文字通り「闘うか逃げるか(差し迫った)反応」。それの対極がpause-and-plan responseは「立ち止まって考える反応」。

No.2　オ　第1段落まとめの1文。「心は大切であるが，体も(考慮に)入れられる必要がある」と考えて③を選択する。on board「かかわって，参加して」という意味。他の選択肢は，①　get along with～で「～とうまくやる」。　②　get it outで「(悩み事を)打ち明ける」。　④　get you downで「あなたをがっかりさせる」。　カ　空所を含む文は「ストレスはあなたに～で短期の目標や結果に焦点を当てさせるが，自制は心に全体像を持つことを要求する」であるから，③「即時の」が入る。　キ　「これら国全体のストレスは私たちの生理機能や自制に損害を与えている」と読みとるのが自然。④のtake a toll「被害・打撃を与える」を選択する。これら国全体のストレスとは，1文前の「ここ10年の出来事－テロリストの攻撃，インフルエンザの流行から環境災害，自然災害，失業，経済破綻と言えるようなものまで」を指す。

No.3　A「もしこれ(アメリカ人が集団的自制心を失っていること)が事実であるとしたら，専門家が主張するアメリカ人の中核的価値観(個人主義)の喪失とほとんど関係がないだろう」。集団的自制心の喪失とアメリカ人の価値観の喪失の関連を考えて空所Aに入るものを選択する。　B 「そして(アメリカ人が集団的自制心を失っていることは)今日の社会におけるストレスや不安の増加と大いに関係があるのだろう」。空所Aはlittle，空所Bはmoreが当てはまる。　No.4　アメリカ人のストレスが自制心を害している具体例を挙げている。　C 「9/11の攻撃後，数か月間は飲酒・喫煙・麻薬の使用率が増加したのは驚くべきことではない」。　D 「同様のことが2008年と2009年の経済危機真っ最中に起きた。ストレスに対処するために，より頻繁に不健康なものを飽食し，喫煙者はより多くの煙草を吸い禁煙をやめたとアメリカ人は報告した」。空所Cはincreased，空所Dはunhealthyが当てはまる。

【4】ア　⑨　　イ　②　　ウ　⑤

〈解説〉ペアワークをより効果的にする方法についての記述である。

ア　ペアのうちの1人が不完全な指示書を持っているとあるので，何時にパーティが始まるのか確信がないと続けるのが自然。　イ　両方の生徒が同じハンドアウトを持っていたら会話はどのようになるかと述べている部分なので，artificial「人工的な」が当てはまる。pointlessは「不毛の」という意味。　ウ　本物のコミュニケーションギャップを装うことができるのは，「～な図表，ところどころ場所が欠けている地図，部分的に欠けている絵，時刻表，その他視覚的補助となるものを通して」と考えincomplete「不完全な」が当てはまる。

【5】No.1　ア　④　　イ　⑤　　ウ　①　　エ　②　　No.2　オ　②　カ　③　　キ　①　　ク　④

〈解説〉No.1　ア　第2段落目の終わりに，「(ラジオ番組の)これらの場面を通して筆者はフランス国民の頑固な論争家のイメージに触れた」とあるので，「フランス人シェフのモーリスは客を誰でも議論の相手と見立てる」と考える。　イ　「筆者がフランスに引っ越したとき，日々のニュースの中で固定観念に合致する人の声がこだました」となる。⑤のstereotype「固定観念に合致する人」とは勿論ここでは論争好きなフランス人を指す。　ウ「(ラジオやテレビでフランス人の論争好きを目の当たりにしてきた)筆者は，夫の学校時代の友人エレナ・デュランの家で夫のエリックと夕食会に招待された晩，初めてフランス人一人ひとりが論争好きであることを体験で知った」となる。on a personal levelは「個人的に，個人個人で」の意味。　エ「～が進むにつれて」と見当がつけられるのでdinnerが当てはまる。　No.2　選択肢の大意は，①「議論に巻き込まれ友人を怒らせたくなかったので，私はすぐに『わからない』と返答した。驚いたことに数分で，やがて来る休日に誰がどこに行くというような悪気のないものに話題が変わった。私はエレナと親友のジュリエットが腕を組んでコーヒーを取りに台所へ行き，笑い声がアパート中に響いたとき，いつものように仲良しであるのを当惑しながら見た」。　②「ジュリエットとエレナは例年のゴルフイベント(実は春にエレナ宅の裏庭で開催されるのだが)の是非について大議論を始めた。エレナは反対。ジュリエットは賛成。他の客もどちらかの立場に立ち始めた。声は大きくなり，手振りまで始まった」。　③「アメリカ文化においては，食事の席でのこのような議論は，誰かが憤慨して席を離れ，ドアをバタンと閉め，戻ってこないという結果になりがちなので好ましくないとされている。ジュリエットが私の方を真っすぐ見つめ『あなたはどう思う？』と私に尋ねたとき，私はますます落ち着かなくなった」。　④「もちろん食事の席で意見の食い違いはどんな文化の中でも起こり得るが，エレナとジュリエットが公衆の面前で猛烈な論争しても友情に何の影響も残さなかったことは，フランス文化に特徴的な出来事である」。

【6】(1)　ア　⑥　　イ　⑤　　(2)　ウ　③　　エ　④　　(3)　オ　③　　カ　①

〈解説〉(1)「効果的な伝達者であるのに係る技術は文化によってかなり異なる」という意味。主語skillに呼応する動詞を語群から選ぶとvary「異なる」。それを修飾する副詞がdramatically「劇的に」。文末から

from one culture to another「文化によって」という意味のまとまりが考えられる。be(ing)はinvolved inではなく，an effective communicatorに組み合わせることに気づくかどうか。並べ替えると空所は，involved in being an effective communicator vary dramatically fromとなる。

(2) 「メッセージの正確な伝達の責任は明確に伝達者に置かれる」という意味。合衆国や他のアングロサクソン文化におけるgood communicationについて述べている文であるから，accurate transmission of the messageというまとまりで主語を組み立てる。accountability for～は「～に対する責任」という意味。並べ替えると空所は，accountability for accurate transmission of the message is placedとなる。

(3) 「メッセージはしばしば暗黙のうちに伝えられ，聞き手に言外の意味を読み取ることを要求する」という意味。こちらはアジアの国々におけるメッセージの伝達についての文である。convey「伝える」，implicitly「暗黙のうちに」，require＋人＋to ～「人に～するよう要求する」とread between the lines「行間を読む」を組み合わせる。並べ替えると空所は，conveyed implicitly, requiring the listener to read between the linesとなる。

【7】Two tourists are asking a mother and her son how to get to Kenrokuen by bus.

〈解説〉「兼六園行きのバス」はthe bus bound for Kenrokuenという表現も考えられる。

【8】(For example,) when Japanese speakers are invited to a party, they may first accept the invitation to avoid directly refusing it. However, they will make up a plausible excuse later and will not attend it. (33 words)

〈解説〉調和を重視し遠回しにものを言う日本人が，アメリカ人を困惑させる例を挙げる。解答例は「日本人はパーティに招待されると直接断るのを避けるため，一旦は承諾するものの，後になるともっともらしい言い訳をして参加しない」。その他に「そのうち(近いうちに)また会おう」「近くまで来たら寄ってください」などの日本人が社交辞令でよく使う表現について書くこともできる。

2017年度　実施問題

【中高共通】

【1】(Listening Test)

Part A　Listen to the description and choose the item that fits it. Then mark the number ①, ②, ③, or ④ on your answer sheet. Each description will be read once.

(1) ① automatically　② desperately　③ extremely
　④ immediately

(2) ① deficiency　② difference　③ difficulty
　④ dignity

(3) ① confident　② frightened　③ important
　④ surprised

(4) ① inspiration　② instruction　③ intonation
　④ introduction

(5) ① associate　② estimate　③ improve
　④ motivate

Part B　Listen to the sentences and write down the whole sentence. Each sentence will be read twice.

No.1　The deadline is next Thursday.

No.2　Put it back where it belongs.

No.3　let's get started.

No.4　Could you clear your desks?

No.5　Theres should be eight kinds of hahdouts in total.

(☆☆☆◎◎◎)

【2】Look at the drawings and choose the most suitable word or phrase for the situation. Then mark the number ①, ②, ③, or ④ on your answer sheet.

(1)

ア

① APPLIANCE

② CONFIDENTIAL

③ PRESCRIPTION

④ SECURITY

(2)

A nurse：イ

① I'd better get a shot.

A child：ウ

① Don't shoot out.

② It'll be over in no time.	② How's it doing?
③ Just be a patient.	③ I hate needles.
④ Please give me a hand.	④ You may feel a little prick.

(☆☆◎◎◎)

【３】Choose the best item from ① to ④ below each question to fill in the blank.

(1) [　ア　] agree that global warming is a serious problem.

① Most of people　② Most people　③ The almost people
④ The most of people

(2) [　イ　] the fact that the weather was so bad, we were lucky to be able to get to the summit.

① Even　② For　③ Given　④ Nevertheless

(3) Being both spoilt and lazy, the student [　ウ　] the teachers for his failure in the entrance exams.

① accused　② blamed　③ charged　④ criticized

(4) My son looked unwell, so I took his temperature. It was two degrees above [　エ　].

① normal　② ordinary　③ regular　④ usual

(5) This department store gives its employees 5 % discount on every item as a special [　オ　].

① benefit　② fee　③ market　④ profit

(6) Mr. Yamada is the chief of the project [　カ　] consumes a quarter of the yearly budget of the company.

① it　② what　③ which　④ who

(☆☆☆◎◎◎)

【４】Read the following passage and answer the questions below.

Rick began to formulate an idea --- the development of a course that would equip students with high self-esteem, relationship skills and conflict management skills. As Rick began to research what such a course should contain, he ran across a study by the National Institute of Education in which 1,000 thirty-year-olds had been asked if they felt their high school education had equipped them with the skills they needed for the real world. Over 80 percent responded, "[ク]."

These thirty-year-olds were also asked what skills they now wish they had been taught. The top answers were relationship skills: How to get along better with the people you live with. How to find and keep a job. How to handle conflict. How to be (オ). How to understand the normal development of a child. How to handle (カ). And how to intuit (キ).

Inspired by his vision of creating a class that might teach these things, [ア]. In his quest for information on what should be included in the course, he asked over 2,000 students in 120 high schools the same two questions:

1. If you were to develop a program for your high school to help you cope with what you're meeting now and what you think you'll be meeting in the future, what would that program include?
2. List the top ten problems in your life that you wish were dealt with better at home and in school.

Whether the students were from wealthy private schools or inner-city ghettos, rural or suburban, the answers were surprisingly the same. Loneliness and not liking themselves topped the list of problems. In addition, they had the same list of skills they wished they were taught as the ones compiled by the thirty-year-olds.

Rick slept in his car for two months, living on a total of sixty dollars. Most days he ate peanut butter on crackers. Some days he didn't eat at all. [イ].

His next step was to make a list of the nation's top educators and leaders in counseling and psychology. He set out to visit everyone on his list to ask for their expertise and support. While they were impressed with his approach --- asking students directly what they wanted to learn --- they offered little help.

"You're too young. Go back to college. Get your degree. Go to graduate school, then you can pursue this." They were [ケ] encouraging.

Yet Rick persisted. By the time he turned twenty, he had sold his car, his clothes, had borrowed from friends and was thirty-two thousand dollars in debt. Someone suggested he go to a foundation and ask for money.

His first appointment at a local foundation was a huge disappointment. As he walked into the office, [ウ]. The vice president of the foundation was a huge dark-haired man with a cold, stern face. For a half hour he sat without uttering a word while Rick poured his heart out about his mother, the two thousand kids and plans for a new kind of course for high school kids.

When he was through, the vice president pushed up a stack of folders, "Son," he said, "I've been here nearly twenty years. We've funded all these education programs. And they all [コ] . Yours will, too. The reasons? They're obvious. You're twenty years old, you have no experience, no money, no college degree. Nothing!"

As he left the foundation office, [エ]. Rick began a study of which foundations were interested in funding projects for teenagers. He then spent months writing grant proposals --- working from early morning until late at night. Rick worked for over a year laboriously writing grant proposals, each one carefully tailored to the interests and requirements of the individual foundations. Each one went out with high hopes and each one came back --- rejected.

Proposal after proposal was sent out and rejected. Finally, after the 155th grant proposal had been [サ] down, all of Rick's support began to crumble.

(Source: *Chicken Soup For The Soul "Rick Little's Quest"* Adapted from Peggy Mann)

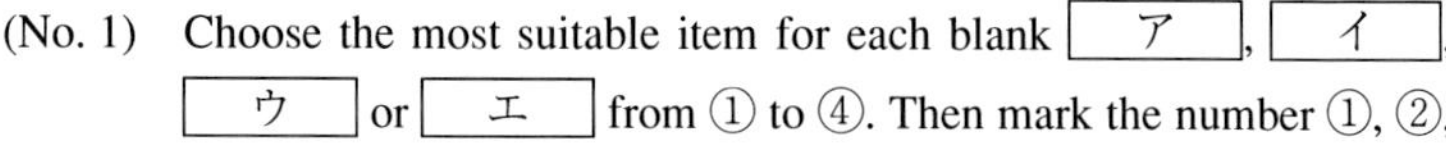
(No. 1) Choose the most suitable item for each blank [ア], [イ], [ウ] or [エ] from ① to ④. Then mark the number ①, ②,

③ or ④ on your answer sheet.

① Rick dropped out of college and set across the country to interview high school students

② Rick had few resources but he was committed to his dream

③ Rick vowed to prove this man wrong

④ Rick was literally shaking with fear

(No. 2) Choose the most suitable item from ① to ④ for each blank (オ), (カ) and (キ).

① a good parent ② financial management ③ fund-raising ④ the meaning of life

(No. 3) Choose from ① to ④ the most appropriate item for the blanks [ク], [ケ], [コ] and [サ].

[ク] ① Absolutely not ② Of course ③ Quite a few ④ Whatever

[ケ] ① less than ② more or less ③ more than ④ no more than

[コ] ① failed ② succeeded ③ true ④ wrong

[サ] ① broken ② fallen ③ settled ④ turned

(No. 4) Answer the question below in English.

If you were to develop a program for junior high or high school students to help them cope with what they'll be meeting in the future, what would that program equip students with?

Complete the first sentence using one of the three options below. Then, write the reason in 50 words or more.

[conflict management skills / high self-esteem / relationship skills]

I think the program would equip them with____________________
This is because ____
____
____
____

(☆☆☆◎◎◎)

【5】The following is a part of the chapter "Report on the Future Improvement and Enhancement of English Education (Outline): Five Recommendations on the English Education Reform Plan Responding to the Rapid Globalization." Choose the most suitable word from ① to ⑨ for each blank [ア] though [ウ].

By starting foreign English activities from the middle grades of elementary school, students can build a foundation for communication skills and raise their [ア] in English as they become familiar with the sounds of the language. In upper grades, students are to develop basic communication skills including the skills of listening to and speaking about daily topics using basic phrases, while also obtaining the mindset for reading and writing. These educational processes should be established as a [イ] in curricula so that we can develop a coherent learning program. The number of English classes and position of English education in elementary schoo will be further studied from a technical [ウ] in comprehensive discussions on the curriculum.

① basics	② common	③ improvement
④ interest	⑤ knowledge	⑥ subject
⑦ term	⑧ perspective	⑨ principle

(☆☆☆◎◎◎)

【6】Read the following article consisting of nine paragraphs and answer the questions below.

My sister and her husband bought an unfinished house a little while ago. Since then, we haven't been able to talk about anything else. The sole topic of [ア] for the past two months has been bathroom tiles: ceramic, granite, marble, metal, stone, wood, glass, and every type of laminate known to man. Rarely have I seen my sister in such anguish. "There are just too many to choose from," she exclaims, throwing her hands in the air and returning to the tile catalog, her constant [イ].

I've counted and researched: My local grocery store stocks 48 varieties of yogurt, 134 types of red wine, 64 different cleaning products, and a grand total of 30,000 items. Amazon, the Internet bookseller, has two million titles available. Nowadays, people are bombarded with options, such as hundreds of mental disorders, thousands of different careers, even more holiday destinations, and an infinite variety of lifestyles. There has never been more [ウ].

When I was young, we had three types of yogurt, three television channels, two churches, two kinds of cheese (mild or strong), one type of fish (trout), and one telephone provided by the Swiss Post. The black box with the dial served no other [エ] than making calls, and that did us just fine. In contrast, anyone who enters a cell-phone store today runs the risk of being flattened by an avalanche of brands, models, and contract options.

And yet selection is the yardstick of progress. [カ]

In his book of the same title, psychologist Barry Schwartz describes why this is so. First, a large selection leads to inner paralysis. [キ]

Second, a broader selection leads to poorer decisions. If you ask young people what is important in a life partner, they reel off all the usual qualities: intelligence, good manners, warmth, the ability to listen, a sense of humor, and physical attractiveness. But do they actually take these criteria into account when choosing someone?

[ク]

Finally, large selection leads to discontent.

[ケ]

So what can you do? Think carefully about what you want before you inspect existing offers. Write down these criteria and stick to them rigidly. Also, realize that you can neber make a perfect decision. Aiming for this is, given the flood of possibilities, a form of irrational perfectionism. Instead, learn to love a "good" choice. Yes, even in terms of life partners. Only the best will do?

In this age of unlimited variety, rather the [オ] is true: "Good enough" is the new optimum (except, of course, for you and me).

(SOURCE: "*The Art of Thinking Clearly*" by Rolf Dobelli)

(No. 1) Choose the most suitable word from ① to ⑥ for each blank [ア] through [オ].

① appreciation　② choice　③ companion
④ conversation　⑤ opposite　⑥ purpose

(No. 2) Place these four passages in their appropriate locations [カ] through [ケ].

① How can you be sure you are making the right choice when two hundred options surround and confound you? The answer is: You cannot. The more choice you have, the more unsure and therefore dissatisfied you are afterward.

② In the past, a young man from a village of average size could choose among maybe twenty girls of similar age with whom he went to school. He knew their families and vice versa, leading to a decision based on several well-known attributes. Nowadays, in the era of online dating, millions of potential partners are at our disposal. It has been proven that the stress caused by this, mind-boggling variety is so large that the male brain reduces the decision to one single criterion: physical attractiveness. The consequences of this selection process you already know - perhaps even from personal experience.

③ It is what sets us apart from planned economies and the Stone Age. Yes, abundance makes you giddy, but there is a limit. When it is exceeded, a surfeit of choices destroys quality of life. The technical term for this is the paradox of choice.

④ To test this, a supermarket set up a stand where customers could sample twenty-four varieties of jelly. They could try as many as they liked and then buy them at a discount. The next day, the owners carried out the same experiment with only six flavors. The result? They sold ten times more jelly on day two. Why? With such a wide range, customers could not come to a decision, so they bought nothing. The experiment was repeated several times with different products. The results were always the same.

(☆☆☆☆◎◎◎)

【7】Rearrange the words of the underlined parts and complete the sentences. Answer the number of words that come second and seventh.

(1) Naomi could not sleep that night. She [① about ② awake ③ be ④ chance ⑤ her ⑥ lay ⑦ thinking ⑧ to] the first woman to sail single-handed and non-stop around the

world.

second　[　ア　]　　seventh　[　イ　]

(2)　The most difficult part of the voyage would be Cape Horn. Naomi knew that she had to sail round it no later than March [①　be　②　good　③　in　④　of　⑤　order　⑥　sure　⑦　to　⑧　weather].

second　[　ウ　]　　seventh　[　エ　]

(3)　The cultivation of the human [①　is　②　needed　③　resources　④　science　⑤　support　⑥　to　⑦　which] and technology innovation is not to be done in a day.

second　[　オ　]　　seventh　[　カ　]

(☆☆☆◎◎◎)

解答・解説

【中高共通】

【1】Part A　(1)　④　(2)　③　(3)　①　(4)　②　(5)　④

Part B　No. 1　The deadline is next Thursday.　No. 2　Put it back where it belongs.　No. 3　Let's get started.　No. 4　Could you clear your desk?　No. 5　There should be eight kinds of handouts in total.

〈解説〉Part A　音声を聞いてその説明に当てはまる単語を選ぶ問題。スクリプトは公開されていないが，解答の選択肢を見るとそれほど難しい語はない。1度しか読まれないので，集中して聞くことが必要である。　Part B　聞き取りに注意すべき語を中心に解説する。

No.1　nextの[t]音は発音されないか，発音されても弱い。　No.2　Putの[t]音とitの[i]音はつながり，itの[t]音は発音されず全体として「プリッバック」のように聞こえる。it belongsのitの[t]音は発音されないか，発音されても弱い。　No.3　get startedはgetの[t]音が消えて「ゲッスターティドゥ」のように聞こえる。 No.4 Could youはCouldの[d]音とyouの[j]音がつながり，「クヂュ」のような独特な響きの音になる。 No.5 should beはshouldの[d]音が消えて「シュッビー」のように聞こえる。

【2】(1) ア ② (2) イ ② ウ ③

〈解説〉(1) 空所アの下に「権限を与えられた人のみ(関係者のみ)」とあることから判断する。 (2) イ 注射を打つ看護師のセリフなので，①「私は注射を打ってもらったほうがよい」は間違い。④のgive＋人＋a handは「人に手をあげる→人を手伝う」という意味。手を差し出すわけではない。ウは患者の子どものセリフなので，④「あなたはちょっとチクっと感じるかもしれない」は間違い。①shoot outは「撃ち抜く」という意味で，shot「皮下注射」と紛らわしい。

【3】(1) ア ② (2) イ ③ (3) ウ ② (4) エ ①
(5) オ ① (6) カ ③

〈解説〉(1) Most of the peopleはその人たち(ある特定のグループ)の中の「ほとんどの人たち」という意味で使われるが，一般的な「ほとんどの人たち」という場合はMost peopleを用いる。③のalmostは副詞なので名詞(people)を修飾しない。 (2) ①Evenは副詞，④Neverthelessは接続副詞でともに目的語をとらない。②Forは「～という事実のおかげで」という意味になり，主文の内容とつじつまが合わないので不可。「天候が非常に悪いという事実を考慮すると，頂上に着くことができたのは幸運だった」と考え，given「～を考慮すると」(前置詞)が正解。
(3) blame＋～(人)＋…「…を～のせいにする」という意味。
(4) above normalで「普通以上の」。 (5) as a special benefit「特別な恩恵として」。④profitはビジネスや何かの行為をして得た「利益」や「得」という意味。 (6) 空所のあとは「会社の年間予算の4分の1を使う」とありprojectがどういうプロジェクトなのか説明しているので，projectを先行詞(人以外)と考え，関係代名詞を選ぶ。

【4】No. 1　ア　①　　イ　②　　ウ　④　　エ　③　　No. 2　オ　①　カ　②　　キ　④　　No. 3　ク　①　　ケ　①　　コ　①　　サ　④

No. 4　(I think the program would equip them with) high self-esteem. (This is because) it is necessary to live a fulfilling life. People with high self-esteem tend to try new things without being afraid of failure. On the other hand, low self-esteem results in a negative attitude toward everything. Providing students with the opportunity to learn how to build their self-esteem is very important for their mental growth.

〈解説〉(No.1)　アの直後に(Rickが考えた)コースに何が含まれるべきかについて情報を探し求めて「彼は120校の高校で2,000人以上の生徒に同じ2つの質問をした」とあるので，①「Rickは大学を中退し，国中で高校生に面接することを始めた」になる。「生徒に質問をする」と「生徒に面接する」が同じ内容を表す。　イ　直前に「Rickは2か月間，車中で寝て，合計60ドルで生活した。ほとんどの日をクラッカーにピーナッツバターを塗ったものを食べた。何も食べない日もあった」と，かなりお金がない状態で調査を続けた様子が記述されているので，②「Rickは資金がほとんどなかったが，夢にのめり込んだ」が続く。

ウ　直後の文に「財団法人の副会長は，大柄で黒髪の男で，冷たく厳しい顔をしていた」とあり，威圧感もあり，顔つきも怖そうだと読み取れるので，④「Rickは文字どおり恐怖で震えていた」が入る。

エ　第9段落で，財団法人の副会長は教育プログラムに資金を出してきたが，すべて失敗し，Rickのアイディアも失敗するだろうと述べている。空所のあとで「どの財団法人が10代の若者のプロジェクトに資金を出すことに関心があるかRickは調査を始めた」とあり，副会長に断られたが，それでも自分のアイディアを捨てきれず，資金を出してくれる他の組織を探していることから考える。③のthis manとはRickに資金を出すことを断った財団の副会長のこと。「この男が間違っていたと証明することをRickは誓った」のである。　(No.2)　オの直後に「子どものふつうの成長の理解のし方」とあるので，親と子どもの記述だと見当をつけ，「良い親のなり方」にする。　カ　handle financial managementで「財務管理(収支の管理)」。　キ　intuit the meaning of life「人生の意味を直観で理解する」。　(No.3)　ク　第1段落2文目に「30歳の人1,000人に，高等教育は現実社会で必要とする技能を生徒に身につけさせたか尋ねた調査に出会った」とあり，その調査で80%以上の人が「～」と返答したとある。その内容を受けて，第2段落1文目に「これらの30歳の人たちはまた，(過去に)どんな技能を教えてもらいたかったと，(今)望んでいるかと尋ねられた」とある。wishは仮定法でS＋had＋過去分詞が続くので，現実社会で必要とする技能を教えてもらわなかったという過去の事実に反して仮定していることから判断する。　ケ　第6段落で全国のトップの教育者やカウンセリングや心理学のリーダーたちに相手にされず，「それら(彼らに言われたこと)は決して勇気を与えるものではなかった」と考える。①「決して～ない」，②「多かれ少なかれ」，③「かなり多数の」，④「わずかに」。

コ　第9段落で，「財団法人の副会長は教育プログラムに資金を出してきたが，すべて～だった。Rickのアイディアも[　コ　]だろう」とあり，そのあとでその理由として，「君は20歳だし，経験も金も学位も何もない」と述べていることから判断する。　サ　第11段落で助成金の申請書を次から次に送ったが断られ，最後の155通目の申請書が[　サ　]されたとき，「Rickを支えていたものが崩れ始めた」とあるので，最後も断られたと考え，turn downにする。　(No.4)　選んだ選択肢をなぜ身につける必要があり，身につけるとどういう利点があるかなどを，簡潔にまとめる。

【5】ア　④　　イ　⑥　　ウ　⑧

〈解説〉「今後の英語教育の改善・充実方策について(報告)」(平成26年9月，英語教育の在り方に関する有識者会議)の英訳からの出題である。

ア　小学生の中学年の児童なので，「英語のコミュニケーション技能の基礎を築き，英語への～を高める」となる。英語を学び始めるときは，英語に関心を持ってもらい基礎を築くことから始めると考える。

イ　(小学校中学年はコミュニケーション技能の基礎を築き，高学年はリスニングとスピーキングを含む基本的なコミュニケーション技能を磨き，リーディングとライティングに対する取り組み方を獲得するといった)「これらの教育プロセスは，一貫した学習プログラムを開発できるようにカリキュラムの～として築かれるべきだ」とあり，どの時期にどの技能を学ぶのか一貫したテーマが必要だと考える。
ウ 「英語の授業数や小学校における英語教育の地位は，(教師や文部科学省の役人など教育の専門家によって)カリキュラムについての包括的な議論の中で，専門的な観点からさらに研究されるだろう」とする。

【6】No. 1 ア ④ イ ③ ウ ② エ ⑥ オ ⑤
No. 2 カ ③ キ ④ ク ② ケ ①
〈解説〉(No.1) ア 空所の直前の文で，「未完成の家を買って以来，他のことについは何も話し合うことができなかった」とあり，具体的には浴室のタイルをセラミックにするのか，花崗岩にするのか，大理石なのかなどが「会話」の話題になっていることから判断する。
イ the tile catalogueの直後に比ゆ的に述べているので，この2か月間，あまりにも多くの品ぞろえが記載されているtile catalogueをいつも見て，どうするか悩んでいるのでher constant companion「彼女のいつもいる仲間」だと考える。 ウ 第2段落は地元の食料品店の品ぞろえの多さや，アマゾンやネット上の本屋の蔵書の多さや，精神疾患の数の多さ，休日の目的地の多さなどいろいろなところで，選択肢が増えているという流れなので，「今日よりも多くの選択肢があったことはない」と考え，There has never been more choice (than today).とする。
エ serve a purpose「目的にかなう，目的を果たす」という意味。(自分が若かったころは)「ダイヤルのついた黒い箱は電話をかけるという目的以外は果たさず，それで私たちは十分だった」となる。 オ 選択肢が多いことがいい結果を生むわけではなく，かえって麻痺して悪い決定をしてしまうことが多いという流れを踏まえ，最後に結論として，「『まあまあ』が一番ふさわしい新たな基準である」とあるので，無限に近い選択肢とは「反対に。そこそこの」といった意味の選択肢が一番ふさわしいと考える。 (No.2) カ 第3段落に筆者の小さい頃は選択肢がなかったが，それで満足だった。しかし今は雪崩のようなブランドやモデルや契約のオプションが多すぎて，第4段落初めに「それなのに選択(できること)は進歩の尺度となっている」と続く。③の最初のitはselectionを指し，「それ(選択できること)が，計画経済と石器時代を分けているものである」と考える。 キ 第5段落2文目に心理学者のBarry Schwartzの本の記述として，「豊富な選択肢(品ぞろえ)は精神の麻痺につながる」とあり，そのあとにそれがどういうことなのか，具体的に述べているものが続くと見当をつける。④はスーパーマーケットのオーナーが，ゼリーを24種類そろえたときと6種類そろえたときで，売り上げを比較したところ，6種類そろえたときのほうが10倍売り上げが上がり，客は品ぞろえが豊富だと(精神が麻痺して)決定できず，何も買わないという結果に至ったとあり，具体例になっている。 ク 第6段落にBarryの本の2つ目の記述として，「品ぞろえが多くなれば，判断はよりまずくなる」とあり，人生の伴侶を選ぶとき，知性や行儀のよさなどいろいろな基準を挙げているが，本当に考慮しているかと問題を提起している。②では，昔は平均的な規模の村では家族構成もわかっているような同年代の男女が結婚をしたとある。今はonline datingで何百万人もいる人から選ぶので，男性の脳は結局，身体的魅力という1つの基準で選ぶという結果になるとあり，品ぞろえが多くなると判断はまずくなるという具体例になっている。
ケ 第7段落最初の文に「最後に品ぞろえが豊富だと結局，不満になる」とある。①の3文目に「選択肢を多くもてばもつほど，もっと確信がなくなり，その結果あとで不満になる」とあり，最初の文を補足する内容になっていることから判断する。

【7】(1) ア ② イ ⑧ (2) ウ ⑤ エ ② (3) オ ⑦ カ ④

〈解説〉(1)「彼女は目を覚ましたまま横になり，単独で世界一周を航海する最初の女性になる機会について考えていた」となる。lie awake

「目を覚ましたまま横になる」, lie doing「～しながら横になる」, think about「～について考える」, chance to do「～する機会」をそれぞれ意味のまとまりとして組み合わせ, lay awake thinking about her chance to beとする。 (2)「ナオミは確実に良い天候であるために, 3月までにホーン岬を迂回して航海しなければならないことを知っていた」となる。in order to doは目的を表して「～するために」, sure ofは「～を確信して」, good weather「良い天候」をそれぞれ意味のまとまりとして組み合わせ, in order to be sure of good weatherとする。 (3) human resources「人材」をひとまとまりにし, The cultivation of the human resources is not to be done in a day.「人材育成は1日でなされるものではない」という大まかな文の骨組みを作る。選択肢に関係代名詞のwhichがあるので, (人でない)名詞を後ろから修飾する節を考え, (The cultivation of the human) resources which is needed to support science (and technology innovation ～)「科学技術の革新を支えるために必要とされる人材育成は～」とする。

2016年度　実施問題

【中高共通】

【1】(Listening Test)

Part A　Listen to the description and choose the item that fits it. Then mark the number ①, ②, ③ or ④ on your answer sheet. Each description will be read once.

(1)　This is a drawing that helps you find your way around

①　list　②　map　③　note　④　passport

(2)　This is a very large round object in space that moves around the sun or another star

①　circle　②　dish　③　planet　④　spaceship

(3)　This is a period of time during which students are taught.

①　class　②　gym　③　homework　④　watch

(4)　This is to take and use something that belongs to somebody else, and return it to them at a later time.

①　borrow　②　lend　③　rent　④　purchase

(5)　This is to buy a product from another country and bring it to your country.

①　export　②　import　③　support　④　transport

Part B　Listen to the sentences and write down the whole sentence. Each sentence will be read twice.

No.1　Make groups of four.

No.2　Come to the front.

No.3　Who wants to try?

No.4　I want someone to read this page.

No.5　May I ask you a favor(favour)?

(☆☆◎◎◎)

【２】Below are the typical phrases used in certain situations. Look at the drawings and choose the phrase most likely to be heard in the situation. Then mark the number ①, ②, ③ or ④ on your answer sheet.

(1)

① Go ahead!

② Go for it!

③ Keep out!

④ Make progress!

(2)

① How much is the commission?

② How would you like your bills?

③ May I have small change?

④ Will that be cash or charge?

(☆☆◎◎◎)

【3】Choose the best item from ① to ④ below each question to fill in the blank.

(1) Even a child can operate the hard disk recorder by [ア] the instructions in the manual.

① doing ② following ③ going ④ looking

(2) "[イ]*gengo-katsudo* in English?" "Language activities."

① How do you call ② How do you tell ③ What do you call ④ What do you say

(3) The more cigarettes a person smokes per day, the [ウ] the health risk will be.

① greater ② more great ③ more greater ④ more greatest

(4) The municipal authorities are making [エ] to reduce the number of crimes in this area.

① a unique attempt ② an unique attempt ③ attempt an unique ④ unique attempt

(5) Since my son started to live alone, he had to get used [オ] by himself.

① a cook ② cooking ③ to cook ④ to cooking

(6) A proverb says, "If you run after two hares, you will catch [カ]." That is, if you try to do two things at the same time, both trials will end up in failure.

① both ② either ③ neither ④ never

(☆☆☆◎◎◎◎)

【４】 Read the following passage and answer the questions below.

It is granted only to the heart (ア) <u>that</u> abounds with integrity, trust, generosity, and love to realize true prosperity. The heart ①<u>that</u> is not possessed of these qualities cannot know prosperity, for prosperity, like happiness, is not an outward possession but an inward realization. Greedy people may become millionaires, but they will always be wretched, and mean, and poor, and will even consider themselves outwardly poor so long as there is another person in the world who is richer than they are, while the upright, the open-handed, and the loving will realize a full and rich prosperity, even though their outward possessions may be small.

When we contemplate the fact ②<u>that</u> the universe is abounding in all good things, material as well as spiritual, and compare it to the blind eagerness to secure a few gold coins or a few acres of dirt, it is then ③<u>that</u> we realize how dark and ignorant selfishness is. It is then that we know ④<u>that</u> self-seeking is self-destruction.

Nature gives all, without reservation, and loses nothing;[　イ　]. If you would realize true prosperity do not settle down, as many have done, into the belief that if you do right, everything will go wrong. Do not allow the word "competition" to shake your faith in the supremacy of righteousness. I do not care what people may say about the "laws of competition," for I know the unchangeable law, which shall one day put them all to rout and which puts them to rout even now in the heart and life of the righteous — and knowing this law, I can contemplate all dishonesty with undisturbed repose, for I know where certain destruction awaits it.

Under all circumstances, do that which you believe to be [　エ　], and trust the law ; trust the Divine Power that is imminent in the universe, and it will never desert you, and you will always be protected. By such a trust all your losses will be converted into gains, and all curses that threaten will be transmuted into blessings. Never let go of integrity, generosity, and love, for these, coupled with energy, will lift you into the truly prosperous state. Do not believe the world when it tells you that you must always attend to "number one" first, and to others afterward. To do this is not to [ウ] at all but only of one's own comforts. To those who practice this, the day will come when all will desert them, and when they cry out in their loneliness and anguish, there will be no one to hear and help them. To consider one's self before all others is to cramp and warp and hinder every noble and divine impulse. Let your soul expand, let your heart reach out to others in loving and generous warmth, and great and lasting will be your joy and all prosperity will come to you.

Those who have wandered from the highway of righteousness guard themselves against competition. Those who always pursue the right do not have to trouble about such defense. This is no [オ] statement. There are people today who, by the power of integrity and faith, have defied all competition, and who, without swerving in the least from their methods, when competed with, have risen steadily into prosperity, while those who tried to undermine them have fallen back defeated.

To possess those [カ] qualities which constitute goodness is to be armored against all the powers of evil and to be doubly protected in every time of trial ; and to build oneself up in those qualities is to build up a success which cannot be shaken and to enter into a prosperity which will endure forever.

(SOURCE : "*As a Man Thinketh*"by James Allen)

(No. 1) Choose the same use of the underlined word (ア) <u>that</u>, from the underlined words ① to ④ in the passage.

(No. 2) Choose from ① to ④ the most appropriate words for the blanks [イ] and [ウ].

[イ] ① those grasping all lose everything

② those grasping all lose nothing

③ those losing all grasp nothing

④ those losing nothing grasp everything

[　ウ　]　① think of all circumstances　② think of one's self
③ think of others　④ think of your heart

(No. 3)　Choose from ① to ⑥ the most appropriate word for the blanks [　エ　], [　オ　] and [　カ　].

① empty　② inward　③ outward　④ poor　⑤ right
⑥ warm

(No. 4)　Choose from ① to ④ the most appropriate title for the passage.

① The Realization of Prosperity
② The Secret of Abounding Happiness
③ The Two Masters, Self and Truth
④ The Way out of Undesirable Conditions

(☆☆☆☆◎◎◎)

【5】The following is a part of the chapter "Five Proposals and Specific Measures for Developing Proficiency in English for International Communication (Provisional translation)." Choose the most suitable word from ① to ⑨ for each blank [　ア　] through [　ウ　].

Foreign language proficiency required in global society can be defined as capability of smooth communication with people of different countries and cultures using foreign languages as a tool. The capability of smooth communication [　ア　], for example, confident and active attitude toward communication with people of different countries and cultures as well as accurate understanding of partner's thoughts and intentions based on his/her [　イ　] and social background, [　ウ　] and reasoned explanation of one's own views, and convincing partners in course of debates.

① alive　② certification　③ cultural　④ implies
⑤ legal　⑥ logical　⑦ relation　⑧ speech
⑨ textbook

(☆☆☆◎◎◎)

【6】Read the following passage consisting of six paragraphs and answer the questions below.

Consider Ashwini Doshi, who I first met several years ago when, as a graduate student, she applied for a research assistant job in our department. Despite my openness, I was really taken aback when she walked into my office for the job interview. Ashwini is a beautiful woman, but she is only three and a half feet tall. Her voice is that of a little girl, but her ideas are those of a mature adult. I'm embarrassed to say that I didn't hire her for the position. [[ア]]

Born in Mumbai (formerly Bombay), Ashwini grew up in a household of nineteen — her father, his three brothers, their wives, all of their children, and her grandparents. She was born normal size, but by the time she was a year old, it was clear that she wasn't growing properly. [[イ]]

Ashwini was fortunate that her family was so open-minded and loving. [[ウ]]

Ashwini sincerely feels there's nothing she can't do and has demonstrated this time and again. [[エ]] Out of necessity, she figures out ingenious solutions to all the physical obstacles that face her every single day.

When I asked Ashwini about the problems she faces, she had a hard time coming up with any. She just doesn't see them. When [オ], she cited the difficulty of finding a driving school willing to accept her as a student. After years of depending on rides from friends and on public transportation, she decided to learn to drive and [カ] a set of pedal extenders so she could reach the gas and brake pedals. It took dozens of calls before she found a driving school that would take her.

What is most impressive is that Ashwini always delivers more than 100 percent of what she's [キ] upon to do. Her only regret? She actually wishes she had [ク] even more risks when she was younger. Despite all she has overcome, Ashwini still thinks she took the safe path. She embraces the idea that life isn't a dress rehearsal, and that you only get one chance to do the best job. Ashwini is the ideal model of someone who never misses an opportunity to be fabulous.

(SOURCE : "*What I Wish I Knew When I Was 20*" by Tina Seelig)

(No. 1) Place these four passages in their appropriate locations [　ア　] through [　エ　].

① In many families, someone so different would have caused great embarrassment and, so, been hidden away. But they didn't do this to Ashwini. In fact, she went to the best schools in Bombay and always excelled. She has a remarkably positive attitude, and from a young age felt strangely empowered by her differences. Ashwini still thinks of herself as a normal person living an extraordinary life.

② She came to California all by herself to attend graduate school. In addition to the cultural differences and her physical limitations, she didn't know anyone when she arrived. Many of her friends encouraged her to stay put, saying life would he much easier for her in India. But she persisted. Once she arrived at Stanford, the only accommodation she received was a small step stool in her apartment that would enable her to reach the stove.

③ The doctors in India weren't able to provide guidance on her care, so her parents sent X-rays of her tiny skeleton to specialists in the United States. The only medical option was to put bone extensions in each of her extremities, a process that would have required extensive surgery over six years. She also would have been bedridden for months at a time, which was out of the question for this very active young girl.

④ This happens to Ashwini a lot. People are so surprised by her appearance that it usually takes several interactions before they're comfortable enough to see past her physical differences. I'm fortunate that she decided to take my course, because it gave me an opportunity to get to know her quite well. When another position became available in our group, I jumped at the chance to hire her. Ashwini's work was exemplary, she was a terrific team player, and she always went way beyond what was expected.

(No. 2) Choose the most suitable word from ① to ⑤ for each blank [オ] through [ク].

① called ② gone ③ pressed ④ purchased

⑤ taken

(☆☆☆☆◎◎◎)

【7】Rearrange the words of the underlined parts below and complete the sentences. Answer the words that come second and sixth.

(1) It is still early spring. You Should [①as ②clothes ③get ④not ⑤so ⑥to ⑦warm ⑧wear] a cold.

(2) Some Japanese people are eager to hear about [①about ②countries ③from ④other ⑤people ⑥think ⑦what] them, but they don't have enough communication skills.

(3) A: You speak English as if you were a native speaker. How did you learn English?

B: The best way [①a foreign language ②is ③it ④to go ⑤to learn ⑥to the country ⑦where] is spoken.

(☆☆☆☆◎◎◎)

【8】The Hokuriku Shinkansen line started its operation on March 14,2015. It is said that a new means of transportation has many influences on our lives. What do you think is the greatest of them? Why do you think so? Please write your opinion in 50 words or more in English.

(☆☆☆☆◎◎◎)

解答・解説

【中高共通】

【1】Part A　(1)　②　(2)　③　(3)　①　(4)　①　(5)　②

Part B　No.1　Make groups of four.　No.2　Come to the front.

No.3　Who wants to try?　No.4　I want someone to read this page.

No.5　May I ask you a favor (favour)?

〈解説〉Part A　例年リスニング問題が出題されている都道府県の場合，日頃から市販の教材などを活用して十分に訓練しておきたい。また，このタイプの問題では，放送が開始される前に質問と選択肢に必ず目を通しておくことが重要である。いずれの問題も基礎的な単語を説明するものであり難易度は高くないが，1回しか放送されないので集中して臨む必要がある。　Part B　この問題では，全ての単語を聞き取る必要があるが，2回読まれるので，聞きのがしても，あわてずに2回目に聞きとるようにする。各英文は短く難易度も高くないが，日頃からディクテーションの訓練をしておきたい。

【2】(1)　②　(2)　②

〈解説〉(1)　正解の②は「頑張れ」，①は「さあ，早く」，③は「立入禁止」の意味である。いずれも基本的な表現なので覚えておきたい。④のmake progressは「上達する」の意味だが，この場合のようなかけ声としては不適である。　(2)　外貨両替所のスタッフの発言として適切なのは「紙幣の内訳はどうしますか」を意味する②である。①および③も両替の際に用いる表現だが，お客の側の発言である。④は「お支払いは現金ですか，それともカードですか」の意味であり，買い物の際に店員が使用する表現である。

【3】(1) ② (2) ③ (3) ① (4) ① (5) ④ (6) ③

〈解説〉いずれも習得しておくべき基礎的な表現や文法の問題である。
(1) follow the instructions「指示に従う」は取扱説明書などでよく見られる表現である。 (2) 英語で何と言うのか質問する場合，How do you say ～ in English?ということはできるが，正解の③以外の選択肢の表現は使われない。 (3) The比較級＋the比較級の構文において，greatの比較級を選択する基本的な問題である。 (4) make an attemptは「試みる」の意味である。形容詞uniqueのuの発音は母音ではないため，前置詞をanでなくaとすべきことに注意が必要である。 (5) get used to ～「～に慣れる」やbe used to ～「～に慣れている」は基本的な表現だが，～を名詞または動名詞とすべきことに注意が必要である。 (6)「二兎を追う者は一兎も得ず」の英訳で，③以外の選択肢は不適切である。

【4】ア ① イ ① ウ ③ エ ⑤ オ ① カ ② キ ①

〈解説〉ア アと同様にthatがwhichに代えることのできる関係代名詞として使われているのは①のみである。 イ 正解は①「全てをつかもうとする者は全てを失う」の意味である。 ウ 空欄ウを含む文の主語であるTo do thisは直前の文のbelieve以下の部分を指していることから，最も適切な選択肢は③である。「これをすることは，他の人のことをまったく考えずに自分自身の満足のみを考えること」の意味である。 エ 空欄エを含む節は「あなたが正しいと思うことをしなさい」の意味である。 オ 正解は①empty「空虚な，無意味な」の意味の形容詞である。 カ 正解は②inward「心の中の」の意味の形容詞である。 キ 全体を読めば適切なタイトルが①「成功の実現」であることはわかるが，最初と最後のパラグラフに注目すると，冒頭の文ではrealize true prosperity，末尾の文ではenter into a prosperityという表現が使われており，大きなヒントとなる。

【5】ア　④　　イ　③　　ウ　⑥

〈解説〉文部科学省がとりまとめた「国際共通語としての英語力向上のための5つの提言と具体的施策」の英訳の抜粋であるが，読んだことがなくても解答可能な問題である。　ア　The capability of smooth communicationを主語とする動詞を入れるべきであり，④implies「意味する」以外の選択肢は不適切である。　イ　全ての選択肢を当てはめると，cultural and social background「文化的・社会的背景」とする③が最も適切であることは容易にわかる。　ウ　イと同様，全ての選択肢を当てはめると，logical and reasoned explanation「論理的で筋の通った説明」とする⑥が最も文脈に合う。

【6】No.1　ア　④　　イ　③　　ウ　①　　エ　②
No.2　オ　③　　カ　④　　キ　①　　ク　⑤

〈解説〉No.1　ア　選択肢④の最初の文の主語Thisは，空欄アの前に述べられている，私がAshwiniの外見に戸惑い彼女を採用しなかったことを指している。したがって，アに入るのは④である。　イ　第2パラグラフの冒頭の文ではAshwiniの病気が判明した時のことを述べていることから，その後の経過について説明している③を入れるのが最も適切である。　ウ　第3パラグラフの冒頭の文ではAshwiniの家族のことに言及しており，一般的な家族についての説明から始まる①を入れるのが自然である。　エ　第4パラグラフの冒頭の文では，Ashwiniが何事にも挑戦することが述べられており，これについて具体的に説明している②を入れると文脈に合う。　No.2　オ　when (she was) pressedは「迫られて，やっとのことで」の意味である。カ　正解は「購入する」の意味の動詞の過去形である。　キ　call upon (on) to doは「～するよう頼む」の意味である。　ク　take a risk (risks)は「危険を冒す」の意味である。

【7】(1)　2番目　⑦　　6番目　④　　(2)　2番目　⑤　　6番目　⑥
(3)　2番目　①　　6番目　⑦

〈解説〉(1)　正しい語順はwear warm clothes so as not to getである。so as not to doは「～しないように，～するといけないから」の意味である。(2)　whatで始まる名詞節を作る。people from other countriesがひとかたまり。think aboutのaboutを忘れないように。正しい語順はwhat people from other countries think aboutである。　(3)　The best wayに続くのはto learn a foreign languageで，それとto go to the country where it (is spoken)をbe動詞で結べばよい。正しい語順はto learn a foreign language is to go to the country where itである。

【8】I think the greatest change is that the number of people visiting Ishikawa has increased. There are many places to see, but it used to take about four hours to travel from Tokyo to Ishikawa. Now it only takes two and a half hours. If many tourists visit Ishikawa, positive economic outcomes are expected. (54 words)

〈解説〉「北陸新幹線が私たちの生活にもたらす最も大きな影響とその理由」について，解答者の考えを自由に述べればよい。語数は50語以上で上限は設けられていないが，適切な語数で簡潔に説明することが求められる。解答例では，最も大きな変化として石川県を訪れる人が増えたことを述べた上で，観光客が増えればプラスの成果が期待できるとの理由を示している。

2015年度　実施問題

【中高共通】

【リスニング放送原稿(ここから)】

Part A

(1) This is a vehicle that hangs from and is pulled by a moving cable which carries passengers up and down a mountain.

(2) This is a book that teaches a particular subject and is used especially in schools and colleges.

(3) This is a quality of mind or spirit that enables a person to face any difficulty.

(4) This is a small device containing powder that burns or explodes and produces bright colored lights and loud noiscs, used especially at cerebrations.

(5) He is a new star in the professional league of Japanese-style wrestling, in which the people taking part are extremely large.

Part B

No.1 Give it a try.

No.2 Please read this section aloud.

No.3 Let's move on to the next topic.

No.4 What day of the week is it today?

No.5 We need a volunteer to come up to the front.

【リスニング放送原稿(ここまで)】

【1】(Listening Test)

Part A Listen to the description and choose the item that fits it. Then mark the number ①, ②, ③ or ④ on your answer sheet. Each description will be read once.

(1) ① bullet train ② cable car ③ express train
④ street car

(2) ① dictionary ② notebook ③ novel
④ textbook

(3) ① activity ② courage ③ dialect
④ gesture

(4) ① firework ② homework ③ housework
④ teamwork

(5) ① Endo Shota ② Honda Keisuke ③ Matsui Hideki
④ Tsuda Kentaro

Part B Listen to the sentences and write down the whole sentence. Each sentence will be read twice.

(☆☆◎◎◎)

【2】Below are the typical phrases used in certain situations. Look at the drawings and choose the phrase most likely to be heard in the situation. Then mark the number ①, ②, ③, ④ or ⑤ on your answer sheet.

(1)

(2)

① Any more fares, please?

② Anything to declare?

③ Are you being served?

④ Could I have the bill, please?

⑤ Keep the change.

(☆◎◎◎)

【3】Choose the best item from ① to ④ below each question to fill in the blank.

(1) [　　] thirty years since he died, but many people remember him as a great politician.

① He has been　② He has passed　③ It has been

④ It has passed

(2) Although the highway bus I took was supposed to arrive by six o'clock, it [　　] by more than forty minutes.

① had delayed　② had to delay　③ was delayed

④ was delaying

(3) "I can't believe that she got married to such a rude man!" "I can't, either. As the proverb goes, [　　]."

① a friend in need is a friend indeed
② between two stools one falls to the ground
③ the face is the expression of the mind
④ there is no accounting for taste

(4) I had a hard time deciding which of the two models to choose, but I think I will buy this car because it is [　　] to that one in handling.

① better　② particular　③ senior　④ superior

(5) After a fire damaged its main factory, Detroit Industry had to [　　] its plan to expand production of its new model.

① react　② recollect　③ reconsider　④ respond

(☆☆☆◎◎◎)

【4】Read the following passage and answer the questions below.

In recent decades, we have come to believe firmly in the power of information and communications technology as a reformer of pedagogy. This has been evidenced by the large-scale acquisition of IT equipment by educational establishments－on the assumption that a significant part of the teaching would become virtual and be delivered online. However, change has been much slower than anticipated. For example, the PISA results show that the use of utility software in educational institutions is slight, and that the pace of growth has been slow. In some countries the use has actually declined.

Information and communications technology has had a much greater impact on the lives of young people outside of educational institutions, and [　ア　] is possibly one of the few areas in which the pupils' know-how may clearly exceed that of teachers. Teachers may well not even be aware of (　オ　). The fascination of chat and games environments is very strong for young people. Transforming fan fiction into educational fiction and reality is therefore a great challenge and an opportunity.

Technology has also had a fundamental impact on competence in the world of employment, the media and many other sectors of society. Basic IT skills have become a part of general knowledge comparable to literacy, but [　イ　] to have improved at all. The utilisation of information technology is still too often isolated in a separate content area in educational institutions.

In view of the demands of employment markets and the need for lifelong learning skills, basic IT competence should be one of the primary goals of comprehensive education, just like (　カ　) and the elements of mathematics. The development of these skills cannot be excluded from education that is common to all because then [　ウ　]. The present inability of education systems to include basic training in technology use as part of an all-round education is a serious threat to (　キ　) and the guarantee of equal opportunities to young people in terms of coping with the technological demands of further study and the employment sector.

Succcssful pedagogical applications of technology require considerable inputs in the development of so-called human technology. This requires, above all, investments in multidisciplinary research into applications of the latest research on learning and information technology, and the productisation of the results in school contexts. The latest results of pilot studies of human technology applications show that [　エ　] in a way that reaches the everyday reality of all teachers. Technology per se is no longer an obstacle.

<u>With wireless technology becoming more commonplace and the costs rapidly (　A　), new opportunities are being created for (　B　) learning environments and (　C　) them outside traditional school premises.</u> Different technologies also merge and create new potential for innovative combinations of image and sound. In future, the pedagogisation of technology, based on strong research, must be used to create new opportunities for replacing and improving learning processes in such a way that technology is perceived not as a threat to (　ク　) but as an important prop for its development. The importance of technology as a transformer of power, a promoter of interactive

structures in educational institutions, and an enabler of collaborative modes of operation provides an example of a human-technology approach that requires the coordinated development of research and school practices and operational cultures.

The significance of various assessments as a basis for decision-making in education policy is growing. Thus, producing the information on which the assessments are based will be [コ critical]. It is increasingly important to ensure that the production of information meets strict scientific [サ criteria], i.e. that it is impartial, independent and methodologically transparent.

(SOURCE : "Facing the Future" by Jyrki Loima)

(No. 1) Place these three sentence fragments in their appropriate locations [ア],[イ],[ウ] or [エ]. Then mark the number ①, ② or ③ on your answer sheet. One location will be left empty. Mark the number ④ for the empty space.

① it is possible to produce pedagogically functional information technology applications

② the different home conditions of children would play too great a role

③ the resources of schools to support the development of these skills do not appear

(No. 2) Choose the most suitable phrase from ① to ④ for each blank (オ), (カ), (キ) and (ク).

① educational equality

② reading literacy

③ the teacher's profession

④ their pupils' expertise

(No. 3) Choose the best combination from ① to ④ in order to fill in the blank (A), (B) and (C), and complete the underlined sentence.

① A : falling B : taking C : updating

② A : falling B : updating C : taking

③　A : taking　　B : updating　　C : falling

④　A : taking　　B : falling　　C : updating

(No.4) Choose the most suitable meaning from ① to ④ for [コ　critical], [サ　criteria].

①　criticizing　　②　important　　③　serious

④　tolerant

①　assessments　　②　interests　　③　standards

④　results

(No. 5) Answer the question below using 30 words or more of English.

When you teach English in junior high school or senior high school, how will you make use of ICT in your class?

* ICT : information and communications technology

(☆☆☆☆☆◎◎◎)

【５】The following is a part of the chapter "Foreign Language Activities" in the Courses of Study. Choose the most suitable word from ① to ⑨ for each blank [　ア　] through [　ウ　].

To form the [　ア　] of pupils' communication abilities through foreign languages while developing the understanding of languages and cultures through various [　イ　], fostering a positive attitude toward communication, and [　ウ　] pupils with the sounds and basic expressions of foreign languages.

①　accuracy　　②　conveying　　③　deepening

④　experiences　　⑤　familiarizing　　⑥　foundation

⑦　joy　　⑧　phrases　　⑨　situations

(☆☆☆◎◎◎)

【6】Read the following article consisting of seven paragraphs and answer the questions below.

Have you always wanted to have your own garden and grow fresh, healthy food but didn't know quite where to start? Which vegetable varieties to go for, how far from one another to place the seeds and how much water to use? That's also how Claire Reid felt back in 2002, at 16, when her father asked her to plant a garden during her school holidays.

[ア] So Reid then decided to put her young mind to work.

"I wanted to come up with an idea that if I only wanted to plant a meter of spinach, I only needed to buy a meter of spinach," recalls Reid.[イ]

Launched in 2010, Reid's Johannesburg-based startup produces a paper strip that comes pre-packaged with seeds and organic fertilizers.[ウ]

[エ]

There are 11 official languages in South Africa so the young [オ] uses simple pictures on the products' packaging to overcome language and literacy [カ]. "It tells you exactly where to water, all the nutrition is already in there,"says Reid, who sells her planting strips throughout South Africa. "Birds can't eat the seeds out of the [キ]; water can't move the seed; and you only need to plant as much as you have [ク] for."

Looking ahead, Reid is determined to see Reel Gardening grow, even outside South Africa. "We are hoping to be live in the UK, selling on the 1st of May," she says.

(SOURCE : CNN International Edition February 25, 2014)

(No. 1) Place these four passages in their appropriate locations [ア] through [エ].

① Reid says her biodegradable strips use 80% less water than traditional gardening methods, because they require water only at the exact location of each seed. And that's one reason why she shares her product with people in urban slums where water is less available. So far, more than 120 community and school gardens have sprouted up with Reid's help.

② "I was overwhelmed by the amount of seed I had to buy, the amount of fertilizer, the wastage," recalls Reid. Reid quickly realized that gardening was not made easy for beginners. She was frustrated that she had to measure manually the correct distance between the seeds, as well as to pay a small fortune to buy what she needed, since everything came in bulk—not to mention the badly written instructions.

③ These are spaced at the right depth and distance apart so they can be easily planted and maintained. The tapes, which are sold in reels, are packed by hand and cost $1 per meter. "We are passionate about starting a planting revolution," says Reid, whose packaged seed strips grow vegetables, herbs and flowers. "So we enable anyone to be able to grow vegetables — with little space, little education and little water"

④ After giving it some thought, Reid used baking flour and liquid fertilizer to stick seeds, in calculated intervals, onto newspaper strips. She then went on to plant the strips in furrows. The experiment worked and Reid was encouraged by a school teacher to present her idea into an expo for young South African scientists — Reid's project won the gold medal. "I was a 16 year old girl that was barely passing science in school and the concept of me becoming a businesswoman was quite absurd," says Reid. Yet, that high school idea has grown today to become Reel Gardening, an award-winning patented invention aiming to simplify food gardening and make it more effective.

(No. 2) Choose the most suitable word from ① to ⑤ for each blank [オ] through [ク].

① entrepreneur　② obstacles　③ qualification

④ soil ⑤ space

(☆☆☆☆◎◎◎)

【7】Rearrange the words of the underlined parts below and complete the sentences. Answer the words that come second and seventh.

(1) If you want to lose weight effectively, you have to [① activity ② addition ③ calorie intake ④ in ⑤ increase ⑥ physical ⑦ reducing ⑧ to].

(2) My dream is to run a small company of my own, but I haven't yet got as [① as ② I ③ money ④ much ⑤ need ⑥ start ⑦ to] a new business.

(3) A : "Mr. Tanaka, you have been teaching at a vocational high school for many years. What is important in career education?"

B : "In career education, we must repeatedly tell students [① belief ② choose ③ occupation ④ our ⑤ own ⑥ that ⑦ they ⑧ whatever], they should take pride in their choice."

(☆☆☆☆◎◎◎)

【8】Imagine you have a foreign student from another country in your class whose parents do not speak Japanese. You would like to meet his or her parent for some reason. Write a letter to the parent in English. The letter should be 50 words or more and include the following information; the time and place to meet, the reason.

(☆☆☆☆◎◎◎)

解答・解説

【中高共通】

【1】Part A　(1)　②　(2)　④　(3)　②　(4)　①　(5)　①

Part B　No.1　Give it a try.　No.2　Please read this section aloud.　No.3　Let's move on to the next topic.　No.4　What day of the week is it today?　No.5　We need a volunteer to come up to the front.

〈解説〉Part A　放送が一度しか流れない場合は，聞き逃すことを避けたいので，日頃からCD等でリスニングの能力を養っておく。

(1)　vehicleは「乗り物」という意味。その後にくる関係代名詞節の「移動ケーブルからつるされながら引っ張られ，山を登ったり下りたりして乗客を運ぶ」から，どういう「乗り物」なのか判断する。

(2)　a bookのあとの関係代名詞節の「ある特定の教科を教え，特に(小・中・高の)学校や大学で使われる」から，どういう「本」なのか判断する。　(3)　a quality of mind or spiritのあとの関係代名詞節の「人がいかなる困難にも立ち向かうことを可能にする」から，どういう「心や精神の特質」なのか判断する。　(4)　deviceは「仕掛け」という意味。a small deviceのあとの関係代名詞節の「特に祝い事で使われ，燃えたり，爆発して，明るい色の光や大きな音を出す」から，どういう「小さな仕掛け」なのか判断する。　(5)　Japanese-style wrestling「日本式レスリング」やpeople taking part are extremely large「参加する人は非常に大きい」から相撲取りだと判断する。

Part B　放送が2度流れる場合は，1回目で集中して聞き取りをすること。1回目で聞き取れない箇所があっても，2回目の放送でその部分を解消すればよいので，あまりこだわらずにそれ以降の部分を聞き逃すことのないようにする。2回目の放送が終わったら，メモ欄，下書き欄を活用して解答を作成する。　No.1「試しにやってみてください」。give it a tryをワンセットで覚える。itは前に出てきた事柄を指す。

No.2「このセクションを音読してください」。read aloudは「音読する」，

section「(書物の)節」。　No.3 「次の話題に移りましょう」。
No.4 「今日は何曜日ですか」。weekをmonthにして，What day of the month is it today?は「今日は何日ですか」という意味。　No.5 「私たちは前に出てくれる志願者が必要です」→「だれか前に出てきてくれる人はいますか」。

【2】(1)　ア　②　　(2)　イ　③

〈解説〉(1)はイラストの中のCUSTOMSという掲示から会話の場所は「税関」で，発言者の男性は税関の役人で他は旅行者だと判断できる。
(2)は背景にたくさんの服が掛かっていて，SIZEの表示があることから会話の場所は「服売り場」で，発言者の女性は店員で右側の女性は客だと判断できる。選択肢はそれぞれ，①「切符を拝見します」，②「何か申告するものはありますか」，③「御用は承っておりますでしょうか」，④「お勘定をお願いできますか」，⑤「おつりはいりません」。

【3】(1)　③　　(2)　③　　(3)　④　　(4)　④　　(5)　③

〈解説〉(1)　It has been ～ since S＋V …で「…以来～経ちます」という意味。ある出来事があってから現在に至るまでどれくらい経っているかを表す表現。④はThirty years have passed since S＋V …の形なら同じ意味になる。　(2)　delayは「～を遅らせる」という意味。空欄の直前のitはhighway busで，高速バスは何かによって「遅らされた」と考え受け身にする。「私が乗った高速バスは6時に着くことになっていたが，40分以上遅れた」。　(3)　最初の会話文で「彼女があんな無作法な男と結婚したなんて信じられない！」とあり，次の会話文は「私もそう思う。ことわざに言うとおり，～」という内容。proverb「ことわざ」。「人の好みはさまざま」という意味のことわざを選ぶ。①「まさかの友が真の友」，②「虻蜂取らず」，③「顔は心の鏡」，④「蓼食う虫も好き好き」。　(4)　2つの車のモデルのどちらを選ぶかで，この車を買う理由としてbut以降に「あの車より操縦の点で～」とある。空欄の直後にtoがあることから判断する。superior to～「～よりまさって」。空欄の直後がtoではなくthanなら①のbetterが正解になる。　(5)「火事で本社工場が損害を被り，Detroit Industryは～」とあることから，生産を拡大する計画を考え直すと判断する。①「反応する」，②「思い出す」，③「再考する」，④「返答する」。

【4】No.1　ア　④　　イ　③　　ウ　②　　エ　①　　No.2　オ　④　カ　②　　キ　①　　ク　③　　No.3　②　　No.4　コ　②　サ　③　　No.5　I will use a digital textbook. It will help the students to understand the contents with some pictures and sound, and they will enjoy studying and expressing their opinion in English. (31 words)

〈解説〉No.1　ア　空欄の前に等位接続詞のandがあるのでS＋V ～ and S＋V ～.の文だと考える。andの前のSはInformation and communications technologyで，Vはhas had，andのあとのSは同じInformation and communications technologyで省略されていて，Vはisなので，このままで完成された文になっている。　イ　空欄を含む文で，前半は「基本的なIT技術は読み書き能力に匹敵する一般常識の一部になっている」とあり，本来ならそれに見合う環境が整っているはずだが，そのあとに「しかし～はまったく改善されていなかったようだ」と続くことから判断する。appear to have done「～したようだ」。③「これらの技術の育成を支える学校資源」。　ウ　空欄を含む文の前半で「これらの技能(読解力や数学の初歩)の育成は，全員に共通の(全員が共通に受ける)教育から除外することはできない」とあり，because以下に理由が述べられている。②を入れて「(もし除外されるなら)子どもの家庭環境の違いが大きな役割を果たす(大きく関与する)だろう」と考える。エ　ヒューマン・テクノロジーの応用を予備的に研究した最新結果では，すべての教師の日々の現実に関わる方法で何を示しているのかを考える。①「教育に実用できるようにITを応用することは可能である」。No.2　オ「情報通信技術は生徒の知識が教師の知識を明らかにまさっているだろう分野の1つ」とあり，その後で「教師は多分～に気づいていないだろう」とあることから判断する。本文ではinformation and

communications technology「情報通信技術」とIT(information technology)は同じ意味で使われている。may well do「たぶん～だろう」，expertise「専門知識」。④は「彼らの生徒たちの専門知識」。
カ 「基本的なIT能力は～のような包括的教育の主要な目的の1つ」とあり，包括的教育の例としてjust like以降に，空欄と「数学の初歩」がandで結ばれていることから判断する。②は「読解能力」。
キ 「教育制度が現在，全人教育の一環としてテクノロジーを使えるよう基本訓練を含めることができないことは～への深刻な脅威である」とあり，学校で基本訓練ができなければ家庭で訓練するしかなく，家庭環境の違いから不平等が生まれると判断する。①は「教育の機会均等」。 ク 「将来，説得力のある研究に基づいたテクノロジーの教育化(テクノロジーを教育に活かすこと)は，テクノロジーが～への脅威ではなく，それの発展の重要な支えとして認識されるようなやり方で学習過程を変えて改善する新しい機会を作り出すために使われなければならない」とあることから判断する。③は「教師という職業」。
No.3 下線部の訳は，「ワイヤレス技術はもっと一般的になり，費用は急速に<u>下がって</u>(A)，学習環境を<u>最新のものにし</u>(B)，その環境を伝統的な学校の敷地から外に<u>出す</u>(C)ための新しい機会が作り出されている」となる。文頭のwith＋～(目的語)＋…「～を…して」は付帯状況を表す。 No.4 コ critical「重大な」。①「批判する」，②「重要な」，③「深刻な」，④「寛容な」。 サ criteriaはcriterion「基準」の複数形。①「評価」，②「関心」，③「基準」，④「結果」。 No.5 質問文は「中学校か高校で英語を教えるとき，授業でどのように情報通信技術を使いますか」。情報通信技術の何を使うのかを述べ，その後にそれが生徒にどういう効果があるのか述べるとよい。解答のほかに，インターネットを使って(use the internet)，世界の人と交流する(interact with students from other countries)や，デジタル教材を使って(use digital resources)，発音練習をする(practice pronunciation)などが考えられる。

【5】ア　⑥　　イ　④　　ウ　⑤

〈解説〉小学校学習指導要領(平成20年3月)第4章　外国語活動　第1　目標の英訳版からの出題である。ア　接続詞while「～と同時に」の前後で分けて考える。whileのあとにはdeveloping the understanding ～とfostering a positive attitude ～とあるので，「～の基礎を作り」，それを土台にしながら同時に「～の理解を深めたり」，「～への積極的な態度を育てる」と考える。　イ　空欄の直前に形容詞のvariousがあるので名詞の複数形が入る。「～を通して言語と文化の理解を深める」とあることから判断する。　ウ　空欄の直前が等位接続詞のandなのでA , B, and Cになり，developing ～とfostering～ともう1つingがくると考える。pupilsのあとにwithがあることから判断する。familiarize ～ with …「～(人)を…に慣れさせる」になる。

【6】No.1　ア　②　　イ　④　　ウ　③　　エ　①　　No.2　オ　①　カ　②　　キ　④　　ク　⑤

〈解説〉No.1　ア　第1段落では，Claire Reidが16歳のときにお父さんから庭に植物を植えるように頼まれたとき，どんな植物を植え，種をどのくらいの間隔で置き，どのくらいの水を使うのか感じた，とある。②はReidが種と種の間の正確な距離を手で測定しなければならないことに困惑していることや，種がまとめて売られているので買うときにちょっとした額を払わなければならないことにいら立っていることなど，その16歳のときの様子を具体的に回想している。　イ　空欄の前のReidの回想で，1メートル分のほうれん草だけを植えたいなら，1メートル分のほうれん草だけを買えば良いという考えを思いつきたかったとあり，④で実際に膨らし粉と液体の肥料を使って新聞の切れ端に計算された間隔で種をくっつけて，あらかじめ種の数を決めたとあることから判断する。baking flour「膨らし粉」。　ウ　ヨハネスブルクに本社があるReidの新興企業は種と有機肥料があらかじめひとまとめになった紙片を製造しているとあり，③で具体的にこれら(種と有機肥料)は適切な深さと距離で離して置かれるので，容易に植えて維持管理ができる。またリールで売られ，1メートル1ドルなど，商品の説明が続く。　エ　③の最後に「場所も知識も水もほとんどいらず，だれでも野菜栽培ができます」とあり，①で「生分解可能な紙片は，伝統的なガーデニングの方法よりも80％少ない水を使用する」と，そのうちの水の話題を具体的に掘り下げて述べている。　No.2　オ　young entrepreneurで「若き起業家」。　カ　overcome「乗り越える，打ち勝つ」の目的語なので「打ち勝つ」対象となるものを選ぶ。obstacle「障害」。　キ　「鳥は～から掘り出して種を食べることができない」から判断する。　ク　「あなたが持っている～と同じ量だけ植える必要がある」から判断する。

【7】(1)　2番目　⑥　　7番目　⑦　　(2)　2番目　③　　7番目　⑥
(3)　2番目　⑤　　7番目　⑦

〈解説〉(1)　「もしあなたが効率よくやせたいなら」とあるので，主節では効率よくやせる方法を述べる。have toのあとは動詞の原形なのでincreaseが続き，何を増やすのか目的語になるphysical activityにする。in addition to「～に加えて」の前置詞(to)のあとは名詞かそれに準ずる動名詞など。lose weight「やせる」。並べ替えはincrease physical activity in addition to reducing calorie intakeとなる。　(2)　「私の夢は自分自身の小さな会社を経営すること」の次に，「でも私はまだ～を得ていない」とあり，最後にa new businessとあるので，新しい事業を始める資金のことだと判断する。問題の直前と選択肢にasがあるので，as much money asをgotの目的語にする。後半のasを接続詞ととらえ，後ろにS＋V～を作る。並べ替えはmuch money as I need to startとなる。
(3)　career educationは「キャリア教育」という意味。キャリア教育で重要なことをBのセリフで作る。tell＋目的語(人)＋目的語(事)ととらえ，2つ目の目的語をour own belief that ～「～という私たち自身の信念」にする。選択肢の後にカンマ(,)，そのあとにS＋V～が来ているので，どういう信念かを接続詞that以下に，譲歩節を導く関係形容詞を使ってwhatever＋名詞＋S＋V～, S＋V～を作る。「たとえ彼ら(学生)がどんな職業を選ぼうとも，彼らは自分の選択に誇りを持つべきだ」となる英語を作る。並べ替えはour own belief that whatever occupation they chooseとなる。vocational high school「職業訓練学校」，occupation「職業」，take pride in「～に誇りを持つ」。

【８】I'd like to talk to you about your son's behavior. He is not doing very well in classes these days. It seems that he has some problems and cannot concentrate on his study. I'd like to meet you at five o'clock on Friday in the principal's office. If this is inconvenient for you, please let me know. (57 words)

〈解説〉基本的に英語は一番伝えたいことを最初に述べるので，まず会って何を話し合うのかその目的を書く。次になぜその話題について話し合いたいのかを続け，最後に日時と場所を述べて，都合を尋ねる。都合が悪い場合は連絡する旨を伝えておくといい。話し合う目的としてほかに，a request for parent volunteers「ご父兄のボランティア参加依頼」，your child's educational progress「子どもの学力向上」，bullying「いじめ」などがある。

2014年度　実施問題

【中高共通】

【1】(Listening Test Part 1) Listen to the description and choose the word that fits it. Then mark the number ①, ②, ③, or ④ on your answer sheet. Each description is read <u>once</u>.

(1) ① blackboard ② Internet ③ keyboard ④ screen
(2) ① emotion ② idea ③ mind ④ reason
(3) ① conversation ② liquid ③ river ④ wind
(4) ① diet ② duty ③ ministry ④ tax
(5) ① *bonsai* ② *fusuma* ③ *yukikaki* ④ *yukizuri*

(☆☆◎◎◎)

【2】(Listening Test Part 2) Listen to the sentences and write them down. Each sentence is read <u>twice</u>.

(☆☆☆◎◎◎)

【3】Choose the best item from ① to ④ to fill in the blank of each sentence. Then mark the number ①, ②, ③, or ④ on your answer sheet.

(1) There is something noble [　　] Catherine.
① about　② in　③ on　④ with

(2) Elementary school students need to become [　　].
① literacy　② literal　③ literate　④ literature

(3) It is most [　　] that she will refuse the offer.
① hardly　② highly　③ largely　④ likely

(4) The noise [　　] from a nearby construction site made it difficult for the students to concentrate on their study.
① produce　② produced　③ producing　④ productions

(5) [　　] he studied a little harder for the test, he might have made a better

score.

① Eventually　② Had　③ If　④ Since

(6) A steam engine is driven by water which has been [　　].

① evacuated　② evaded　③ evaluated　④ evaporated

(7) I am not rich, [　　] do I wish to be.

① and　② neither　③ nor　④ not

(8) The bread my mother makes is much better than [　　] which you can buy at a store.

① it　② one　③ that　④ those

(9) "We're going to have a meeting at three tomorrow. Does it [　　] for you?"

① convenient　② make　③ suit　④ work

(10) A proverb says, "Birds of a [　　] flock together."

① color　② feather　③ friend　④ kind

(☆☆☆◎◎◎)

【4】Read the following passage and answer the questions below.

For a long time, a big part of my identity was "bachelor uncle." In my twenties and thirties I had no kids, and my sister's two children, Chris and Laura, became the objects of my ((1) a　　). I reveled in being Uncle Randy, the guy who showed up in their lives every month or so to help them look at their world from strange new angles.

It wasn't that I spoiled them. I just tried to impart my perspective on life. Sometimes that drove my sister crazy.

Once, about a dozen years ago, when Chris was seven years old and Laura was nine, I picked them up in my brand-new Volkswagen Cabrio convertible. "Be careful in Uncle Randy's new car," my sister told them. "Wipe your feet before you get in it. Don't mess anything up. Don't get it dirty."

I listened to her, and thought, as only a bachelor uncle can: "That's just the sort of [オ <u>admonition</u>] that sets kids up for failure. Of course they'd eventually get my car dirty. Kids can't help it." So I made things easy. While my sister was outlining the rules, I slowly and deliberately opened a can of soda, turned it over, and poured it on the cloth seats in the back of the convertible. My message : People are more [キ] than things. A car, even a pristine gem like my new convertible, was just a thing.

As I poured out that Coke, [ア]. Here was crazy Uncle Randy completely rejecting adult rules.

I ended up being so glad I'd spilled that soda. Because later in the weekend, little Chris got the flu and threw up all over the backseat. He didn't feel guilty. He was relieved ; he had already watched *me* christen the car. He knew it would be OK.

Whenever the kids were with me, we had just two rules :

1) No whining.

2) Whatever we do together, don't tell Mom.

Not telling Mom made everything we did into a pirate adventure. Even the mundane could feel magical.

On most weekends, [イ] and I'd take them to Chuck E. Cheese, or we'd head out for a hike or visit a museum. On special weekends, we'd stay in a hotel with a pool.

The three of us liked making pancakes together. My father had always asked : "Why do pancakes need to be round?" I'd ask the same question. And so we were always making [カ <u>weirdly</u>] shaped animal pancakes. There's a sloppiness to that medium that I like, because every animal pancake you make is an unintentional Rorschach test. Chris and Laura would say, "This isn't the shape of the animal I wanted." But that allowed us to look at the pancake as it was, and imagine what animal it might be.

I've watched Laura and Chris grow into terrific young adults. She's now twenty-one and he's [ク]. These days, I am more grateful than ever that I was a part of their childhoods, because I've come to realize something. It's unlikely that I will ever get to be a father to children over age six. So my time with Chris and Laura has become even more precious. They gave me the gift of being a presence in their lives through their pre-teen and teen years, and into adulthood.

Recently, [　ウ　]. After I die, I want them to take my kids for weekends here and there, and just do stuff. Anything fun they can think of. They don't have to do the exact things we did together. They can let my kids take the lead. Dylan likes dinosaurs. Maybe Chris and Laura can take him to a natural history museum. Logan likes sports : maybe they can take him to see the Steelers. And Chloe loves to dance. They'll figure something out.

I also want my (　2　) and (　3　) to tell my kids a few things. First, they can say simply : "Your dad asked us to spend this time with you, just like he spent time with us." I hope they'll also explain to my kids how hard I fought to stay alive. I signed up for the hardest treatments that could be thrown at me because I wanted to be around as long as possible to be there for my kids. That's the message I've asked Laura and Chris to deliver.

Oh, and one more thing. If my kids mess up their cars, [　エ　].

(Source : "*The last Lecture*" by Randy Pausch)

(No.1)　Place these four sentence fragments in their appropriate locations [　ア　] through [　エ　]. Then mark the number ①, ②, ③,or ④ on your answer sheet.

① Chris and Laura would hang out at my apartment
② I asked both Chris and Laura to do me a favor
③ I hope Chris and Laura will think of me and smile
④ I watched Chris and Laura, mouths open, eyes widening

(No.2)　Choose from ① to ④ the most suitable meaning for the underlined parts [オ admonition], [カ weirdly].

[　オ　]　① disgust　② praise　③ surprise　④ warning

[　カ　]　① delightfully　② fortunately　③ instantly

④ unusually

(No.3) Choose from ① to ④ the most appropriate words for the blanks [キ], [ク].

[キ] ① characteristic ② important ③ serious ④ worldwide

[ク] ① seventeen ② nineteen ③ twenty-one ④ twenty-three

(No.4) When the sentences below are true, mark ①. And when the sentences are wrong, mark ②.

(1) The author wanted Chris and Laura not to make mistakes.

(2) Chris and Laura had a good time with the author when they were young children.

(3) The author believes Chris and Laura will let his kids sign up for the hardest treatment.

(No.5) Fill in the blanks (1) with appropriate words starting with the given letters.

(No.6) Fill in the blanks (2), (3) with appropriate words.

(☆☆◎◎◎)

【5】The following is a part of 2011 White Paper on Education, Culture, Sports, Science and Technology. Fill in the blanks with suitable words starting with the given letters.

The Courses of Study have been stipulated as the general standard for the Curriculum ranging from kindergartens to upper secondary schools, to ensure that children can receive the ((1) s) level of education wherever they are in Japan. The Courses of Study for kindergartens, elementary schools, and lower secondary schools were revised in March 2008, and those for upper secondary schools and schools for special needs education, etc. were revised in March 2009. These revisions are aimed at fostering a "zest for life" with emphasis on seeking balance between academic ability, ((2) r) in humanity, and sound body. Accordingly, the revisions focus on development of abilities to think, make decisions, and ((3) e　　) oneself, as well as acquisition of knowledge and skills, and include an increased number of classes and enhance the contents of education.

(☆☆☆◎◎◎)

【6】Read the following and answer the questions below.

(A) In releasing the newly revised Red List, which evaluates extinction risks of each individual species, on Aug. 28, the Environment Ministry announced that the Japanese river otter has become extinct. The ministry also announced that the Japanese black bear in Kyushu has become extinct.

① The Red List is revised roughly every five years. The new list has classified 3,430 species of mammals, birds, insects, plants, etc., as critically endangered, an increase of 419 from the previous Red List. This shows environmental conditions for plants and animals are deteriorating rapidly.

② In 1993, the Act for the Conservation of Endangered Species of Wild Fauna and Flora went into force. But clearly Japan is lagging in measures to protect and increase the population of an endangered species. The possibility cannot be ruled out that the number of extinct species will increase. The government should consider drastically changing the law and improving measures to protect endangered species to maintain Japan's biodiversity.

③ Under the law, agents assigned to protect endangered species, including the Environment Ministry, are not given the needed authority to provide adequate protection for species under threat. The law also fails to cover oceanic fish and mammals, such as whales.

④ The report means that Japan has lost two mammals important to its ecosystem. Pollution was not solely responsible for the extinction of the Japanese river otter, hunting for furs took its toll as well.

(F) Human activity, such as [　オ　] projects and the failure to manage forests properly, is also contributing to the extinction of species. In writing a new strategy for securing [カ] , the national government should present a clearer vision, and map out in detail the efforts and strategies it intends to implement to provide greater protection to endangered species. It's also important to devise ways to heighten public [キ] and involve them in conservation programs. Banning the [ク] and sale of more endangered species should also be implemented.

(SOURCE : The Japan Times Weekly October 6, 2012)

(No.1) Arrange ①～④ in order so that they make sense.

(A)→(B)[ア]→(C)[イ]→(D)[ウ]→(E)[エ]→(F)

(No.2) Choose the most suitable word from ① to ⑤ for each blank [オ]through [ク]in paragraph (F)

① acquisition ② awareness ③ biodiversity
④ development ⑤ possibility

(☆☆☆◎◎◎)

【7】Rearrange the words of the underlined parts below and complete the sentences. Answer the words that come second and seventh.

(1) I'm sorry to bother you, but I'd really like to know when and how my school was founded. I would [<u>① answer ② appreciate ③ if ④ it ⑤ my ⑥ question ⑦ would ⑧ you</u>].

second[ア] seventh[イ]

(2) It's been fifteen years since I moved into this house, and many electorical appliances broke down after fifteen years' use. I had to buy a new washing machine, but [<u>① I ② in ③ recorder ④ repairing ⑤ succeeded ⑥ tape ⑦ the ⑧ video</u>].

second[ウ] seventh[エ]

(3) I couldn't sleep well last night. I wish [<u>① another ② had ③ in ④ let ⑤ me ⑥ room ⑦ sleep ⑧ you</u>].

second [オ] seventh[カ]

(☆☆☆◎◎◎)

【8】Fill in each blank with one or a few appropriate English sentences.

(1) Teacher : Which do you like better, fiction or nonfiction?

Student : What are you talking about?

Teacher : They are categories of literature. ______________________

Student : I see. Now I can guess what nonfiction is. It includes facts and is about real people, places, and events. Then I like nonfiction better.

(2) Teacher : You shouldn't just search the Internet when you write a report.

Student : Why not?

Teacher : This is what you have to keep in mind when you search the Internet on your own.

____

Student : You mean we should visit two or more websites just to make sure.

(☆☆☆◎◎◎)

【9】Imagine that you have a foreign student in your class and that he or she asks you one of these questions. You need to answer the question in English. How would you answer it? Choose one of the two questions and answer in not less than 50 words.

(1) What is "*Tanabata*?"

(2) What is "*Omisoka*?"

(☆☆☆◎◎◎)

解答・解説

【中高共通】

【1】(1) ④　(2) ③　(3) ②　(4) ③　(5) ④

〈解説〉説明を聞いて何について述べているかを選択する問題。傾向としては教室に関連した物，日本的な物，石川県に関連する事物や人名などが出題されることが多いようである。また選択肢なしで，日本語で解答を記述する問題も過去には出ているので，出題形式は今後年度により多少変化があるかもしれない。対策としては初級～中級の英会話番組を聞く，教材CDで聞き取り練習をする，などの方法でよいだろう。

【2】No.1　Raise your right hand.　No.2　How've you been doing?
No.3　That's all for today.　No.4　Let's give her a round of applause.
No.5　Turn over the paper and pass it forward.

〈解説〉こちらは聞き取った文を書き取る問題。傾向としては教室で使われる表現が出題されることが多いようだ。レベルとしては初級～中級までの会話程度だが，教室での表現はいずれ使用する機会が増えると考えられるので，馴染みのない人は，そういった表現を集めた教材をさらっておく必要があるだろう。スペルミスなどがないよう，くれぐれも注意されたい。

【3】(1) ①　(2) ③　(3) ④　(4) ②　(5) ②　(6) ④
(7) ③　(8) ③　(9) ④　(10) ②

〈解説〉(1)　there is something ～ about で，「…(人)にはどこか～なところ(雰囲気)がある」という意味になる。問題文では「どことなく高貴な雰囲気がある」となるが，他にgraceful「優雅な」，artificial「わざとらしい」，intellectual「知的な」，feminine「女っぽい(男性について言う場合)」などいろいろな形容詞で表現される。　(2)　同じ語幹を持つものを集めた選択肢。いずれも文字に関わりがある。それぞれ，①「識字能力」，②「文字(上)の，文字どおりの，逐語的な」，③「読み書きできる」，④「文学，文献」。「小学生は～になる必要がある」という文なので，「読み書きできるようになる」とする③。　(3)　①②③はいずれも程度を表す副詞で，修飾すべき形容詞または副詞がなく，名詞句が続くので，形容詞 likely「ありそうな」が適切。most likely that … で「恐らく・十中八九そうなるであろう」という意味合いになる。「彼女はたぶんオファーを断るだろう」　(4)　The から site までが主語を形成する名詞句なのでエは noise を修飾する語で②か③。noise と construction site の関係から noise は「発せられる」と受け身の意味になるため②が適切。　(5)　文後半が仮定法過去完了の形の受けになっているので前半は過去完了時制でなければならない。If だと仮定法過去になり不可。If he had studied = Had he studied で，②。　(6)「蒸気機関は[蒸発した]水で動かされる」で④。他選択肢はそれぞれ原形で①「非難させる」，②「～から逃げる」，③「評価する」。　(7)　前半が I am not rich, という否定文で，後半が do I wish と倒置されているので，nor do I という形を思い出してほしい。「私は裕福ではないし，そうなりたいと願ってもいない」　(8)　空欄はパンを示す代名詞。it だとすでに言及されている「どれかのパン」を意味することになり不適，one は限定されない名詞を受けるため，「母のつくるパン」「パン屋で買えるパン」と限定された物を示すことができないこと，bread は不可算名詞なので one とは置き換えられないこと，から不適，those も複数形であるから，one 同様，可算名詞の代わりにしかなれない。the + 名詞の繰り返しを避けるために置かれる代名詞は that，と覚えておこう。　(9)　疑問文で Does が置かれており，空欄には動詞原形が入るはずなので形容詞の①は不可。It works for [人].で「[人]にとって，それで構わない，都合が良い」という意味になり④があてはまる。make，suit は他動詞なので，原則として前置詞を後ろに置かない。

(10)　birds of a feather で「同じ羽毛の鳥」，つまり同種のものという意味。諺の意味は「同じ羽毛の鳥が一カ所に集まるように，趣味や行動様式の似た者は仲間になりやすい」で，日本語で言えば「類は友を呼ぶ」に対応する。

【4】(No.1) ア ④ イ ① ウ ② エ ③ (No.2) オ ④ カ ④ (No.3) キ ② ク ② (No.4) (1) ② (2) ① (3) ② (No.5) (1) affection (No.6) (2) niece (3) nephew

〈解説〉(No.1) ア 母親から「叔父さんの車を汚さないで」と警告されていたのに当の叔父が自分で汚してしまった，という状況。子供たちの反応として，「驚いた」というのが自然なので，それを描写した④が適切。 イ 空欄の後に，筆者と子供たちがあちこち出かけて行く様子が書かれており，子供たちが筆者を訪問したか筆者が子供たちの家を訪れたか，という状況が想像できるが選択肢にあるのは前者で①。 ウ 空欄の後に「自分が死んだら彼らに，私の子どもたちを週末あちこちへ連れて行ってほしいのだ」とあるので「私は Chris と Laura に頼みごとをした」の②。 エ 文の前半に，筆者の車と子供たちについてのエピソードとして，子供たちが車を汚すことに筆者が寛容だったことが書かれていることから判断できる。「ChrisとLauraが私のことを思って笑ってくれるといいなと思う」 (No.2) オ admonition は「警告」で④と同義。set someone up for ～で「仕立て上げる，はめる」の意味。筆者は「これは子供たちを失敗に陥れるたぐいの警告だな」と思ったわけである。 カ 筆者の父が「どうしてパンケーキは丸くなくてはならないんだ？」と言っていた点から，「変な，普通でない」形のパンケーキを作ったと想像でき，「変わった」の④。 (No.3) キ people と things を対比しており，「特徴的な」の①，「真面目な」の③，「世界規模の」の④はあてはまらない。「人は物よりも大事だ」で important が適する。 ク 第3段落に when Chris was seven years old and Laura was nine, とあり，Chris が Laura より2歳年下だとわかる。 (No.4) (1) 第4段落に，That's just the sort of admonition that sets kids up for failure. Of course they'd eventually get my car dirty. Kids can't help it. とあり，筆者が子供の失敗に寛容だったことがわかる。

(2)　文全体に，叔父と甥，姪が頻繁に交流していたことが描かれており，子供たちも楽しく過ごしていたことがうかがえる。　(3)　困難な治療法にサインしたのは筆者であることが，最後から2番目の段落に書かれている。子供たちがサインすることについては言及がない。
(No.5)　(1)「愛情の対象」はobjects of my affection で，(1)にはaffection が入る。　(No.6)　自分が叔父という立場から見れば子供たちは姪と甥。

【5】(1)　same　(2)　richness　(3)　express
〈解説〉文部科学白書第2章「子どもたちの教育の一層の充実」の「総論」からの抜粋で，元の文は「子どもたちが全国どこにいても一定水準の教育を受けられるようにするために，幼稚園から高等学校までの教育課程の大綱的基準として学習指導要領等を定めています。平成20年3月に幼稚園教育要領，及び小学校，中学校の学習指導要領を，21年3月に高等学校と特別支援学校の学習指導要領などを改訂しました。これらの改訂では，知・徳・体のバランスを重視した「生きる力」を育むため，知識や技能の習得とともに，思考力・判断力・表現力などの育成を重視し，教科等の授業時数の増加と教育内容の充実を図っています。」とある。白書は毎年公表されるので，教育関連の箇所だけでも文科省のウェブサイト等で眼を通しておくとよいだろう。

【6】(No.1)　ア　④　イ　②　ウ　③　エ　①
(No.2)　オ　④　カ　③　キ　②　ク　①
〈解説〉(No.1)　ア　ニホンカワウソと九州ツキノワグマの絶滅の報告について書かれている段落(A)の直後は，(A)の内容を受け，「この報告は，日本が，日本の生態系にとって重要な2種の哺乳類を失ったということを意味している」と書いている④。また③冒頭の Under the law, …の the law は②で言及された the Act for the Conservation of Endangered Species of Wild Fauna and Flora を指していると推定できるので，④→②→③→①の順番が判断できる。　(No.2)　オ　空欄の語と and で結ばれた the failure to manage forests properly「森林の適切な管理の失敗」とは並列的な関係にあるので，自然破壊に関連した語が空欄に入ると考えられ，自然破壊の結果を招くことが多い development「開発」があてはまる。　カ　securing は「確保する，守る」であるから「生物多様性を保つ」とする biodiversity が適切。　キ　public awareness「普及啓発，国民の意識向上」は自然環境問題への取組のキーワードのひとつ。ク「さらなる絶滅危惧種の[ク]と販売の禁止」という文脈なので acquisition「捕捉」があてはまる。

【7】(1)　ア　④　　イ　⑤　　(2)　ウ　⑤　　エ　⑥　　(3)　オ　②　カ　①

〈解説〉(1)　I would [appreciate it if you would answer my question]. で，2番目が it，7番目は my である。　(2)　… but [I succeeded in repairing the video tape recorder]. で2番目に succeeded，7番目には tape が入る。(3)　I wish [you had let me sleep in another room]. で2番目が had，7番目が another である。

【8】(1)　Fiction refers to stories about imaginary people and events. など。

(2)　Make sure the website you find is reliable. など。

〈解説〉文脈を読み取る力がまず必要であるが，書く内容としては常識的なものであればよいだろう。生徒に教師が説明するという設定なので，難解な単語や言い回しは避け，簡潔に言い表すことは言うまでもない。こういった説明文は，日常身の回りの物を使って日頃から練習が可能なので，いろいろなものを即座に英語で説明できるよう自己訓練をしておきたい。

【9】(1)　*Tanabata* is a star festival held on July 7th. The legend goes that two stars, *Orihime* and *Hikoboshi*, separated by the Milky Way, can meet only on the night. In the festival we decorate bamboo trees with strips of colored paper on which we write down our wishes or prayers. など。　(2)　*Omisoka* is the last day of the year. By this day we clean our houses, cook special dishes for the New Year's Day and prepare ourselves to greet the new year. Most families spend the night together. They watch special TV programs and eat ***toshikoshisoba***, buckwheat noodles, wishing for a healthy long life. など。

〈解説〉日本の事物についての説明は，いきなり試みてもすっきりした文にすることは難しいだろう。石川県では日本的な事物に関する説明の問題が例年のように出題されているので，うまく書けない人は外国人向けの説明が書かれた物などを利用してコツをつかんでおきたい。これも，いろいろな事物について何度も書いて練習することが最も大事である。

2013年度　実施問題

【中高共通】

【1】(Listening Test Part 1) Listen to the description and identify what or who it is. Answer in Japanese. Each description is read once.

(☆☆☆◎◎◎)

【2】(Listening Test Part 2) Listen to each sentence and write down the whole sentence. Each sentence is read twice.

(☆☆☆◎◎◎)

【3】Choose the best item from 1) to 4) to fill in the blank of each sentence.

(1) Susanna enjoyed the movie a lot but her friend found it (　　).

1) bore　2) bored　3) bores
4) boring

(2) Please let me know as soon as you (　　) a report on the accident.

1) draw up　2) drew up　3) had drawn up
4) will draw up

(3) This document (　　) been written out by Jim alone, for his writing skill is unbelievably awful.

1) cannot have　2) mustn't have　3) need have
4) should have

(4) Much to her disappointment, Christine prepared for the exam for all she was worth only (　　).

1) failed　2) failing　3) to be failing
4) to fail

(5) He knows that he is in a really tough situation (　　) way he turns.

1) however　2) where　3) whichever

4) whoever

(6) Tiffany was wondering what (　　) her dress, perfume and necklace that she was wearing would have on him.

1) affect　　2) defect　　3) effect

4) infect

(7) This parking area is designated exclusively for the (　　).

1) disability　　2) disable　　3) disabled

4) disabling

(8) Mr. Goodwin is an old fox, so to speak, (　　) you should watch out when negotiating with him in business.

1) although　　2) because　　3) however

4) therefore

(9) "Let's go out for lunch."

"Sorry. I have too much work. I'll have to (　　)."

1) take a chance　　2) take a hedge　　3) take a paid leave

4) take a rain check

(10) "Do you think he can pass the next bar exam?"

"(　　)"

1) Beats me　　2) Got it　　3) I'm just getting by

4) Take it into court

(☆☆☆☆◎◎◎)

【4】Read the following passage and answer the questions below.

I have also wondered if a small, densely populated nation such as Britain could be made viable and Gaia-friendly in the long term by (① d　　) it into three parts. One third would be given for cities, industries, ports, airports and roads; the second third would be for intensive farming, enough to grow all we need; and the last third would be given entirely to Gaia and left to evolve wholly without interference and management.

[　A　]. Dense, compact cities, free of suburban sprawl, the kind now favoured by the architect Richard Rogers in his book *Cities for a Small Planet*(1997); these would need comparatively little land and they might even be tight enough for walking to be the preferred method of transport. In a radio interview another distinguished architect, Norman Foster, reminded us that over 75 per cent of energy usage is in buildings and transport; dense, well-planned cities encourage its easy and painless ②reduction.

[B]. For longer-distance travel, to ease that ③peripatetic itch we all seem to have, we could use sailing ships again. I am not thinking of those magnificent wooden, four-masted vessels, (④ w) operation required dozens of sailors. I imagine a high-tech automated sailing vessel, like a modern aircraft, that would travel a planned path chosen and updated to maximize the thrust of the wind. It would take longer than a jet but, as is often said, it is usually better to travel than to arrive. From the personal experience of thirteen transatlantic journeys on passenger ships to and from North America, it is far more pleasant to go by ship than by air, but, if air travel is demanded, then why not giant sailing airships that rode the trade winds? [C].

We are, unconsciously, evolving to a state where much of our time is spent using low-energy (⑤ d). What a stunningly good invention was the mobile telephone: it ⑥exploits the universal tendency of humans to chatter and obliges us to consume hours of the day at minimal energy cost—it is one of the greenest inventions ever. Small computers of great efficiency are now stealing into our lives to make us spend our time at minimal energy cost, playing games or surfing the net. An ultra-high-tech low-energy civilization may well be possible, but it would be wholly different from the present-day vision of a low-energy world of sustainable development and renewable energy where the multitude tries to survive on food from organic small-holders farming a protesting Earth.

Whatever form future society takes it will be tribal, and hence there will be the privileged and the poor. [D]: vegetables grown in soil and cooked with meat and fish. We are in our present ⑦mess because the luxuries of whole-house heating and private transport by car have become necessities and far beyond the Earth's capacity to provide. ⑧ Vigilance would be needed to constrain the growth of luxuries that threaten Gaia. I have to stress that the well being of Gaia must always come before that of ourselves: [X].

(Source: "*The Revenge of Gaia*" by James Lovelock)

(No.1) Place these three sentence fragments in their appropriate locations [A] through [D]. One location will be left empty. Please write "4" for this empty space.

1) This being so, there would in our high-tech world surely be a fashion among the rich for eating real food

2) Most of us prefer an urban existence, provided that predatory lowlife is kept invisible

3) They could be made of aircraft materials and use steam as the lift gas

(No.2) Choose from 1) to 4) the most suitable meaning for the underlined parts ②⑥⑦⑧.

② 1) agreement 2) control 3) decrease 4) shortage

⑥ 1) takes advantage of 2) takes care of 3) takes no notice of 4) takes part in

⑦ 1) messages 2) mistakes 3) problems 4) wastes

⑧ 1) angry voice 2) careful attention 3) complete honesty 4) illegal act

(No.3) Fill in the blanks ①④⑤ with appropriate words starting with the given letters.

(No.4) Paraphrase the underlined words ③ into the following. Write a suitable word to fill in the blank space below, whose initial letter is 'd'.

= strong (d) to travel

(No.5) Choose the most suitable sentence from 1) to 4) below for the blank space [X].

1) we accept this fate or plan of our own destiny within Gaia

2) we are to avoid the unpleasant changes it forecasts

3) we cannot exist without Gaia

4) we have to expand our instinctive recognition of life to include the Earth

(☆☆☆☆◎◎◎)

【5】The following is the overall objectives in the new course of study for high schools foreign languages (English). Fill in the blanks with suitable words starting with the given letters.

To develop students' communication abilities such as accurately understanding and appropriately conveying (① i), ideas, etc., deepening their understanding of language and culture, and fostering a (② p) attitude toward communication through foreign languages.

(☆☆☆☆◎◎◎◎)

【6】Read the following and answer the questions below.

The role of the critical period in second language acquisition is still much debated. For every researcher who holds that there are maturational constraints on language acquisition, there is another who considers that the age factor cannot be separated from factors such as motivation, social identity, and the conditions for learning. They argue that older learners may well speak with an accent because they want to continue being identified with their first language cultural group, and adults rarely get access to the same quantity and quality of language input that children receive in play settings.

(A) After years of classes, learners feel frustrated by the lack of progress, and their motivation to continue may be diminished. School programs should be based on realistic estimates of how long it takes to learn a second language. One or two hours a week will not produce very advanced second language speakers, no matter how young they were when they began.

(B) When the objective of second language learning is native-like mastery of the target language, it is usually desirable for the learner to be completely surrounded by the language as early as possible. However, as we saw in Chapter 1, early intensive exposure to the second language may entail the loss or incomplete development of the child's first language.

(C) Many people conclude on the basis of studies such as those by Patkowski or Newport and Johnson that it is better to begin second language instruction as early as possible. Yet it is very important to bear in mind the context of these studies. They deal with the highest possible level of second language skills, the level at which a second language speaker is indistinguishable from a native speaker. But achieving a native-like mastery of the second language is not a goal for all second language learning, in all contexts.

(D) When the goal is basic communicative ability for all students in a school setting, and when it is assumed that the child's native language will remain the primary language, it may be more efficient to begin second or foreign language teaching later. When learners receive only a few hours of instruction per week, learners who start later (for example, at age 10, 11, or 12) often catch up with those who began earlier. We have often seen second or foreign language programs which begin with very young learners but offer only minimal contact with the language. Even when students do make progress in these early-start programs, they sometimes find themselves placed in secondary school classes with students who have had no previous instruction.

(Source: "*How Languages are Learned*" by Lightbown and Spada)

(No.1) Arrange (A) to (D) in order so that they make sense.

(No.2) Choose the most suitable words from 1) to 4) for the blanks (a) and (b) so that the following passage is consistent with the text above.

Even people who know nothing about the critical period research are certain that, in school programs for second or foreign language teaching,

'(a)'. However, both experience and research show that older learners can attain high, if not 'native', levels of proficiency in their second language. Furthermore, it is essential to think carefully about (b) of an instructional program and the context in which it occurs before we jump to conclusions about the necessity - or even the desirability - of the earliest possible start.

(a) 1) earlier is worse 2) less is worse 3) older is better
4) younger is better

(b) 1) the evolution 2) the goals 3) the impact
4) the integration

(☆☆☆◎◎◎)

【7】Rearrange the words of the underlined parts below and complete the sentences.

(1) It (saw / his school / that / he / at / was) a computer at the first time.

(2) She believed that education was important. For that reason, she (her baby / be / to / by / wanted / adopted) college graduates.

(3) The first thing he did was ask all the product teams to (were / explain / they / the products / making / if) were really necessary.

(☆☆☆◎◎◎)

【8】Fill in each blank with one or a few appropriate English sentences.

(1) Teacher: Have you ever heard about the National Aeronautics and Space Administration?

Student: Umm.... What is it?

Teacher: NASA is the acronym for it. ____________________

Student: Thank you for explaining to me what acronyms mean. We can use them all the time because they save us time in both writing and speaking. Actually, I've heard about NASA many times and I'm interested in rockets and space vehicles.

(2) Students: I'm not very good at writing essays. Could you give me some advice?

Teacher: I think you should learn about stages in the writing process. The first stage is prewriting－Plan what you are going to write about. The second one is drafting－Write down your ideas in rough. What do you think comes next?

Student: Well, let me see.... Revising?

Teacher: Yes, the third one is revising－____________________________

The fourth one is editing－Find and fix mistakes. All of these stages are important before writing your final copy.

(☆☆☆☆◎◎◎◎)

【9】If you were asked about the following words by people with little knowledge about Japanese schools how would you explain it to them? Choose one and explain it in 50 or more words in English.

(1)　Hokenshitsu (保健室)　　(2)　Kyushoku (給食)

(☆☆☆◎◎◎)

解答・解説

【中高共通】

【1】No.1　黒板　　No.2　舌　　No.3　ハチ　　No.4　風呂敷
No.5　高峰譲吉

〈解説〉英文を聞いて，何について説明しているかを答える問題である。日本語で解答することに注意したい。説明文が一度しか読まれないので，集中して聞くようにしよう。日頃から何かを英語で説明する習慣をつけておけば，英文がすっと入ってくるであろう。

【2】No.1　Could you repeat it again?　　No.2　Long time no see! How have you been?　　No.3　We are landing soon. Please fasten your seat belts.

No.4　Japan should open up her markets to foreign countries.

No.5　I must show you how to use the computer.

〈解説〉ディクテーション問題である。文が二回ずつ読まれるので，一回目で書き取れなかった箇所は二回目で埋めることができる。音が連結する箇所やアクセントが置かれない語は聞き取りにくいであろうが，語彙は比較的易しく文も短いので，しっかり押さえておきたいところである。

【3】(1)　4)　　(2)　1)　　(3)　1)　　(4)　4)　　(5)　3)　　(6)　3)

(7)　3)　　(8)　4)　　(9)　4)　　(10)　1)

〈解説〉(1)　「映画がつまらない」という意味になればよい。適切なのは4)のboringである。2)のboredは「(人が)つまらない，退屈している」という意味である。　(2)　時に関する接続詞(whenなど)をとる節は，未来のことでも現在形で書くという文法規則がある。したがって，答えは1)である。なお，条件節の場合もこの規則があてはまる。

(3)　文脈から考えると，「～のはずがない」というフレーズが入ることが予測される。各助動詞がそれぞれどんな意味で使われるかを確認しておこう。　(4)　ここではto不定詞がある種「運命」といった意味合いを持っている。意訳すると，「大変がっかりしたことに，クリスティンの試験勉強は実を結ばなかった」となる。　(5)　適切な複合関係詞を選ぶ問題である。直後に名詞をとれるのはwhateverまたはwhicheverなので，正解は3)である。　(6)「どんな効果があるか」という意味にするには，3)のeffectを選ぶのが一番適切である。それ以外の選択肢はネガティブな意味合いを含むので，この問題の文脈には合わない。　(7)　the＋形容詞で「その形容詞の性質を持つ人」という意味になる場合がある。2)のdisableは動詞，4)のdisablingは形容詞であるが，意味が異なることにそれぞれ注意しよう。　(8)　空欄前後をうまく結ぶ語を入れればよい。「だから，それゆえ」といった語が一番しっくりくるので，正解は4)である。なお，thereforeは副詞であり，前に関連する文や発話が必要であることに注意したい。　(9)　英検準一級などで頻出のイディオムである。take a rain checkで「また今度にする」という意味になる。招待を断るとき，決まり文句としてよく使用される。また，他の選択肢も重要なイディオムなので確認しておこう。それぞれtake a chance「思い切ってやってみる」，take a hedge「立ち去る」，take a paid leave「有給休暇をとる」，となる。　(10)　相手の問いに答えられないときの表現でBeats me. = It beats me.「知らない，分からない」というものがある。初見だと意味をとりにくいので，こういった表現集に少し目を通せるとよい。他の表現の意味は，それぞれGot it.「分かった」，I'm just getting by.「(近況を尋ねられて)なんとかやっています」，take it into court「裁判沙汰にする」，となる。

【4】No.1　A　2)　B　4)　C　3)　D　1)　No.2　②　3)　⑥　1)　⑦　3)　⑧　2)　No.3　①　dividing　④　whose　⑤　devices　No.4　desire　No.5　3)

〈解説〉No.1　文章の適切な箇所に文を挿入する問題である。文章の内容とその展開をしっかり理解することが要求される。まず，Aには「国を3つのパーツ(都会，農地，未開の地)に分ける」という考えを受けて「我々の多くは都会を好むだろう」で始まる2)が入る。Bには何も入れなくても理解に支障がないので，4)が適切である。Cに関しては，直前の文中のairshipsを受けたtheyで始まる3)が適切であろう。最後にDについては，直前の文中のthe privilegedと1)のthe richが同義語として使われていると考えられ，繋がりが見えるのでこれが正解である。さらに空欄直後のvegetables以下と1)のreal foodも同じものを指していると思われる。　No.2　類義語を選ぶ問題である。極端に難解な語彙は含まれていないので，日々の勉強でカバーしておきたい。対策としては，英作文をするときに一つの意味を複数の方法で表現する練習をすることなどが挙げられる。　No.3　①　空欄後のthree partsがヒントとなる。3つのパーツに「分ける」ので，divideが適切であろう。前置詞byに合わせて動名詞にすることがポイントである。 ④ 空欄直後のoperation「操作」は，空欄直前のvesselsの操作のことである。したがって，所有格の関係代名詞whoseを入れるとよい。 ⑤ 空欄に続く文中のmobile telephoneがヒントになるであろう。これと類似した語が入る。「道具」などのキーワードを連想できれば正答は近い。

No.4 peripateticは形容詞で「歩き回る」の意味で，itch「かゆみ，欲望」の意味を知っていれば答えやすいであろう。itchの元々の意味とそれから派生した意味を一定の文脈において連想できるかどうかがカギとなる。 No.5 コロンに続く文を選ぶので，答えは直前の文の言い換えであることが予想される。直前の文は「地球の幸福はいつもヒトの幸福に先立つべきである」という意味なので，それを端的にパラフレーズしている3)が正解である。

【5】① information ② positive

〈解説〉学習指導要領に関する問題である。外国語科の目標にあたる。ヒントがあるとはいえ初見で完答することは難しいので，学習指導要領の重要な部分だけでも英語で読んでおくことが好ましい。対応する日本文は「外国語を通じて，言語や文化に対する理解を深め，積極的にコミュニケーションを図ろうとする態度の育成を図り，情報や考えなどを的確に理解したり適切に伝えたりするコミュニケーション能力を養う。」である。

【6】No.1 (C) → (B) → (D) → (A) No.2 (a) 4) (b) 2)

〈解答〉No.1 内容に即して段落を並べ替える問題。各段落がどんな内容であるか，また他の段落とどうつなげられるかについて考えながら読むとよい。臨界期と言語習得の関係について書かれた第一段落には第二言語習得の先行研究について書かれた(C)を続けるとよい。その後は言語習得の目標について書かれている(B)と(D)を選べばよいが，筆者の主張は(D)の方なので，そちらを(B)の後に置くとよい。最後に，(A)の結論へとつながる。 No.2 (a) 研究に知識のない人は年齢が若い方が外国語または第二言語の学習によいと考えている。 (b) 前文で大人の学習者の到達レベルについて述べられていることから，学習の目標the goalsが適当。

【７】(1) was at his school that he saw　(2) wanted her baby to be adopted by　(3) explain if the products they were making

〈解説〉(1) Itが形式主語になった強調構文である。 (2) her babyがto以下されて欲しかったという形をつくればよい。 (3) ifを「～かどうか」という意味でとる。また，関係代名詞のthatが省略されていることに気付けば，正解できるはずである。

【８】(1) Acronyms are abbreviations made up from the first letters of the words in a phrase. など。 (2) Change your draft by adding new information or making improvements. など。

〈解答〉(1) 生徒の応答として，「acronyms『頭字語』の意味を説明してくれありがとう」とあるので，頭字語の定義を簡単に説明すればよい。 (2) 動詞reviseは「～を改訂する」「～を復習する」という意味である。ここではessay「レポート」を書く段階として，下書きを見直し，情報を付け加えたり，改善したりすることを助言すればよい。

【９】(1) It is one of the rooms at school where students get emergency medical treatment. The nursing teacher is usually in the room. Some students go there for health counseling and some go for school life counseling from the teacher. We can say that the ***hokenshitsu*** has an important function in supporting students at school. (54語)など。 (2) It is the school-provided lunch for students. In Japan most elementary and junior high schools and some senior high schools provide it. The menu is set each month and a nutritious and balanced meal is usually brought from the regional school lunch center. Recently local products are often used for school lunch (52語)など。

〈解説〉(1)か(2)を選び，それについて50語程度で説明する問題。日本についての知識が少ない人にむけて説明するので，各語の基本的な役割について言葉を尽くして説明することが大切である。

2012年度　実施問題

【中高共通】

【1】(Listening Test Part 1)　Listen to the description and identify what or who it is. Answer in Japanese. Each description is read once.

(☆☆☆◎◎◎)

【2】(Listening Test Part 2)　Listen to each sentence and write down the whole sentence. Each sentence is read twice.

(☆☆☆◎◎◎)

【3】Choose the best item from 1) to 4) to fill in the blank of each sentence.

(1)　Most company bosses say that they are opposed (　　) a lot of overtime.

1)　employees work　　2)　employees working

3)　for employees to work　　4)　to employees working

(2)　Each meal comes with soup or salad and a dessert at no extra (　　).

1)　charge　2)　fare　3)　fee　4)　toll

(3)　When you hear the name of the book you are looking for (　　), please come to the counter.

1)　call　2)　called　3)　calling　4)　to be called

(4)　Interest rates have moved from their historic lows. Still, rates are not high enough to (　　) many investors to buy bonds.

1)　deduce　2)　induce　3)　introduce　4)　reduce

(5)　The provider has demonstrated that the quality of learning online is (　　) to the quality of traditional learning programs.

1)　comparable　2)　comparing　3)　comparison

4)　comparative

(6)　Mary thought her friends had forgotten her birthday. Little (　　) that they were planning a surprise party for her.

1) did she know 2) has she known 3) she had known

4) she would know

(7) Taro studied in France for a year and liked it so much that he decided to stay there ( ). Now he lives in Paris and works for a company there.

1) as scheduled 2) by chance 3) for good

4) in exchange

(8) The organization named "Protection of Scenic Sites" insisted that the government ( ) the preservation of scenery within 100 meters of historical buildings.

1) aim 2) measure 3) object 4) target

(9) "Could I use your phone?" "Be my ( )."

1) client 2) customer 3) guest 4) visitor

(10) "I'm afraid I've broken your vase. I was so careless. I do hope you'll forgive me." "Oh, ( ). Anyone can make mistakes."

1) allow me to express my gratitude 2) don't let that worry you

3) I'd like to ask you a favor 4) there is some apology needed

(☆☆☆☆◎◎◎◎◎)

【4】Read the following passage and answer the questions below.

For almost six decades now research and practice in English language teaching has identified the "four skills" — listening, speaking, reading, and writing — as of paramount importance. In textbooks and curricula in widely varying contexts, ESL classes around the world tend to focus on one or two of the four skills, sometimes to the exclusion of the others. And a visit to the most recent <u>① TESOL</u> Convention will offer you a copious assortment of presentations indexed according to the four skills.

It is perfectly appropriate to so identify language performance. The human race has fashioned two forms of (② p) performance, oral and written, and two forms of receptive performance, aural (or auditory) and reading. There are of course offshoots of each mode. Lumped together under nonverbal communication are various visually perceived messages delivered through gestures, facial expressions, proximity, and so forth. Graphic art (drawings, paintings, diagrams) is also a powerful form of communication. And we could go on. But for learners of a second language, some attention to the four different skills does indeed ③ pay off as learners discover the differences among these four primary modes of performance along with ④ their interrelationships.

With all our history of treating the four skills in separate segments of a curriculum, there is nevertheless a more recent trend toward skill integration. ＜　X　＞ That is, rather than designing a curriculum to teach the many aspects of one skill, say, reading, curriculum designers are taking more of whole language approach whereby reading is treated as one of two or more interrelated skills. ＜　Y　＞ A lesson in a so-called reading class, under this new ⑤ paradigm, might, for example, include:

(1) A pre-reading discussion of the topic to activate schemata.

(2) Listening to a lecture or a series of informative statements about the topic of a passage to be read.

(3) A focus on a certain reading strategy, say, (⑥ s　　).

(4) Writing a paraphrase of a section of the reading passage.

This class, then, models for the students the real-life integration of language skills, gets them to perceive the relationship among several skills, and provides the teacher with a great deal of flexibility in creating interesting, motivating lessons.

Some may wish to argue that the integration of the four skills diminishes the importance of the rules of listening, of speaking, of reading, and of writing that are unique to each separate skill. Such an argument rarely holds up under careful scrutiny of integrated-skill courses. ＜ Z ＞ If anything, the added richness of the latter gives students greater motivation that converts to better retention of principles of effective speaking, listening, reading, and writing. Rather than being forced to plod along through a course that limits itself to one mode of performance, they are given a chance to diversify their efforts in more meaningful tasks. Such integration can, of course, still utilize a strong, principled approach to the separate, unique characteristics of each separate skill.

So you may be wondering why courses weren't always integrated in the first place. There are several reasons:

(1) In the pre-CLT days of language teaching, the focus on the forms of language almost predisposed curriculum designers to segment courses into the separate language skills. It seemed logical to fashion a syllabus that dealt with, say, pronunciation of the phonemes of English, stress and (⑦ i　　), oral structural patterns (carefully, sequenced according to presumed grammatical difficulty), and variations on those patterns. These "language-based" classes tended to be courses in "baby linguistics" where a preoccupation with rules and paradigms taught students a lot about language but sometimes at the (⑧ e　　) of teaching language itself.

(2) Administrative considerations still make it easier to program separate courses in "reading" and "speaking," etc., as a glance at ⑨ current intensive and university English courses reveals. Such divisions can indeed be justified when one considers the practicalities of coordinating three-hour-per-week courses, hiring teachers for each, ordering textbooks, and placing students into the courses. It should be noted, however, that a proficient teacher who professes to follow principles of CLT would never conduct, say, a "Reading" class (⑩ w　　) extensive use of speaking, listening, and writing in the class.

(3) Which leads to a third reason that not all classes are integrated: There are certain specific purposes for which students are studying English that may best be labeled by one of the four skills, especially at the high-intermediate to advanced levels. In an academic setting such as a university, for example, specialized workshops, modules, tutorials, or courses may be constructed ⑪ explicitly to improve certain specialized skills. Thus a module in listening

comprehension might include instruction on listening effectively to academic lectures, to fellow students in the classroom, to audio programs where there are no visual cues, to the consultative register used in the professor's office, and even to fellow students in casual conversation. Such a course might encompass phonological, morphological, syntactic, lexical, ⑫ semantic, and discourse elements.

(Source : "*Teaching by Principles*" by H. Douglas Brown)

(No. 1) Why does the author advocate integrated-skill courses? Choose one of the sentences that give the reason and write the first and the last words of that sentence.

(No.2) Choose from 1) to 4) the most suitable meaning for the underlined parts ③ ⑤ ⑨ ⑪ ⑫.

③ 1) bring success after a long time
2) develop into a bad situation
3) gradually become less efficient 4) have a right

⑤ 1) a level of quality, skill, ability, or achievement by which someone or something is judged
2) a particular way of thinking about something, which is generally accepted
3) a set of ideas about right and wrong, which influences you to behave in a particular way
4) an area of knowledge, interest, or thought

⑨ 1) existing in large numbers 2) happening or existing now
3) influenced by the newest ideas 4) liked by a lot of people

⑪ 1) boldly 2) carefully 3) clearly 4) intentionally

⑫ 1) dealing with words 2) relating to the meanings of words
3) relating to the system of speech sounds
4) relating to the way words are arranged in order

(No.3) Fill in the blanks ② ⑥ ⑦ ⑧ ⑩ with appropriate words starting with the given letters.

(No.4) Where should this sentence be placed? Choose the most suitable place from < X > to < Z >.

A course that deals with reading skills, then, will also deal with related listening, speaking, and writing skills.

(No.5) What does ① TESOL stand for? Fill in the blanks. → Teaching of English to Speakers of (　　)(　　)

(No.6) Paraphrase ④ their interrelationships. Fill in the blanks. → the fact that the four (　　) have something to do with (　　)(　　)

(☆☆☆☆◎◎◎◎)

【5】The following is the overall objectives in the new course of study for junior high schools foreign languages (English). Fill in the blanks with suitable words starting with the given letters.

To deepen the understanding of languages and cultures through foreign language learning; to foster a positive (① a　　) to attempt communication; and to (② d　　) basic communication abilities in listening, speaking, reading, and writing.

(☆☆☆◎◎◎◎)

【6】Read the following and answer the questions below.

(A) According to the popular image of science, everything is, in principle, predictable and controllable; and if some event or process is not predictable and controllable in the present state of our knowledge, a little more knowledge and, especially, a little more know-how will enable us to predict and control the wild variables.

(b) If I throw a stone at a glass window, I shall, under appropriate circumstances, break or crack the glass in a star-shaped pattern. If my stone hits the glass as fast as a bullet, it is possible that it will detach from the glass a neat conical plug called a *cone of percussion*. If my stone is too slow and too small, I may fail to break the glass at all. Prediction and control will be quite possible at this level. I can easily make sure which of three results (the star, the percussion cone, or no breakage) I shall achieve, provided I avoid marginal strengths of throw.

(c) Curiously enough, the more precise my laboratory methods, the more unpredictable the events will become. If I use the most homogeneous glass available, polish its surface to the most exact optical flatness, and control the motion of my stone as precisely as possible, ensuring an almost precisely vertical impact on the surface of the glass, all my efforts will only make the events more impossible to predict.

(d) This view is wrong, not merely in detail, but in principle. It is even possible to define large classes of phenomena where prediction and control are simply impossible for very basic but quite understandable reasons. Perhaps the most familiar example of this class of phenomena is the breaking of any superficially homogeneous material, such as glass. The Brownian movement of molecules in liquids and gases is similarly unpredictable.

(e) But within the conditions which produce the star-shaped break, it will be impossible to predict or control the pathways and the positions of the arms of the stars.

(F) If, on the other hand, I scratch the surface of the glass or use a piece of glass that is already cracked (which would be cheating), I shall be able to make some approximate predictions. For some reason (unknown to me), the break in the glass will run parallel to the scratch and about 1/100 of an inch to the side, so that the scratch mark will appear on only one side of the break. Beyond the end of the scratch, the break will veer off unpredictably.

(No.1) Arrange (b)～(e) in order so that they make sense.

(No.2) What is this passage about? Choose the most suitable word from the text for the blank.

→ what science can and cannot (　　)

(☆☆☆◎◎◎◎)

【7】Rearrange the words of the underlined parts below and complete the sentences.

(1) Nothing(me / more / gives / along / than / pleasure / a stroll / taking) the path around a Japanese garden and enjoying nature in all its seasons in Kyoto.

(2) In discussing tax reform, the government needs to give consideration not only to the future level of the consumption tax but (tax's function / to / how / strengthen / income / to / the / also) of redistributing income.

(3) It's important for companies nowadays to thoughtfully change, and as soon as something is going well, it's (for / next / is / time / looking / start / what / to).

(☆☆☆◎◎◎◎)

【8】Fill in each blank with one or a few appropriate English sentences.

(1) Student : It takes a long time to learn English.

Teacher : ______________________

Student : Oh, I know that proverb well. I'll try to memorize a few words at a time.

Teacher : That's wonderful.

(2) Teacher : ______________________

Student : Really? How can I guess? How do the parts work? Could you give me an example?

Teacher : Sure. The Greek prefix ‘tele-’ means ‘far off’, and a suffix ‘-scope’ means ‘see’. So a telescope is a piece of equipment to make distant objects look larger and closer.

Student : Wow, it's useful to know roots of English words.

(☆☆☆◎◎◎)

【9】If you were asked about the following words by people with little knowledge about Japanese culture, how would you explain them? Choose one of them and explain it in 50 or more words in English.

(1)　Undokai　(運動会)　　(2)　Nengajo　(年賀状)

(☆☆☆☆◎◎◎◎)

解答・解説

【中高共通】

【1】(No.1)　ぶどう　(No.2)　くも　(No.3)　鏡　(No.4)　てるてる坊主　(No.5)　中谷宇吉郎

〈解説〉スクリプト無し。聞き取った内容をもとに，それが何(誰)についての描写であるかを推測する問題。英文は1度しか流れないので，注意して聞かねばならない。

【2】(No.1)　Last night, I went to the airport to meet my friend.

(No.2)　Leaves were blowing about in the light wind.　(No.3)　Rent is collected once a month.　(No.4)　I'd have called her if I'd had her number.

(No.5)　Could you tell me what kind of transportation is available?

〈解説〉聞き取った英文をそのまま書き出す問題。英文は2回流れるので，落ち着いて取り組みたい。聞き取れなかった情報があっても，他の情報から推測して解答することが可能である。一方で，聞きとれた情報であっても，前後の情報との整合性・時制などに十分注意して正確な解答を心掛けたい。

【3】(1)　4　(2)　1　(3)　2　(4)　2　(5)　1　(6)　1　(7)　3　(8)　4　(9)　3　(10)　2

〈解説〉(1)　形容詞opposedの用法を問う問題。be opposed to ～「～に反

対する」　(2)　ここでは，サービスに対する料金を表す語がふさわしいので，chargeが適当。　(3)　ここに入るcallは，bookを叙述する過去分詞形にするのがふさわしい。英文の意味は「探している本の名前が呼ばれるのが聞こえたら，カウンターまでおこし下さい」である。
(4)　induce (人) to ～「(人)を説得して～する気にさせる」　(5)　形容詞であり「匹敵する」を意味するcomparableがふさわしい。
(6)　否定を表すlittleが文頭にあるので，倒置文を選択しなければならない。時制は過去にあるので，did she knowが適当。　(7)　英文の意味を考えると，for good「永久に」が適当である。　(8)　target「～を目標にする」を入れるのがふさわしい。　(9)　be my guest「どうぞご自由に」　(10)　don't let that worry you「そのことがあなたを悩ませるようにはするな」は，「そのことを気にしないでください」と解釈することができるので，2がふさわしい。

【4】(No.1)　the first word : This / If / Rather　the last word : lessons / writing / tasks　(Thisとlessons，Ifとwriting，Ratherとtasksのいずれかの組み合わせ)　(No.2)　③　1　⑤　2　⑨　2　⑪　3　⑫　2
(No.3)　②　productive　⑥　scanning　など　⑦　intonation
⑧　expense　⑩　without　(No.4)　Y　(No.5)　Other Languages
(No.6)　skills … each other

〈解説〉(No.1)　当てはまる英文が3つ存在するので，いずれかを選べればよい。第4パラグラフ1文目のThis … lessons. か，第5パラグラフ3文目のIf … writing. か，第5パラグラフ4文目のRather … tasks. が解答にふさわしい。　(No.2)　辞書の意味をしっかりと表している選択肢を選べばよい。　③　pay off「物や事がうまくいく」　⑤　paradigm「理論的枠組み」　⑨　current「今の，その時の」　⑪　explicitly「明白な，明示的な」　⑫　semantic「意味に関する」
(No.3)　②　空欄の後ろの箇所で，リーディングがreceptive performanceであると述べられていることをヒントに，ライティングがどのようなperformanceであるかを対比的に考える。　⑥　リーディングストラテジーには様々あるが，scanning(必要な情報を集めるための読み)はその中でも基本的なストラテジーなので，抑えておきたい。　⑦　空欄の前部にstressがあることから，英語を発音する他の要素としてintonationを連想することができる。　⑧　解答にあたって，“language-based”のクラスでは，言語そのものの規則を教えることを優先させていることを理解する。　⑩　CLTの理念を支持する教師は，「リーディング」の授業において，スピーキング・リスニング・ライティングなどの他の技能をも扱うのである。二重否定になっていることに注意する。(No.4)　空欄Yの前文は，リーディングを他のスキルと関係づけて扱うカリキュラムについて述べている。設問にある文は，この前文をわかりやすく言い換えている。　(No.5)　TESOLは，Teaching of English to Speakers of Other Languagesの略称である。基本的知識として，押さえておきたい。　(No.6)　④　their interrelationshipsのtheirはfour skillsを示している。have to do with ～「～と関係がある」

【5】①　attitude　　②　develop

〈解説〉日本語文は，「外国語を通じて，言語や文化に対する理解を深め，積極的にコミュニケーションを図ろうとする態度の育成を図り，聞くこと，話すこと，読むこと，書くことなどのコミュニケーション能力の基礎を養う」となっている。「態度」としてattitude,「養う」としてdevelopが適当である。

【6】(No.1)　d → b → e → c　　(No.2)　predict

〈解説〉(No.1)　トピックは，科学が予想できることとできないことについてである。まず，与えられたAの段落で，知識とノウハウがあれば，様々な変化を予測でき，制御できると述べられている。これを受けて，dのThis view以下が続き，ガラスを割るという現象について話が移る。その内容を詳しく述べたbが次に続く。石の大きさや投げ方によってどのようにガラスにひびが入るかが説明されている。しかし，ひびがどのように枝分かれするかというような細かい部分は予測できないという内容のeが次に続き，予測できないことが多くあることが述べられたcが最後に入る。　(No.2)　この文章のキーワードは事象を予測できるかどうかであるので，predictが適当である。

【７】(1)　(Nothing) gives me more pleasure than taking a stroll along (the path ….)　(2)　(… but) also how to strengthen the income tax's function (of redistributing income.)　(3)　(…, it's) time to start looking for what is next.

〈解説〉(1) 「日本庭園の周りを散歩し，京都のすべての季節の自然を楽しむことほど，私に喜びを与えてくれるものはない(＝庭園を散歩し，楽しむことが，私の一番の喜びである)」，Nothing is more A than B「BほどAなものはない，Bが一番Aである」の表現。take a stroll「散歩をする」　(2)「税制改革を討議する上で，政府は，消費税の今後の動向を考慮するだけでなく，所得税の再分配機能をどのように強めていくかということも考慮する必要がある」　(3)「現在，企業にとってよく考えて変化することは重要であり，何かうまくいったらすぐに，次に何が起こるか予期し始めるべきである」 it's time to ～「～すべきとき」，look for ～「～を探す，予期する」

【８】(1)　Rome was not built in a day. / Little things make a big difference.　など　(2)　If you know the meaning of a word's parts, you can probably guess what it means.　など

〈解説〉(1) 「英語を学ぶのは大変であるが，何事もすぐには成し遂げられない」，または「小さなことの積み重ねで達成される」という意味のことわざが入ることを，前後の教師と生徒の会話から読み取る。proverb「ことわざ，格言」，Rome was not built in a day.「ローマは一日にして成らず」，Little things make a big difference.「ちりも積もれば山となる」　(2)　生徒にどのような例があるか聞かれた教師の答えとして，telescopeという語を部分に分けて，それぞれの部分の意味から語の全体の意味を予測できることを説明している。よって，語の小さ

く分けた部分の意味を知っていれば，その語の意味を予測することができる，という内容が教師の最初の発言として入ることが読み取れる。

【9】(1)　Undokai is an annual event in most schools in Japan. It is usually held on a good day in spring or autumn. Students take part in competitive sports, fun games or track and field events. Parents and relatives of the students often attend Undokai. At some schools, students practice Japanese traditional dance and perform it in Undokai.　(57語)

(2)　Nengajo is special postcards of New Year's greeting. Some have a lottery number at the bottom. The cards are sent to friends or relatives on New Year's Day. People start to write in the end of November and mail by the middle of December so that they will be surely delivered on January 1st.　(54語)

〈解説〉日本の文化について，英語で説明する問題。このような自由英作文では，難しい表現を使うのではなく，易しくとも自分の知っている表現を使って説明する方がよい。　(1)　運動会についての説明。運動会はいつ，どこで，どのような内容が行われるのか，また，家族や親戚も集まって応援に来る学校の一大イベントであることも説明すると，運動会がどのようなものか伝わると思われる。　(2)　年賀状についての説明。年賀状は，新年のあいさつのために送られる伝統的な日本の慣習であること，元日に友人や親戚から届くものであること等だけではなく，元日に届くようにするためには，11月の終わりから書き始め，12月の中旬までには投函しなければならないこと等の情報も入れることで50語ほどの説明になると思われる。

2011年度　実施問題

【中高共通】

【1】(Listening Test Part 1) Listen to the description and identify what or who it is. Answer in Japanese. Each description is read twice.

(☆☆☆◎◎◎)

【2】(Listening Test Part 2) Listen to the passage and answer the questions. They are both read once.

(☆☆☆◎◎◎)

【3】Choose the best item from (a) to (d) to fill in the blank of each sentence.

(1) If there is not ( ) room for the wisdom tooth, it will become embedded against the tooth in front of it.

(a) enough (b) few (c) many (d) very

(2) The boys always worked so hard that no one was really surprised when they ( ) all the other teams.

(a) beat (b) gained (c) got (d) won

(3) He has to somehow come to ( ) with his feelings and get over the shock.

(a) life (b) place (c) senses (d) terms

(4) Banks ( ) a profit from the difference in the interest paid to depositors and charged to borrowers.

(a) deprave (b) deprive (c) derive (d) drive

(5) Dobermans are not outside dogs. They are ( ) to cold weather and absolutely need human attention.

(a) sensible (b) sensitive (c) sensual (d) sensuous

(6) Because the bacteria is highly infectious, the disease is ( ) widespread in the southern hemisphere.

(a) fast　(b) fairly　(c) quickly　(d) slowly

(7) If you ( ) the magazine you ordered by tomorrow, please let me know.

(a) didn't receive　(b) haven't received　(c) won't receive

(d) wouldn't receive

(8) We have to ( ) how to deal with the recent sharp rise in commodity prices.

(a) consider about　(b) discuss about　(c) mention about

(d) talk about

(9) "They say you have a family. Is that right?"

"( ) I'm still single."

(a) In no case.　(b) That's not the case.　(c) This is it.

(d) You got it.

(10) "Are you telling me paragliding is not dangerous?"

"( )"

"OK, I'll give it a try!"

(a) Hold your tongue.　(b) Make my wishes.

(c) Read my lips.　(d) Take my word for it

(☆☆◎◎◎)

【4】Read the following passage and answer the questions.

What lessons have we learned from the historic legislation known as No Child Left Behind? The most gratifying is that more kids are learning their lessons. How do we know? Because our schools are now required to find out how each student is doing every year in the key building-block subjects of reading and math. Now that we have annual assessment data that are disaggregated by student group, we can diagnose and correct weaknesses in <u>① instruction</u> and learning.

Our nation's education report card tells the story. Achievement is up <u>② across the board</u>, especially for those too often "left behind": poor, minority, and special education students. In reading, 9-year-olds made more progress in the last nine years than in the previous 28 years combined. [A] Lesson No. 1: Accountability is a powerful tool and is working to improve learning.

Lesson No. 2: Accountability also makes people uncomfortable. We no longer are able to hide from the facts, which say that only half our minority students ③ stand a chance of graduating from high school on time. The discomfort this has created shows the fundamental power of accountability that is at the core of the No Child law. We would be ④ loath to go back to the days when we tested students every few years and averaged their scores together to mask the staggering achievement gap that plagues our country.

[B]

We've also identified ways that the law can be improved. The policy ⑤ calls made when the law was enacted were based on far less information than we have today. We only had a single snapshot of data in elementary and middle school. We did not ask schools to report on achievement gaps between low-income and minority students and their peers. That all has changed. Now, ⑥ the reauthorization will be guided by these data and a better understanding of the law's strengths and limitations.

Lesson No. 3: The law should encourage continuous improvement in our classrooms, give educators the credit they deserve for the most challenging work, and provide parents and students more customized options. Now that we have annual assessment in all 50 states, we can use systems that give schools and teachers ⑦ credit for an individual student's year-over-year improvement, rather than looking at absolute scores. As secretary of education, I started a pilot program to allow states to use such systems. We can build on this pilot and expand it nationwide.

[C] Research shows that the most powerful way to improve student achievement is to make sure every child is taught by a highly effective teacher. Our most effective teachers should be teaching our most disadvantaged students and be rewarded with better pay and more support. On this issue, too, we can build on the work started through President Bush's Teacher Incentive Fund and expand it to all 50 states.

Parents (⑧) even more information and better options that customize schools to meet the needs of their children. We need more charters, more school choice, more customized technology, and more real-time feedback to catch educational problems, intervene immediately, and better address the needs of our student population. Those will make a real difference.

The one question driving all of our actions should be "Are kids learning?" policymakers have come a long way in 10 years. Talk of class size ratios, modernization of school facilities, and how much money is being spent is now overshadowed by a focus on student achievement. [D] It's an easy way to avoid the hard decisions about what to do with our lowest-performing schools. Lesson No. 4: Watch for special-interest agendas that stall the focus on closing the achievement gap.

That leads to the last lesson, which is the hardest. To really close the achievement gap and provide opportunity to every student, from gifted academic learners to special education students, we must get more serious about this work. Policymakers still have not taken on the most sacred cows in education: (⑨) We intuitively know that no enterprise of any kind can be fully successful without the best use of both. It's time for us to put kids before adults and begin to get really serious about our lessons.

(Source: "Measuring the Value of Accountability" by Margaret Spellings, the Secretary of Education in USA from 2005 to 2009 US.News & world reports, January 2010)

(1) Choose the most suitable sentence from (a) to (d) below for each of the blank spaces [A] to [D].

(a) But there are some who would rather go back to the days of policymaking based on inputs rather than results.

(b) Politicians of both parties, educators, and especially parents now rightfully expect to know the truth.

(c) We can also do a much better job of evaluating and assessing teacher effectiveness.

(d) What gets measured does indeed get done.

(2) Choose the word from (a) to (d) below, which is closest in meaning to the underlined word(s) ①, ②, ③, ④, ⑤ and ⑦.

① (a) information (b) statement (c) studying
(d) teaching

② (a) extensively (b) hopelessly (c) immediately
(d) legally

③ (a) have (b) stay (c) stick (d) support

④ (a) dislike (b) ready (c) reluctant (d) willing

⑤ (a) decisions (b) requests (c) shouts (d) visits

⑦ (a) belief (b) praise (c) responsibility (d) trust

(3) Paraphrase the underlined words ⑥ into the following. Write a suitable word to fill in the blank space below, whose initial letter is 'p'.

= giving legal (p　　) for the law again.

(4) Choose the most suitable item from (a) to (d) below for the blank (⑧) and (⑨).

⑧ (a) catch (b) conceal (c) deserve (d) exchange

⑨ (a) How to effectively use time and people in our schools.
(b) How to make learners autonomous and teachers more motivated in our schools.
(c) How to put more effort into teachers' promotion in our schools.
(d) How to succeed both the classroom and testing standards.

(☆☆☆☆◎◎◎)

【5】Rearrange the words of the underlined parts below and complete the sentences.

(1) Parenthood is by far the toughest job in the world, <u>it / which / why / explain / may / is</u> so often done badly.

(2) Before we decide to go with your competitor, we want to give you an opportunity to renegotiate with us. We would like to request a 30% discount on future purchases on / that / it / so / can / pass / we to our consumers.

(3) The company has decided to enlarge the size of a warehouse will / imported / where / store/ it / the products from China.

(☆☆◎◎◎)

【６】Put the underlined parts into Japanese.

(1) It is an accepted cliche in education that the number one goal of teachers should be to help students learn how to learn. I always saw the value in that, sure. But in my mind, a better number one goal was this: I wanted to help students learn how to judge themselves. Did they recognize their true abilities? Did they have a sense of their own flaws? Were they realistic about how others viewed them? In the end, educators best serve students by helping them be more self-reflective.

(2) A language achieves a genuinely global status when it develops a special role that is recognized in every country. This might seem like stating the obvious, but it is not, for the notion of 'special role' has many facets. Such a role will be most evident in countries where large numbers of the people speak the language as a mother tongue.

(3) We go to the mall because it insulates us from life. We go to the flea market to embrace the ghost of a scavenger past we've sold out in favor of malls and bicentennial celebrations. We think of friends we've had, lovers we've lost, times irretrievable, but things show up at the flea market and make us remember times, places and people we didn't even know we forgot. New things have no history, no frame of reference; they're just products.

(☆☆☆◎◎◎)

【7】Fill in each blank with one or a few appropriate English sentences.

(1) Boy:______

Girl: Americans? I'm not sure. Some people describe them as "open and friendly."

Boy: How about Japanese people?

Girl: Polite and reserved.

(2) Teacher: Please tell us a synonym for "gorgeous."

Student: Synonym? What does that mean?

Teacher:______

Student: Oh, I see. "Beautiful" is a synonym for it.

Teacher: That's right.

(☆☆☆☆◎◎◎)

【8】Write one paragraph starting with the sentence written in the answer sheet. You must write 50 words or more in English.

(☆☆☆◎◎◎◎)

解答・解説

【中高共通】

【1】No.1　カレンダー　　No.2　鼻　　No.3　バスケットボール
No.4　電気　　No.5　長谷川等伯

【2】No.1　b　　No.2　b　　No.3　d　　No.4　c　　No.5　a

〈解説〉リスニングでは，文字を媒体としたリーディングと違い，音声は流れるとともに消えていってしまうので，効率より解答が求められる。そのため，受験する都道府県の出題内容や問題形式の傾向(例えば，放送は2度聞くことができるのか，質問文は問題用紙に記載されているのか，メモはとれるのか等)をあらかじめ把握しておくことは，とても重要である。また，近年は様々な訛りの英語が話される傾向もあるようなので，発音を選り好みせず，色々な英語に耳を慣らしておくとよい。教育に関する用語を英語で覚えておくことも大切である。実際のリスニング試験での一般的な心構えとして，①放送を聞く前に質問文に目を通して聞かれる内容を把握しておく，②全ての単語を無理に聞きとろうとせず，どのような趣旨の英文なのか聞きとることをまずは優先する，③1度目と2度目の放送でそれぞれ何を聞きとればいいのか，目的を明確にして聞く，④必要に応じてメモをとることが必要である。どうしてもわからない場合は深く考えず勘で解答して，次の問題に答える準備をするという思い切りのよさも必要であろう。

【3】(1)　a　(2)　a　(3)　d　(4)　c　(5)　b　(6)　b　(7)　b　(8)　d　(9)　b　(10)　d

〈解説〉(1)　enough：十分な。訳：親知らずに十分な空間がないと，親知らずはその前にある歯に向かって生えてしまうだろう。

(2)　beat：打ち負かす(過去形もbeat)。訳：少年たちはいつも一生懸命頑張ったので，彼らが他の全てのチームを打ち負かしたとき誰も驚かなかった。　(3)　come to terms with～：(困難など)をあきらめて受け入れる。訳：彼はどうにかして自分の感情を受け入れ，ショックから立ち直らなければならない。　(4)　derive A from B：BからAを引き出す(Aには利益や知識などが入る)。訳：銀行は預金者に支払われる利子と債務者に課される利子の差から利益を得ている。　(5)　sensitive：敏感な，～の影響を受けやすい(cf.sensible：分別のある)。訳：ドーベルマンは外で飼う犬ではない。ドーベルマンは寒い気候に影響を受けやすく，人の世話が明らかに必要である。　(6)　fairly：かなり，すっかり。訳：その細菌は非常に伝染しやすく，病気は南半球ですっかり広まってしまった。　(7)　条件を表す節(if～)では，未来のことでも現在時制で表す。If you don't～と同義。訳：もし明日までに注文した雑誌を受け取らなかったら教えてください。　(8)　consider, mention, discussは全て他動詞なので前置詞を伴わない。訳：最近の日用品の値段の急激な上昇にどう対処するか，我々は話し合わなければならない。(9) That's not the case.で「それは本当ではない(＝That's not true)」の意味。 (10) Take my word for it.で「私の言葉を信じて」の意味。

【4】(1) [A] d [B] b [C] c [D] a (2) ① d ② a ③ a ④ c ⑤ a ⑦ b (3) permission (4) ⑧ c ⑨ a

〈解説〉(1) [A] この段落の教訓(lesson)は「アカウンタビリティ(＝学力の伸び等について情報開示すること)は学習を伸ばす」で，選択肢の「測られるもの(＝学力)が真になされる」という内容と一致する。
[B] この段落の教訓は，アカウンタビリティは人をuncomfortableにさせるが，最終的には真実を知りたいと思うようになるというもの。選択肢の内容がちょうど結論文になっている。 [C] この段落の主旨は，教師を評価することで教師の技量が把握でき，より技量のある教師に能力の低い児童を教えさせることで効率のよい教育ができるというもの。選択肢は，その主題文になっている。 [D] この段落の主旨は，政策の結果，学校間に生まれてしまった学力差を隠そうとする人々の思惑に注意しないといけない，というもの。それが選択肢の「結果(results)ではなく，労働の投入量(inputs)に基づいて政策決定していた日々に戻りたい人がいる」という内容と一致。 (2) ① instruction：指導(＝teaching)。 ② across the board：全域にわたって(＝extensively)。学力が全域にわたって上がったとある。 ③ stand：(可能性・希望)を持っている(＝have)。 ④ be loath to V：Vするのに気が進まない(＝reluctant)。 ⑤ call(名詞)：決定(＝decision)。made ～ enactedはThe policy callsを後置修飾している。 ⑦ credit：評判・勤務評定(＝praise)。 (3) 文脈からreauthorizationの意味は，法律の内容を再検討し決めなおすこと，と考えられる。つまり，改めて法的に承認(＝permission)を与えるということ。 (4) ⑧ deserve：望む。両親はさらに多くの情報と，より良い選択肢を望んでいる，とある。 ⑨ 次

文のno enterprise ～ best use of bothのuse of both(＝両方の使い方)が選択肢のuse time and peopleに相当する。

【５】(1)　which may explain why it is　　(2)　so that we can pass it on
(3)　where it will store the products imported

〈解説〉(1)　whichは関係代名詞の非制限用法で，先行詞はParenthood ～ world全体。関係代名詞節内のitはparenthoodを指す。訳：子育ては世界で最も大変な仕事であり，そのことがなぜ子育てがしばしば下手に行われるかを説明しているかもしれない。　(2)　so that S can V：SがVできるように。pass on ～ to …：～を…に与える，回す。訳：貴社の競合相手と我々が提携する前に，再交渉する機会を与えたいと思います。消費者に(その利益を)回せるよう，今後の購入については30％の値引きをお願いしたいと思います。　(3)　whereは関係副詞(＝in which)で先行詞はwarehouse。訳：その会社は中国から輸入された商品を保管する倉庫のサイズを大きくすることに決めた。

【６】(1)　よりよい第一の目標はこういうことだった。つまり，私は生徒が自分自身をどのように評価すべきかを学ぶ手助けをしたかったのだ。　(2)　これは明白なことを述べているように思われるかもしれないが，そうではない。というのも，「特別な役割」という概念には多くの側面があるからである。　(3)　蚤(のみ)の市では様々なものが現れ，自分で忘れていたことさえわからなかった時間や場所や人を思い出させるのだ。

〈解説〉(1)　代名詞thisはコロン(：)以下を指す。help O Vで「OがVするのを助ける」の意味。ここのjudgeは「自分を客観的に眺め，どんな能力があるか見極める」といった意味であることが下線部の後に書いてある。　(2)　seem like ～ は「～のように見える」。the obvious(the＋形容詞)で「明白なこと」。but it is notは後にstating the obviousが省略。forは理由を導く接続詞。facet：面。　(3)　「flea market(＝蚤の市)」はいわゆるフリーマーケットのこと。show up：現れる。makeを使った使役構文(人に～させる)の補語(C)にあたるrememberの目的語はtimes・places・peopleの3つ。we didn't～we forgotは前述の3つの名詞を先行詞とする関係代名詞節。

【7】(1)　How would you best describe Americans?　　(2)　It is a word with the same meaning or almost the same meaning as another word in the same language, such as "pleasure" and "satisfaction."

〈解説〉(1)　下線部に続く会話では，アメリカ人の国民性(open, friendly)と日本人の国民性(polite, reserved)が述べられている。Girlが用いた表現(＝describe)をヒントに質問を作る。　(2)　synonym：同義語。この単語を知らなくても，beautifulがgorgeousのsynonymだという文から，その意味は推測できる。

【8】Should elementary school or junior high school students be allowed to have their own cell-phone? I would answer "Yes." It is because many students already have their own cell phone these days, so it sounds quite unrealistic to prohibit them from having one even at school. Rather than putting it under a total ban, teachers should decide rules or place restrictions on the use of their cell phones. For example, students can use their cell phone in lunchtime and after school, but they must turn it off and put it in their bag during lessons.

〈解説〉携帯電話を許可すべきかどうかは一般の人々の間でも話題になっているホットなテーマ。評価規準は，(1)正確な英語で書かれていること，(2)根拠や具体例等を伴った，まとまりのある内容であること，(3)50語以上の英語で書かれていること，の3点になっている。語数が少なくあまり長い文章は書けないので，まず自分の立場を明確に「はい」か「いいえ」で答えた後に，その根拠や具体例を簡潔に述べよう。奇をてらったような意見を書いてしまうと，説得力をもたせるのが難しくなるので，避けるのが無難。

2010年度　実施問題

【中高共通】

【１】(Listening Test Part1) Listen to the description and identify what or who it is. Answer in Japanese.

Each description is read twice.

(☆☆☆◎◎◎◎◎)

【２】(Listening Test Part 2) Listen to the passage and answer the questions. They are both read twice.

(☆☆☆◎◎◎◎◎)

【３】Choose the best item from (a) to (d) to fill in the blank of each sentence.

(1) The earth (　　) on its axis.

(a) circles　(b) spins　(c) whirls　(d) revolves

(2) "(　　), I was at a loss what to do. Why didn't you come back earlier?" "I should have come back earlier, but I couldn't help it."

(a) With you gone　(b) With you going

(c) With you to go　(d) With you go

(3) He tried to get Sarah (　　) out to the concert, but she was too busy.

(a) come　(b) to come　(c) to coming　(d) coming

(4) "You should talk in a more polite way to the (　　). Your attitude might affect our sales even though our products have the very best qualities'." "I'm very sorry. I promise not to talk like that again."

(a) borrowers　(b) visitors　(c) customers　(d) guests

(5) (　　) that tidal wave five years ago, there would be a beautiful village here.

(a) If it were not for　(b) Without for　(c) Had it not been for

(d) If it had not been

(6) It was his first race, but he ( ) run 10 km. He was proud of himself.

(a) managed (b) was able to (c) could (d) could have

(7) "I came to Japan two months ago, but I still have difficulty using chopsticks."

"Oh, ( ) It's just a matter of time."

(a) you'll keep up with us soon. (b) don't mind.

(c) you'll get the hang of it. (d) getting used to them is not so easy.

(8) "The committee has excellent staff. They were all' playing leading roles, but they haven't come up with a good solution."

"Well, as the saying goes, ( )"

(a) It is better to wear out than to rust out.

(b) Acorns were good until bread was found.

(c) It never rains but it pours.

(d) Too many cooks spoil the broth.

(9) "I can't walk any more. I'll stop here."

"Come on! The top is just 500m ahead. ( ) "

(a) Search me! (b) Keep up! (c) It's a deal!

(d) Good luck!

(10) "Watch your tongue. Some people are very ( ) to criticism and take it to heart."

"That's true. Thanks for your advice."

(a) contingent (b) vulnerable (c) resilient (d) intriguing

(☆☆☆☆◎◎◎◎◎)

【4】Read the following passage and answer the questions.

It's important to praise our children, but it's even more important to be (A) in our praise. The ways parents behave on the sidelines of the athletic field often tells a lot about what qualities they value. Some parents make it clear by the way they behave that to them, winning is everything.

Nine-year-old Robby has gone out for Little League. He's not a great athlete, but he enjoys playing and he's learning some important physical as well as social skills through his participation in the sport. Most of the time he tries hard and does reasonably well. However, one day during a game against another team, (1) his heart doesn't seem to be in it. Robby's mother is standing on the sidelines, frantically screaming for his team to win. Her cheering is particularly intense whenever Robby is up at bat or a ball is coming his way in the outfield. (2) [more / to / screams / more / and / she / he / seems / fumble / the / the] falter.

After the game, which his team loses, his mother says, "It's all right, you know. You tried," but after the way she behaved throughout the game, and because of her tone of voice, Robby knows she doesn't really mean it.

There will always be times when we will be disappointed in our children, and there is no point in trying to hide our feelings. However, what is most important is (B). When things don't go well, and kids know it, we need to take it easy on our own disappointment. What Robby needs is a big hug and reassurance from his mom that she's on his side, no matter who wins. We have to remember that what's important is that our kids are learning the rules of good sportsmanship, working together as a team, giving their best effort, and having fun. After all, (3) it is not our aspirations for our children that will determine their lives, but rather their own goals and dreams for themselves.

We provide a better example for our kids when our feelings and our actions match as closely as possible. (4) This is a somewhat complicated matter, however. On the one hand, we want our children to say what they mean, and mean what they say, at least most of the time. On the other hand, we want them to develop a sense of when total honesty is called for, and when certain things are better left unsaid. We don't want our children to be phony, but we do want them to be polite and considerate of others' feelings. And while it's important to teach them good manners and the formalities of please and thank-you, we want to do more than just teach them to say the right words. We want them to genuinely (D) the thoughtfulness and generosity of others. This is not an easy job, but one of the best ways we can tackle it is by providing our children with a model of behavior that strikes a balance between kindness and frankness, honesty and diplomacy, showing them through our own actions (E).

(Source: Dorothy Law Nolte, *Children Learn What They Live*, Workman)

(1) Choose the most suitable word for the blank (A) from (a) to (e) below.

(a) collective (b) enjoyable (c) reserved (d) sincere
(e) wonderful

(2) Explain the reason for the underlined part (1) in Japanese.

(3) Rearrange the words of the underlined part (2) and complete the sentence.

(4) Choose the most suitable sentence for the blank (B) from (a) to (e) below.

(a) how much complaining we do in our everyday life
(b) that we don't have to be perfect role models for our children
(c) how our children feel about their own efforts
(d) that we should share our disappointment with others
(e) how our children can take responsibility for their behavior

(5) Translate the underlined part (3) into Japanese.

(6) About the underlined part (4), in what ways is it complicated? Explain it in Japanese.

(7) Choose the most suitable word for the blank (D) from (a) to (e) below.

(a) appeal (b) appoint (c) appreciate (d) approach
(e) approve

(8) Choose the most suitable sentence for the blank (E) from (a) to (e) below.

(a) how to handle themselves in stressful situations
(b) how to negotiate these delicate but important social interactions

(c) the way family values are taught and passed down one generation to the next

(d) how to give a condemning look or add a critical edge to our words

(e) how much we can anticipate things in advance

(☆☆☆☆◎◎◎◎◎)

【5】Read the following passage and answer the questions.

In the span of a few days in the spring of 1999, hundreds of thousands of ethnic Albanians fled their homes in Kosovo as Serbian forces drove them into neighboring countries. At the time, I was a new medical school graduate put in charge of ① triaging sick and injured refugees who showed up in a constant stream at an improvised medical aid station in the cold, muddy no-man's-land between Kosovo and Macedonia. As I stood there, I could see thousands of men, women and children who had trudged across the border or arrived in trucks, cars, horse-drawn carts or the arms of fellow refugees. [A] Many families had been abruptly separated during the chaos of expulsion. Once inside the border in refugee camps, desperate mothers and fathers posted paper notes with names and descriptions of their missing children.

Soon after I began working, a new way to help that did not involve scraps of paper became available. Employees at Microsoft's European headquarters in Paris, aware of the tragedy unfolding nearby, offered their services to the U.N.A few weeks after my arrival, I walked into a tent and found a Microsoft team photographing refugees and presenting them with ② computer-generated ID cards. The Microsoft workers hoped to register the refugees for food and shelter assistance and, through cross-checks made in these newly created databanks, to help locate lost family members.

It was odd to see the modern information age materialize in a teeming refugee camp packed (③) people stripped to their bare essentials. Why did computers look so foreign there? Perhaps it was because, before Kosovo, most refugee camps were situated in poorer, less developed places, where computers were a rarity. Perhaps it was because computers and other modern technologies demonstrate humankind's progress, and forced migration reflects its regression. Ultimately, the precision of a computer database seemed ④ incongruous when set against the chaos of relief work, with its rapidly changing environment and unpredictable donations discharged by well-intentioned but often poorly organized do-gooders.

As humanitarian workers try to save lives and relieve suffering, they are increasingly taking advantage not only of information and communications technologies but also of remote sensing operations perfected by the military, forensic identification techniques reminiscent of CSI, and quantitative methods applied routinely by (⑤) (who track the causes of disease outbreaks and devise public health strategies for limiting their toll). Workers are also employing more systematic approaches to planning and delivering aid, enabling the field of humanitarian assistance to evolve into an applied social science. Now the challenge for aid workers and policy-makers is to ensure that these advances help the people who need such assistance the most and to prevent the tools from becoming mere high-tech window dressing framing human catastrophes.

The desire to find quick and accurate ways to come to grips with the scale of a crisis was one of the early spurs to applying new technologies (⑥) relief work. [B] In the summer of 1931, after weeks of heavy rain and flooding, a typhoon stalled over China and sent water from rivers, lakes and canals crashing through levees and flood walls. The massive ⑦ [for / it / to / Chinese authorities / survivors / inundation / difficult / locate / made]. Charles A. and Anne Morrow Lindbergh, arriving in Nanjing on what was to be a vacation tour, used their long-distance Lockheed Sirius airplane to conduct aerial surveys that identified millions of additional victims and thousands more square miles of flooding. Their work helped to guide the Chinese government's response. It also drew international relief aid to the affected regions and evoked a prescient opinion from the New York Times: "This broad sky-survey ... [of] woes is [a] significant [example] of the aid that wings will give in this new age by telling matters that are seen from above the surface of the earth to ... inhabitants far and wide."

[C] Satellite imagery can be combined with computer-based tools known as geographic information systems (GIS) that integrate data from various sources with digital maps. In a humanitarian crisis, a GIS might superimpose data regarding the whereabouts of victims, their health status and other information onto a map or satellite images.

The devastating earthquake and tsunami that struck South Asia in December 2004, which together killed more than a quarter of a million people spread throughout 12 countries, demonstrated the worth of techno-do-goodism, along with the inevitable entanglements that accompany any crisis. The immediate aftermath in the hardest-hit area, the Indonesian province of Aceh, began in disarray. Political sensitivities related to a decades-long conflict between government forces and a rebel insurgency reportedly delayed the public release of some imaging data of the island, barring (⑧) to information that could have helped workers locate survivors in the critical first days.

The Indonesian government also took two days to invite international relief workers to enter the area, which it had recently closed to foreigners during an upsurge in the conflict. Soon, however, hundreds of aid groups began arriving by plane, helicopter and boat. Their services were supplemented by logistical help provided by military forces from multiple nations that delivered thousands of tons of supplies and equipment.

[D] Too many aid workers showed up in some areas, while other places remained underserved. But when I arrived a month later as a health team leader for the International Rescue Committee (IRC), after having worked in tsunami-affected areas of Thailand, the aid effort had already become more organized — ⑨ in [of / of / technology / part / use / because /

the]. In Banda Aceh, the province's capital city, I went immediately to a Humanitarian Information Center (HIC), set up by the U.N.'s Office for Coordination of Humanitarian Assistance.

There I collected GIS maps that depicted the disaster zone at different scales, (⑩) the regional down to the village level. The maps were accompanied by various spreadsheets that compiled the number of displaced, injured, dead and missing persons; coverage areas for various aid groups; the location of hospitals, clinics and pharmacies; and the most common potential disease outbreaks in each area. This data packet (⑪) as a useful guide when I traveled along Aceh's northern coastline to coordinate a vaccination campaign aimed at halting the spread of a small measles outbreak among displaced children and the families that hosted them. (Having studied medicine, I deal primarily with the health issues that arise from large crises, but aid workers providing food, water, sanitation and shelter and working on (⑫) detection and removal also use GIS to support their efforts.)

(Source: *Scientific American*, November 2007)

(1) Choose the most suitable definition from (a) to (e) below for the underlined word ①.

(a) entering or recording in an official list

(b) deciding the order of treatment of

(c) performing surgical techniques

(d) keeping safe from harm or injury

(e) removing someone from a place of danger to a safer place

(2) Choose the most suitable sentence from (a) to (d) below for each of the blank spaces [A] to [D].

(a) The initial relief effort was chaotic.

(b) Their numbers taxed the ability of overstretched United Nations refugee officials to track them.

(c) Recognition of that need dates back to one of the deadliest recorded natural disasters in history.

(d) Today's "sky-surveys" harness satellite and information technology to offer a far broader and more comprehensive picture of disasters.

(3) Why did a Microsoft team give refugees ② computer-generated ID cards? Give two reasons in Japanese.

(4) Choose the most suitable definition from (a) to (e) below for the underlined word ④.

(a) able to be used for a practical purpose or in several ways

(b) causing or likely to cause harm

(c) lacking the power to perform physically demanding tasks

(d) not in harmony or keeping with the surroundings or other aspects of something

(e) not fulfilling or not expected to achieve the intended purpose or desired income

(5) Choose the most suitable word for the blank (⑤) from (a) to (e) below.

(a) bioclimatologists (b) ecologists (c) epidemiologists

(d) ethnologists (e) meteorologists

(6) Write a suitable word to fill in each of the blank spaces (③), (⑥) and (⑩).

(7) Rearrange the words of the underlined parts ⑦ and ⑨, and complete the sentences.

(8) Choose the most suitable word for the blank (⑧) from (a) to (e) below.

(a) access (b) delay (c) donation (d) lack (e) use

(9) Choose the most suitable word for the blank (⑪) from (a) to (e) below.

(a) gained (b) helped (c) identified (d) located

(e) served

(10) To fill in the blank space (⑫), write a suitable word, referring to the definition below.

a type of bomb placed on or just below the surface of the ground or in the water, which detonates on contact with a person, vehicle, or ship

(☆☆☆☆◎◎◎◎◎)

【6】Write two or more paragraphs entitled "How much English should Japanese teachers of English speak in their English classes?" You are expected to write about 100 words in English.

(☆☆☆☆◎◎◎◎◎)

解答・解説

【中高共通】

【1】(1) 虹　(2) 日記　(3) カバ　(4) シェークスピア

〈解説〉リスニング問題では，文字を媒体としたリーディングと違い，音声は流れるとともに消えていってしまうので，より効率の良い解答が求められる。そのため，受験する都道府県の出題内容や問題形式の傾向(例えば，放送は2度聞くことができるのか，質問文は問題用紙に記載されているのか，メモはとることができるのか，など)をあらかじめ把握しておくことがとても重要である。ただ，なかなか対策がとりにくいこともあるが，市販のリスニング教材を一つ選び繰り返し活用することも一つの方法である。教育に関する専門用語を英語で覚えておくことも大切である。実際のリスニング試験での一般的な心構えとして，①放送を聞く前に質問文に目を通して聞かれる内容を把握しておく，②全ての単語を無理に聞きとろうとせず，どのような趣旨の英文なのか聞きとることをまずは優先する，③1度目と2度目の放送でそれぞれ何を聞きとればいいのか，目的を明確にして聞く，④必要に応じてメモをとることが必要である。どうしてもわからない場合は深く考えず勘で解答して，次の問題に答える準備をするという思い切りのよさも必要であろう。さらに，都道府県によって原稿が手に入る(見ることができる)ところとそうでないところがあるので，このように原稿が見られるところは発話の難易度，問題の傾向などをつかむために十分に活用しておくことが望まれる。

【2】(1)　c　(2)　a　(3)　d　(4)　c
〈解説〉【1】の解説参照。

【3】(1)　d　(2)　a　(3)　b　(4)　c　(5)　c　(6)　b
(7)　c　(8)　d　(9)　b　(10)　b
〈解説〉(3)　get は原型不定詞をとるので注意。　(5)　five years agoという過去を示す言葉がある場合は仮定法過去完了になる。　(6)　be able to ～：～ することができる。　(9)　Keep up!：頑張ってください。(「維持する」 などといった意味がある)。　(10)　vulnerable：攻撃を受けやすい。

【4】(1)　d　(2)　母親が，彼のチームが勝つように常軌を逸したように声を張り上げ，特に，彼が打席に立ったり，彼のところへボールが飛んできたりすると，その声援がさらに大きくなるから。
(3)　The more she screams, the more he seems to fumble and　(4)　c
(5)　子どもたちの人生を決めるのは，子どもたちに対する私たちの強い願いではなく，むしろ子どもたちが自分で見つける目標や夢なのである。　(6)　私たちは，子どもたちに本音をいってほしいと思う一方，いつ真正直さが求められ，いつ物事を言わずにいた方がいいのか，という感覚を身につけてほしいとも願うという点で複雑であるということ。　(7)　c　(8)　b
〈解説〉親が子どもをほめるときのこと，子どもがどう本音を言うかということ，子どもと親の感情が重なるときの一例などが挙げられている。

【5】(1)　b　(2)　[A]　b　[B]　c　[C]　d　[D]　a
(3)　・食料と避難所を援助するために，難民を登録するため。　・行方不明の家族の捜索に役立てるため。　(4)　d　(5)　c
(6)　③　with　⑥　to　⑩　from　(7)　⑦　inundation made it difficult for Chinese authorities to locate survivors　⑨　part because of the use of technology　(8)　a　(9)　e　(10)　mine
〈解説〉アルバニア民族に関する話で，難民救助などの話が主な内容となっている。その中で，筆者の働いた経験も盛り込まれている。

【6】省略
〈解説〉採点のポイントとしては，正確な英語で書かれていること，根拠や具体例を伴った，まとまりのある内容であること，2段落以上の構成で，約100語の英語で書かれていることなどになる。

2009年度　実施問題

【中高共通】

【1】(Listening Test Part 1) Listen to the description and identify what or who it is. Answer in Japanese. Each description is read once.

(☆☆☆◎◎◎)

【2】(Listening Test Part 2) Listen to the passage and from the following sentences (a～k), choose three that belong with the passage. The passage and the choices are read twice.

(☆☆☆◎◎◎)

【3】Choose the best item from (a) to (d) below to fill in the blank of each sentence.

(1) Don't look so (　　) when I tell you these things. They are true!

(a) inconsiderable　(b) inconsiderate　(c) incredible

(d) incredulous

(2) Lincoln High School and Milan High School are (　　) the first and second largest high schools in the state.

(a) respectably　(b) respectfully　(c) respectively　(d) responsibly

(3) Bill was slightly bruised, but (　　) unhurt.

(a) except　(b) nonetheless　(c) other than　(d) otherwise

(4) I got (　　) and started shouting at the television.

(a) brought away　(b) carried away　(c) lost away

(d) taken away

(5) "Cathy, breakfast is ready!" "OK, Mom, (　)."

(a) I'll come　(b) I'll go　(c) I'm coming　(d) I'm going

(6) "Don't worry too much. Everybody makes mistakes, and we can learn a lot from them. (　)"

"Yeah, I guess so. Thanks."

(a) A stitch in time saves nine. (b) Every cloud has a silver lining.

(c) Out of sight, out of mind. (d) The squeaky wheel gets the grease.

(7) Ann regretted ( ) her own shopping bag. She didn't get two yen back at the supermarket.

(a) not to have brought (b) not having brought

(c) not that she brought (d) that she should have brought

(8) The new treaty will facilitate financial ( ) between the two countries.

(a) certainties (b) emergencies (c) offenses (d) transactions

(9) "Why are you in such a hurry?" "My wife will be angry ( ) 7:00."

(a) if I don't get home by (b) if I don't get home until

(c) unless I get home by (d) unless I get home until

(10) "Do you think it'll stop raining tomorrow?" "I'm afraid the weather will ( ) today."

(a) be no worse than (b) be no better than (c) not be so bad as

(d) not be so good as

(☆☆☆◎◎◎)

【4】Read the following passage and answer the questions.

In the Army, dominance is achieved by a system of symbols, stripes for the non-commissioned officers and bars, leaves, birds and stars for the commissioned officers. But even without the symbols, the pecking order remains. I have seen privates in a shower room (①) to sergeants without knowing who they were or what their rank was. The sergeants, through their manner and bearing, were able to convey an obvious body-language message of rank.

In the business world, where neither stripes nor other obvious symbols are worn, the same ability to project a sense of superiority is the common attainment of the executive. How does he do it? What tricks does he use to subdue subordinates, and what tricks does he bring out for in-fighting in his own rank?

An attempt to study this was made by two researchers in a series of silent films. They had two actors play the parts of an executive and a visitor, and switch roles for different (②). The scene had one man at his desk while the other, playing the part of a visitor, knocks at the door, opens it and approaches the desk to discuss some business matter.

The audience watching the films was asked to (③) the executive and the visitor in terms of status. A certain set of rules began to emerge from the ratings. The visitor showed the least amount of status when he stopped just inside the door to talk across the room to the seated man. He was considered to have more status when he walked halfway up to the desk, and he had most status when he walked directly up to the desk and stood right in front of the seated executive.

Another factor that governed status in the eyes of the observers was the time between knocking and entering, and for the seated executive, the time between hearing the knock and answering. The quicker the visitor entered the room, the more status he had. The longer the executive took to answer, the more status he had.

It should be obvious that what is involved here is a matter of territory. The visitor is allowed to enter the executive's territory and by that arrangement the executive automatically achieves superior status.

How far into the territory the visitor penetrates, and how quickly he does it, in other words how he challenges the personal space of the executive, announces his own status.

The ‘big boss’ will walk into his subordinate's office unannounced. The subordinate will wait outside the boss' office until he is permitted in. If the boss is on the phone, the subordinate may tiptoe off and come back later. If the subordinate is on the phone, the boss will usually assert his status by standing above the subordinate until he murmurs, ‘Let me call you back,’ and then gives the boss his full attention.

There is a continuous shifting or fighting for status within the business world, and therefore status symbols become a very necessary part of the shift or dance. The executive with the attaché case is the most obvious one, and we all know the joke of the man who carries only his lunch in his attaché case but insists on carrying the case simply because it is so important to the image he must project.

Big business sets up a host of built-in status symbols. A large drug firm in Philadelphia earned enough money through the sale of tranquillizers to put up a new building that would house their rapidly expanding staff. The building could have been designed with any number of offices and workrooms, but quite deliberately the company set up a built-in status symbol in the offices. The corner offices on the very highest floor were reserved for the very highest personnel. [(X)] The last rank had desks out in an open room.

Rank was arrived at by an equation whose elements consisted of time on the job, importance of the job, salary and degree. The degree of MD, for example, gave any man no matter what his salary or time on the job, the right to have a closed office. PhDs might or might not have such an office, depending on other factors.

Within this system there was room for many other elements to demonstrate degree of status. Curtains, rugs, wooden desks as opposed to metal desks, furniture, couches, easy chairs, and of course, secretaries, all set up sub-hierarchies.

An important element in this set-up was the contrast between the frosted-glass cubicles and the clear-glass cubicles. By allowing the world to see in, the man in the clear-glass cubicle was automatically reduced in importance or rank. His territory was that much more open to visual invasion. He was that much more vulnerable.

(Source: Body Language)

(1) Choose the most suitable word form (a) to (e) below to fill in blank spaces (①) to (③).

① (a) deferential (b) defining (c) inaccurate
(d) indifferent (e) infamous

② (a) take (b) taken (c) takes (d) taking
(e) to take

③ (a) assert (b) eliminate (c) emerge (d) modify
(e) rate

(2) Answer the following questions in Japanese.

① In the series of silent films, the audience perceived that the executive was far more important than the visitor in two situations. Describe which two situations made the audience come to their conclusions.

② Describe the difference in behavior, between when the ‘big boss’ visits his subordinate's office and in the opposite case.

③ How can we say that the people who occupy clear-glass cubicles are lower in rank in the business world than those who occupy frosted-glass cubicles?

(3) Arrange the following sentences below so they make sense in the blank (X).

(a) The rank below this had offices without windows at all.

(b) Below them were the men with partitioned cubicles for offices.

(c) The corner offices on the floor below were reserved for the next rank of top personnel.

(d) These had frosted-glass walls and no doors and the next rank down had clear-glass cubicles,

(e) Lesser, but still important executives had offices without corner windows.

(☆☆☆◎◎◎)

【5】Read the following passage and answer the questions.

The more scientists learn about the brain's decay, the more curious they've become about how well people function anyway. Even among people 85 and older, only 18.2 percent live in nursing homes. "In the past, much of the research has focused on disease and decline," says Gene Cohen, director of the Center on Aging, Health and Humanities at George Washington University. "Now we're looking at the concept of potential and how older people often continue to thrive and grow even in the face of the most serious illness." Recent studies of both animal and human ① subjects have found that several factors go hand in hand with better mental performance, including education, professional success, and intellectual, social, and physical activities. A 2003 study reported in the *New England Journal* of Medicine, for example, found that people over 75 who danced, read, or played board games or musical instruments also had a lower rate of dementia.

Much of the work has focused on finding ways to ② bulletproof people against Alzheimer's. In mice, an Alzheimer's vaccine seemed to work, but it proved toxic in humans and trials were (③) (although research on vaccines continues). Beta carotene supplements may delay cognitive decline if taken for many years - but only by a year and a half. Education seems to lower your odds of Alzheimer's - but even some Nobel laureates develop it. Cholesterol-lowering drugs seemed to offer some promise in fending off Alzheimer's, but a 12-year-long study published in January showed they had no effect.

For decades, scientists assumed that humans were born with all the brain cells they'd ever have. Then, in the 1970s, researchers showed that new brain cells and neural pathways form through the end of life. "This was the beginning of the brain ④ plasticity movement," says Cohen, "the understanding that when we challenge our brains, the brain cells sprout new dendrites, which results (⑤) increased synapses, or contact points." More recent research has shown that there isn't an age limit: Training older adults in certain memory tasks, like remembering faces and names, seems to boost those specific abilities - though it won't remind you to bring your shopping list to the store. And the newest evidence suggests that intensive practice in reasoning skills or in distinguishing sounds appears to lead to more generalized improvements in brain function.

In 2006, for example, a controlled clinical study of more than 2,000 older people by researchers at Pennsylvania State University, Indiana University, Johns Hopkins University, and elsewhere found that those who received 10 60-to-75-minute training sessions in reasoning - specifically, in recognizing word, number, and letter patterns and filling in the next item in a series - reported less difficulty with such activities of daily living as understanding instructions on a medication label. The effects still were apparent five years later. This past November, scientists from the University of Southern California and the Mayo Clinic announced that study subjects who spent an hour a day for eight to 10 weeks using a program that asked them to recognize subtle differences in sounds performed better than the ⑥ control group on memory and speed tests, too. Designers of the Brain Fitness Program (made by Posit Science, which founded the study) claim that such ear training causes the brain to convey information more precisely from one region to another - which, in turn, improves other types of thinking.

"The amount of memory improvement was equivalent to going back 10 years in your ability," says Elizabeth Zelinski; professor of gerontology and psychology at USC and a principal investigator on the study, which has not yet been published.

Experts caution that most brain-training products haven't been tested and that ⑦ [are / do / data / exist / what] still shaky. If improvement of daily living tasks is the goal, "we don't yet have the data to suggest ⑧ they accomplish that," says Arthur Kramer, a neuroscientist at the University of Illinois. "Yes, we have data that says you can get better at certain things with practice. [A] We don't know yet." Still, many doctors who work with older people feel they don't have time to wait for the research, and nursing homes and senior centers across the country are adding "brain gyms" and other programs ⑨ [people / help / stay / older / to] mentally active.

"I've learned more about China than you can imagine," says Hortense

Gutmann, 100, who started using E-mail just over a year ago through a new computer-education program for residents of Sarah Neuman Center for Healthcare and Rehabilitation, a nursing home in Mamaroneck, N.Y. She now keeps in (⑩) with relatives there, as well as in Minnesota and Israel, and takes great pleasure in having mastered a new skill.

[B] The market for products like Brain Fitness Program, Nintendo's Brain Age, and MindFit soared to an estimated $80 million in 2007, up from just $2 million to $4 million in 2005, according to SharpBrains.com, a San Francisco-based group that follows the industry. Meanwhile, the Alzheimer's Association recommends any activity that will keep you curious and learning: reading and writing, attending lectures, taking classes, even gardening.

Still, the best workout for your brain may be the old-fashioned kind. As far back as 1999, researchers at the University of Illinois found that older people who started exercising showed faster reaction times and better ability to focus after just six months than did a control group. [C] In a second study reported in 2006, the same team found that the aerobic exercisers actually increased their brain size (⑪) about 3 percent. Last year, researchers at Columbia University found that when people exercised regularly for three months, blood flow increased to a part of the hippocampus, which is important for memory. In studies of mice who exercised on treadmills, increased blood flow to the same part of the brain corresponded with an increase in the production of new brain cells.

The power of exercise seems far more impressive than (⑫) of brain-training software, says Sandra Aamodt, editor in chief of *Nature Neuroscience*, a scientific journal on brain research, and coauthor of the forthcoming book *Welcome to Your Brain*. A recent meta-analysis of numerous exercise studies found that, on average, faithful aerobic exercise might boost someone's cognitive performance from average - say, from 10th place out of 20 people tested - to notably above average - say, to No.5. But cognitive training would boost the same person to eighth out of 20.

[　　D　　] Maybe for the same reason it's so good for the heart: its beneficial effect on blood vessels. "It may be that a pretty significant amount of deterioration in brain function relates to disruptions of the cardiovascular system by microstrokes," in the tiny vessels in the brain, says Aamodt. Exercise may help prevent them. It also stimulates the production of proteins called growth factors, which promote the formation and growth of brain cells and synapses.

(Source: U.S. NEWS & WORLD REPORT, FEBRUARY 11, 2008)

(1) Choose the word from (a) to (e) below which is closest in meaning to the underlined word ①.

(a) examinees　(b) issues　(c) substances　(d) themes
(e) victims

(2) Choose the word from (a) to (e) below which is closest in meaning to the underlined word ②.

(a) cure　(b) deprive　(c) prepare　(d) protect　(e) save

(3) Choose the most suitable word from (a) to (e) below for the blank space (③).

(a) accelerated　(b) forgiven　(c) improved
(d) maintained　(e) suspended

(4) Choose the word from (a) to (e) below which is closest in meaning to the underlined word ④.

(a) artificiality　(b) creativity　(c) flexibility
(d) intellectuality　(e) superiority

(5) To fill in blank spaces (⑤), (⑩), (⑪) and (⑫), write a suitable word.

(6) Choose the most suitable definition from (a) to (e) below for the underlined words ⑥.

(a) a group or class of persons enjoying superior intellectual or social or economic status

(b) a group of persons abnormally dependent on something that is psychologically or physically habit-forming (especially alcohol or narcotic drugs)

(c) a group of participants in a clinical study who have the actual drug or treatment being studied

(d) a group of people who have a form of treatment of particular mental illnesses which involves sending an electric current through the brain

(e) in a test or trial, a group that does not receive the new treatment being studied and which is compared to the group that does receive the new treatment

(7) Rearrange the words of the underlined parts ⑦ and ⑨, and complete the sentences.

(8) Write down the words from the passage which the underlined word ⑧ refers to.

(9) Choose the most suitable sentence from (a) to (d) below for each of the blank spaces [A] to [D].

(a) Consumers aren't waiting for more research, either.

(b) But does it translate to the real world?

(c) Why is exercise so good for the brain?

(d) Now, it's becoming clearer why.

(10) Choose a statement from (a) to (e) below that corresponds to the passage.

(a) Gene Cohen says that many brain scientists have done research only on cures for mental disease and insists that they should encourage patients to garden or read regularly.

(b) If older people take cholesterol-lowering drugs, they can prevent Alzheimer's disease.

(c) The number of a person's brain cells doesn't change all through his life.

(d) Designers of the Brain Fitness Program reached the conclusion that the training of recognizing differences in sounds is closely related to the ability to communicate information with others.

(e) It was found that mice who exercised on treadmills had more blood flow to their hippocampus and produced more new brain cells.

(11) Which of the following would be the best title for this passage?

(a) Fear of Alzheimer's　(b) Keeping Your Brain Fit

(c) Lifelong Learning　(d) Living in a Graying Society

(e) The Secret of Staying Healthy

(☆☆☆◎◎◎)

【6】FY2006 White Paper on Education, Culture, Sports, Science and Technology points out, that "The situation surrounding education has changed greatly since the original Basic Act on Education was promulgated in 1947." Explain one or two of the numeric changes shown in the figure below and what kind of influence you think it has had on our society. You are expected to write about 100 words in English.

Figure ◆ 1-1　Situation at the time of the establishment of the Fundamental Law of Education compared to the present

○ Average life expectancy					
Male	50.06 years (1947)		→	78.53 years (2005)	
Female	53.96 years (1947)		→	85.49 years (2005)	
○ Overall fertility rate	4.54	(1947)	→	1.26	(2005)
○ Proportion of population aged 65 or above	4.8%	(1947)	→	20.1%	(2005)
○ High school attendance rate	42.5%	(1950)	→	97.7%	(2006)
○ University, etc., attendance rate	10.1%	(1955)	→	49.3%	(2006)
○ Percentage of employment by industry		(1950)	→	(2005)	
Primary (agriculture, forestry, and fishing)		48.5%	→	4.8%	
Secondary (mining, construction, and manufacturing)		21.8%	→	26.1%	
Tertiary (service, etc.)		29.6%	→	67.2%	

(Source: *White Paper*, Ministry of Education, Culture, Sports, Science and Technology, 2007)

(☆☆☆◎◎◎)

解答・解説

【中高共通】

【1】(1) バナナ　(2) 救急車　(3) 魔法　(4) ジョン・レノン　(5) 西田幾多郎

〈解説〉(1)　果物で「長く曲がっている」「熟すと皮が黄色」から正解はバナナ。　(2)「緊急時に病人や怪我人を運ぶ自動車」だから正解は救急車。　(3)「特別な言葉や動きによって不可能なことをする秘密の力」だから正解は魔法。　(4)「ビートルズの元メンバーで，『イマジン』などを作ったロックミュージシャン」だから正解はジョン・レノン。
(5)「石川で生まれ，禅と西洋哲学を融合させるような哲学を生み出した，日本の哲学者」だから正解は西田幾多郎。

【2】a　d　j
〈解説〉冒頭に「成功している人はたいてい，話し方が上手」とあるので，まずaが正解。第3段落に「私自身が放送(on the air)などで話してきた人々のことを思い返すと」とあるので，筆者は放送業界に関係があることが分かるので，dも正解。筆者が上げる話し方のポイントの6番目は「相手の立場に立って考え，相手と共感すること」なので，jが正解。

【3】(1)　d　(2)　c　(3)　d　(4)　b　(5)　c　(6)　b　(7)　b　(8)　d　(9)　a　(10)　b
〈解説〉語彙力を問う問題。正解となった単語の意味は以下。
(1)　(d)　incredulous「疑い深い」　(2)　(c)　respectively「それぞれ」　(3)　(d)　otherwise「その他は」　(4)　(b)　carried away「我を忘れて」　(5)　(c)　I'm coming.　呼ばれている方へ行く際に使う。
(6)　(b)　Every cloud has a silver lining.ことわざで，直訳は「どんな雲にも銀の裏がついている」。意味は「憂いの反面には喜びがある」ということ。　(7)　(b)　not having brought「持ってこなかったこと」。後悔している時点よりも，さらに過去のことを表わすために「have＋過去分詞」が用いられている。　(8)　(d)　transactions「取引」
(9)「私が7時までに家に戻らなければ妻は怒るだろう」とすれば自然なので，(a)が正解　(10)「今日の天気より，良くはならないだろう」とすれば自然なので正解は(b)。

【4】(1)　①　a　②　c　③　e　(2)　①　客が部屋に入ったところで立ち止まり，重役と遠く距離を置いた状態で話をしたとき。客がドアをノックしてから重役が応対するまでの時間が長いとき。
②　・上司の場合，部下の部屋へ許可なく入っていき，電話中なら傍らに立ち，部下を見下ろして上司が待っていることを言外に伝える。部下の場合，上司の部屋の外で入室の許可を待つ。上司が電話中なら足音を立てずに立ち去り，後で出直してくる。　③　すりガラスの個室は他人の視線から自分の領域が守られているが，透明なガラスの個室は外から丸見えであり，自分の領域が他人の視線から守られていない分だけ弱い立場ということになるから。　(3)　c→e→a→b→d

〈解説〉「ビジネスの世界で，上司や部下などの序列がどのような仕組みで秩序付けられているか」ということをテーマにした文章。特に(2)の難易度が高い。(2) ①では「客よりも重役の方が立場が上」と感じられるのはどのような場合か，と問われている。②では「上司が部下の部屋を訪ねる」場合と反対に「部下が上司の部屋を訪ねる」場合の振る舞いの違いを説明するよう求められている。③透明なガラスの個室にいる人の方が，すりガラスの個室にいる人よりも序列が下であるのはどうしてなのか説明が求められている。①②③ともキーワードが登場する段落を探し当て，その段落の意味を簡潔に日本語でまとめていけばよい。

【5】(1)　a　(2)　d　(3)　e　(4)　c　(5)　⑤　in　⑩　touch
⑪　by　⑫　that　(6)　e　(7)　⑦　what data do exist are
⑨　to help other people stay　(8)　brain-training products
(9)　[A]　b　[B]　a　[C]　d　[D]　c　(10)　e　(11)　b

〈解説〉いわゆるアルツハイマー病のような，高齢者に見受けられる脳機能の低下に関する，最新の研究についての科学記事。やや難しい論理的な文章では，重要な内容が，文章のどこに書かれているか予測した上で読むと読みやすくなる。ポイントは冒頭の段落と各段落の最初の文である。この文章では，冒頭の段落で，以前の研究では脳機能について，病気や能力の低下に注目してきたが，最近は，高齢になって脳の機能が低下していく中でどのように潜在能力を生かし，成長させていくかをテーマに研究が進められている，ことが述べられている。この大枠にそって，それぞれの科学者のレポートを段落の最初の文に注意しながら読み解いていくとよい。

【6】(解答例)　One of the important numeric changes is the high school attendance rate. It rose from 42.5% in 1950 to 97.7% in 2006. This means the standard of education got higher in this period. I think this high standard of education created the well-educated workforce. Another important change is the percentage of employment of tertiary industry. It also rose 29.6% in 1950 to 67.2% in 2005. Generally speaking, tertiary industry needs well-educated workforce. I think the high standard of education created the well-educated workforce and developed the industry structure. 〈88語〉

〈解説〉解答例の日本語訳は以下。「重要な数的な変化の1つは，高校就学率だ。1950年の42.5%から2006年の97.7%へと上昇している。これは，この期間に教育水準が高まったことを意味する。私は，この教育水準の高さが質の高い労働力を生み出したのだと思う。もう1つの重要な変化は，第3次産業の労働人口の割合だ。これも1950年の29.6%から2005年の67.2%へと上昇している。一般的に言って，第3次産業は質の高い労働力を必要とする。私は，教育水準の高さが質の高い労働力を生み出し，産業構造を発展させたのだと思う。」　採点のポイントは以下の3点。①表に示された数的変化の中の1つ又は2つが，適切な英語で説明されているか。②数的変化が，これまで社会に与えてきた影響について，妥当な説明が，妥当な英語で書かれているか。③100語程度で書かれているか。数的な変化と社会への影響を論理的に説明する英文を書く必要がある。

2008年度　実施問題

【中高共通】

【1】(Listening Test) Listen to the tape and answer the questions.

(☆☆☆◎◎◎)

【2】(Listening Test) Listen to the tape and answer the questions.

(☆☆☆◎◎◎)

【3】Choose the best item from (a) to (d) below to fill in the blank of each sentence.

(1) Music is everything to me. If (　　), I would have nothing.

(a) I was deprived by it　(b) I was deprived of it

(c) it was deprived of me　(d) it was deprived by me

(2) Many Japanese are eager to study English.(　　) soon, bookstores in Japan are filled with English textbooks.

(a) By the new academic year

(b) While the new academic year starting

(c) With the new academic year started

(d) With the new academic year starting

(3) Mr. Grant is applying for the position of head teacher (　　) has been posted on the web since last December.

(a) as　(b) but　(c) who　(d) which

(4) I am a poor correspondent and I seldom,(　　), write to my mother living in Nagano.

(a) if ever　(b) if never　(c) if any　(d) if only

(5) It was a costly success (　　) we lost three lives on our way to the top of the mountain.

(a) such that　(b) in that　(c) so that　(d) except that

(6) Teachers should have objective ( ) when they mark tests.
(a) criteria (b) levels (c) achievements
(d) modifications

(7) "I could hardly understand what Mr. Ito said. He wasn't capable of carrying on a ( ) conversation and made a lot of contradictory statements."
(a) confidential (b) comprehensive (c) coherent
(d) colloquial

(8) Mr. White's speech was perfect. It ( ).
(a) could have been better (b) could have been worse
(c) couldn't have been worse (d) couldn't have been better

(9) Put yourself in my shoes and think of ( ).
(a) how discrimination is like
(b) how it would be like to be discriminated against
(c) what it is like discrimination
(d) what it is like to be discriminated against

(10) Professor Cooper says that although making use of real-life writing in the classroom ( ) is at least the creation of plausible contexts.
(a) is problematic, we should aim at one
(b) is problematic, what we should aim for
(c) is what we should aim, one of which problems
(d) may be a problem, however difficult it

(☆☆☆☆◎◎◎)

【4】Read the passage below and answer the questions.

Growing up as an American preteen in Germany, Erin Maury recalls having to maneuver three modes of (A) on her own ― bus, subway and streetcar ― just to get to her ice skating lessons at the Nuremberg rink. Maury, now 35, said that experience and other aspects of living overseas as a youngster made her more courageous and more open to new ideas as an adult. On the other hand, her husband, Jon, 36, who spent his whole childhood in Whitehall, Pennsylvania, said he was (B) even at the age of 12 to order a pizza over the telephone. Today the couple has opted to (1)<u>replicate</u> Erin Maury's life by raising their two children, Nick and Harper, as expatriates in London. "[①]," said Maury, whose father was a U.S. Army officer and who lived in nine different cities before the age of 18.

In today's global economy, living and traveling overseas have become second nature for many executives, But through a child's eyes, any leap into the unknowns of another culture can be an alarming one. Yet many adults who have spent part or all of their childhood living abroad say they cannot think of (2)<u>[offspring / a better / growing up / their own / as / for / than / childhood]</u> an expat.

"I believe that the exposure I had as a child to different cultures, languages and even foods opened up my eyes to a society larger than just my backyard," said Aimie Vargas, a self-described Army brat who grew up all over the world, "[②]." All of this, experts say, is why (3)<u>expats often run in families.</u>

"I think this is very common — even when (4)<u>it skips a generation</u>," said Ruth Van Reken, an American and author of "Third Culture Kids: The Experience of Growing Up Among Worlds." "My grandparents worked in Iran, so my father was born and raised there," Van Reken said. "I was born and raised in Nigeria, had one child born in Liberia, and raised all my kids there." Van Reken moved back to the United States in 1985 for family reasons and now lives in Indianapolis, Indiana. Her second daughter lives in Ghana and had her first child there. Van Reken's older sister, on the other hand, has lived in America, in the same house, for 35 years. But her sister's daughter is leading the expat life now as the wife of a U.S. Foreign Service officer. Van Reken said that those who grow up as expats often find living in a more "monocultural environment" as adults too bland. "The joy of exploring feels inhibited in this environment, and so people (5)<u>get itchy feet,"</u> she said.

Josephine Huchet is a French woman who grew up in Hong Kong and Singapore and is now raising her own children in London. "I loved discovering new ways of life as a child, and I always felt special when living abroad," she said, describing the frequent dinner parties her parents held at home, to which they invited her father's business associates from all over the world. But even though Huchet wants her children to have some of the same broadening experiences she had − such as meeting and befriending people from different cultures − she does not intend to do everything exactly the same as her parents, such as making (C) business trips and leading an active social life in the evenings. "Living abroad doesn't always bring a family together," she said. "I think it is very tempting to meet a lot of people when you are overseas and for parents to make as many friends as possible because they have no family members by their side.[③]." She said she would "probably do it differently when my girls are older, and I will not go out as much, and I will try to travel with the whole family."

(6)<u>While for some people, growing up as an expat is an experience that reaps loads of multicultural benefits, for others, coping with huge changes in schooling and lifestyle can be unpleasantly disorienting</u>. Robin Pascoe, a Canadian author who has moved her children around the world with her (7)<u>diplomat</u> husband, cited a kind of Murphy's Law that applies to expats: If a parent raises two children overseas, one will typically replicate the lifestyle as an adult, while the other will want to stay (D) and never move again. "Our daughter is the global one, who loved to see the world as she was growing up and wanted to one day be just like Mom and Dad," Pascoe said. "[④]," she said. "From his point of view, his Dad was often away and not available to him, so he naturally would develop an (E) towards it all."

And while some families become expats primarily because of work, others do it primarily for their children. Carrie Levenson-Wahl and her husband, both Americans, have raised their two daughters − now 18 and 20 − in Paris for the last five years to give them the experience of living abroad.

"[⑤]," said Levenson-Wahl, who works at the International School of Paris. "They have a global approach rather then an insular American one."

Vargas, the Army brat, who lived in Brazil and worked in Europe after finishing her education, also wants the expat lifestyle for her family — although she has not quite put it together yet. She and her husband, (8)<u>who grew up in New Jersey and have never lived outside the United States</u>, live in San Francisco. "We both agree that our plans for our family include living abroad and it's. something we hope to do in the next few years," she said. In the meantime, Vargas is trying to replicate the expat lifestyle without actually living abroad. "We're teaching my son English and Portuguese, and we're planning on sending him to the international school in San Francisco, and we also plan to travel as much as possible," she said, "[⑥]."

(Source: Herald Tribune, April 29-30－May 1, 2006)

(1) Choose the most suitable word for the blank (A) from (a) to (e) below.

(a) transaction (b) transcription (c) transformation
(d) transplantation (e) transportation

(2) Choose the most suitable word for the blank (B) from (a) to (e) below.

(a) ambitious (b) bold (c) curious (d) nervous
(e) obstinate

(3) Choose the most suitable definition for the underlined word (1) from (a) to (e) below.

(a) admit having done something wrong
(b) decline to accept something offered
(c) do something again exactly in the same way
(d) feel uncertain about something
(e) prevent something from being active

(4) Rearrange the words of the underlined part (2) and complete the sentence,

(5) Explain the meaning of the underlined part (3) in Japanese.

(6) There is an example of the underlined part (4) in the passage. Describe it in Japanese.

(7) Explain the meaning of the underlined part (5) in Japanese.

(8) Choose the most suitable word for the blank (C) from (a) to (e) below.

(a) familiar (b) flexible (c) forbiden (d) frequent
(e) frustrating

(9) Translate the underlined part (6) into Japanese.

(10) Choose the most suitable definition for the underlined word (7) from (a) to (e) below.

(a) a person that you work with, do business with or spend a lot of time with
(b) a person employed by somebody to find out information about something
(c) a person whose job is to represent his or her country in a foreign country
(d) a person who has an important job as a manager of a company
(e) a person who is in a position of authority in the government or a large organization

(11) Choose the most suitable word for the blank (D) from (a) to (e) below.

(a) cast (b) put (c) quit (d) rid (e) set

(12) Choose the most suitable word for the blank (E) from (a) to (e) below.

(a) antipathy (b) expectation (c) imbalance
(d) implication (e) understanding

(13) The underlined part (8) has one grammatical error. Correct it.

(14) Choose the most suitable sentence from (a) to (f) below for each of the boxes [①] to [⑥].

(a) But I hated the fact that my parents were never around when I was growing up

(b) It's not the same as living abroad, but I'm hoping that at least some of the benefits are transferable this way

(c) I learned young about tolerance, about being different, about having to be confident in oneself and about learning to listen to other people

(d) But my son saw his father's travel — and mine to a lesser degree — as something which impacted profoundly on his life

(e) It was the best thing we could have given them

(f) I never wanted my own children to be afraid of the unknown, and I wanted them to have an appreciation of other cultures

(☆☆☆☆◎◎◎)

【５】Read the following passage and answer the questions.

It's a fair bet that global warming is going to lead to a rise in human sickness and death. But what form they will take is difficult to say. We can be pretty sure that as average temperatures climb, there will be more frequent and longer heat waves of the sort that contributed to the death of at least 20,000 Europeans in August 2003. Other predictions are more (1)<u>tenuous</u>. For example, rising temperatures could — if rainfall and other conditions are right — result in larger mosquito populations at higher elevations in the tropics, which could in (A) contribute to the spread of malaria, dengue and other insect-borne infections.

Early indications are not (B). The World Health Organization (WHO) believes that even the modest increases in average temperature that have occurred since the 1970s have begun to take a toll. Climate change is responsible for at least 150,000 extra deaths a year — a figure that will double by 2030, according to WHO's (2)<u>conservative</u> estimate.

(X)<u>As with so many public-health issues, a disproportionate part of the burden appears to be falling on the poorest of the poor</u>. That doesn't mean, however, that the comparatively wealthy — who account for more than their share of greenhouse-gas emissions — will escape harm.

A look at three key factors affected by warming offers a hint of things to come.

AIR We're used to thinking of industrial and traffic pollution as having a detrimental effect on air quality. But all other things being equal, rising temperature by itself increases the amount of ground-level ozone, a major constituent of smog. (Y)<u>So many studies have linked higher ozone levels to death rates from heart and lung ailments that many cities issue smog alerts to warn those at risk to stay indoors.</u> You can expect more and longer alerts.

It gets worse. Higher levels of carbon dioxide favor the growth of ragweed and other pollen producers over other plants, according to Dr. Paul Epstein at Harvard's Center for Health and the Global Environment. In addition, ragweed chums out more pollen as CO_2 levels rise. Scientists have tied local spikes in asthma and allergy attacks to increases in molds and emissions from diesel engines. Apparently, the molds attach themselves to diesel particles, which deliver them more efficiently deep into the lungs. Add a plentiful helping of dust storms (from, for instance, the desertification of Mongolia or northern Africa) and a rise in drought-driven brush-fires, and you have a made-to-order recipe for increasing respiratory distress worldwide.

WATER Residents of the U.S. Gulf Coast don't have to be reminded that water can be a killer. You can usually evacuate people ahead of a major storm, but you can't evacuate infrastructure. "Thirteen of the 20 largest cities in the world happen to be located at sea level," says Dr. Cindy Parker of the Johns Hopkins School of Public Health in Baltimore, Md. That means that where people are most at risk from floods, so are hospitals and water-treatment plants. As we have seen in New Orleans the health effects of losing those facilities persist long after the water has receded.

Another predicted consequence of global warming is heavier downpours, leading to more floods, The immediate hazard is drowning, but the larger issue is water quality. To take just one example, (Z)<u>more than 700 U.S. cities have sewer systems that regularly overflow into water supplies during heavy rainstorms mixing dirty and clean water and sometimes requiring mandatory boiling to make contaminated tap water safe</u>. A heavy rainfall preceded the majority of waterborne-disease outbreaks in the U.S. over the past 60 years, says Dr. Jonathan Patz of the University of Wisconsin at Madison.

Ocean-water patterns also play a role in human health. Mercedes Pascual and her colleagues at the University of Michigan have been poring over more than a century's worth of data on cholera outbreaks in Bangladesh and tying them to detailed temperature reports of the surface waters of the Pacific Ocean, True, Bangladesh isn't anywhere near the Pacific, but the researchers are using the temperature data as an indication of a larger weather pattern called the El Niño/Southern Oscillation, or ENSO. What they have found is that the severity of an epidemic is linked to water temperature — but only in years of higher-than-normal temperatures on the ocean's surface. More alarming: as the ENSO pattern has become more pronounced since the 1970s, the association with cholera has become even stronger.

INSECTS The news here is not all bad. Ticks, for example, may not be able to survive hotter temperatures in the southwestern U.S. And global warming is unlikely to have much of an effect on malaria, as long as you focus on lowland areas (because those regions already have so many mosquitoes). That picture may change, however, as you move upward in elevation. Malaria has seen a dramatic upswing since the 1970s in highland cities like Nairobi (about 1,680 m above sea level). How much of that can be tied to temperature increases — as opposed to population movement, lapses in mosquito control or the spread of drug-resistant parasites — is a matter of debate. But because each year there are at least 300 million cases accounting for more than 1 million deaths, even a small uptick in the spread or severity of malaria could be devastating.

The tricky thing about all those predictions is that you can't point to any outbreak or any individual's death and say, "This occurred because of climate change." But we know that good public health relies on a long list of factors — the availability of doctors and nurses, effective medicines, clean water, proper sanitation — and that even today, millions of people die every year of what should be preventable diseases. With global warming, you can expect the death toll to be even higher.

(Source; Time, April 3, 2006)

(1) Choose the word from (a) to (e) below which is closest in meaning to the underlined word (1).

(a) accurate (b) explicit (c) likely (d) reliable
(e) uncertain

(2) To fill in the blank (A), choose the most suitable word from (a) to (e) below.

(a) advance (b) detail (c) favor (d) place (e) turn

(3) To fill in the blank (B), choose the most suitable word from (a) to (e) below.

(a) astonishing (b) clear (c) disgusting (d) encouraging
(e) pessimistic

(4) Choose the most suitable definition for the underlined word (2) from (a) to (e) below.

(a) approved by the government or by someone in authority
(b) correct to a very detailed level
(c) purposely low for the sake of caution
(d) larger than it actually needs to be
(e) close to the correct number but not exact

(5) Translate the underlined part (X), (Y) and (Z) into Japanese.

(6) According to the section AIR, which statement below is true? Choose one from (a) to (e) below.

(a) The amount of ground-level ozone is related only to rising temperature.

(b) Smog is mainly made up of CO_2 and ozone, both of which contribute to global warming.

(c) As CO_2 levels increase, ragweed grows faster and produces more pollen.

(d) Even when molds are attached to exhaust gas, they have nothing to do with lung diseases.

(e) With the steep increase in the number of dust storms, the risk of brush-fires is also increasing.

(7) According to the section WATER, which statement below is true? Choose one from (a) to (e) below.

(a) It is best to evacuate people from flooded areas into an infrastructure.

(b) Even after a flood has subsided, it usually has harmful effects on the residents because of the damage to public facilities.

(c) Mercedes Pascual has concluded that ENSO doesn't have any influence on cholera outbreaks in Bangladesh.

(d) An infectious disease is not in the least related to atmospheric or water temperature.

(e) The more distinct the ENSO pattern, becomes, the fewer people suffer from cholera.

(8) According to the section INSECTS, which statement below is true? Choose one from (a) to (e) below.

(a) Harmful insects, such as ticks and mosquitoes, are sure to increase in number along with a rise in temperature.

(b) The incidence rate of malaria has been gradually increasing in Nairobi since the 1970s.

(c) Although over one million people die of malaria every year, people don't have to worry too much about a moderate increase in the number of mosquitoes.

(d) It is difficult to attribute the cause of the spread of malaria in cities at high altitudes to temperature increases only, because there are other factors behind it.

(e) Even today a large number of people die of malaria every year because researchers have not discovered good remedies for it.

(☆☆☆☆◎◎◎)

【6】FY2005 White Paper on Education, Culture, Sports, Science and Technology points out that "Japanese children have a poor desire to learn and have not mastered good learning habits." Write your own ideas about what you should do as a teacher in order to solve these problems. You are expected to write about 100 words in English.

(☆☆☆☆◎◎◎)

解答・解説

【中高共通】

【1】解答略

〈解説〉内容をしっかり聞き取ること。まぎらわしい表現にまどわされないようにする。

【2】解答略

〈解説〉できるだけ詳細にメモをとること。数字・疑問詞などには特に注意する。

【3】(1) (b)　(2) (d)　(3) (d)　(4) (a)　(5) (b)　(6) (a)　(7) (c)　(8) (d)　(9) (d)　(10) (b)

〈解説〉(1) deprive…of～「…から～を奪う」　(2) 分詞構文の付帯

状況。「まもなく新学年が始まるので」という意味。　(3)　先行詞が「校長の立場」なので，関係代名詞はwhichになる。　(4)「私は筆無精で，長野にいる母には，もしあるとしてもめったに手紙を書かない」　(5)　in that～「～という理由で」　(6)　objective criterion「客観的基準」criteriaはcriterionの複数形。　(7)　「彼は筋の通った話ができず，矛盾したことを言った」contradictory「矛盾した」　(8)「それ以上良くならなかっただろう」ということは，「大変素晴らしかった」という意味になる。　(9)　what is …like「…がどんなものか」ここでは形式主語構文を用いている。put oneself in someone's shoes「(人) の身になる」 discriminate against～「～を差別する」　(10)「目指す」という意味で使うaimは自動詞なので，目的語を伴う場合は前置詞が必要となる。problematic「問題の」　plausible「もっともらしい」 context「文脈」

【4】(1)　(e)　(2)　(d)　(3)　(c)　(4)　a better childhood for their own offspring than growing up as　(5)　海外移住者になることが，家系の中で受け継がれていくことが多いということ。　(6)　ヴァン・レケンの姉は，父が海外移住をしていたにもかかわらず，アメリカ国内で35年間も暮らしている，しかし，その娘は現在海外移住をしている。　(7)　じっとしていられなくなる　(8)　(d)　(9)　海外移住者として成長することで多文化の恩恵を大いにこうむる人もいれば，その一方で就学や生活様式の大きな変化に対応することが，不快な精神的混乱につながる人たちもいる。　(10)　(c)　(11)　(b)　(12)　(a)　(13)　have→ has　(14)　①　(f)　②　(c)　③　(a)　④　(d)　⑤　(e)　⑥　(b)

〈解説〉(1)　直後にbus, subway and streetcarとあることから分かる。　(2)　On the other handという書き出しで始まることから，courageousとは反対の意味を持つ単語が入ることが分かる。　(3)「複写する，繰り返す」という意味。　(4)「自分の子どもが海外居住者として成長するよりもよい子ども時代を思いつくことができない」という意味になる。

(5)　run in「流れ込む」　expatはexpatriateのこと。　(6)「世代を飛ばす」という意味にあてはまる文章を探す。同じ段落に書かれている。　(7)　itchy feet「出歩きたくてむずむずしている」　(8)　frequent business trips「頻繁な出張」　(9)　some～, others…「～する人もいれば，…する人もいる」　reap「得る」　cope with～「～に対応する」　disorient「混乱させる」　(10)「外交官」　(11)　stay put「定着している」whileに導かれているので，前の文章とは反対の内容になることが分かる。　(12)　彼の見地から，父は留守がちだし，忙しいので，全てに対して「反感」をもつだろう。　(13)　先行詞はher husbandなので，単数扱いとなる。　(14)　①「子どもたちをエリンが育ってきたように育てることにした」とあるので，その理由が述べられていると考えられる。　②　世界中をまわって経験したことをあげている。それを受けて，「このすべてが」と文章がつながっている。　③「身近に家族がいないから」と書かれている文章を受けている。　④　娘に関して述べた後，heと受けていることから，息子であると分かる。⑤「狭量なアメリカ人よりむしろグローバルなアプローチを身に付けている」と述べていることから，自分たちの判断に対してよい評価をしている。　⑥　サンフランシスコに住んでいながら，子どもに英語とポルトガル語を教えたり，インターナショナルスクールに入れる計画を立てていたりすることに対しての評価をしている。

【5】(1)　(e)　(2)　(e)　(3)　(d)　(4)　(c)　(5)　(X)　非常に多くの公衆衛生問題と同様に，貧しい中でも最も貧しい人々に，割に合わないほど大きな負担がかかっているようである。　(Y)　非常に多くの研究が，オゾン濃度の高さを心肺の病気による死亡率に関連付けてきたので，多くの都市は，危険な状況にある人々には屋内にいるようスモッグ警告を発している。　(Z)　700以上のアメリカの都市では，激しい暴風雨の間にしばしば下水が上水の中に溢れ出し，汚水と浄水が混じるため，時には汚染された水道水を安全なものにするため強制的に煮沸しなければならない事態になる。　(6)　(c)　(7)　(b)

(8)　(d)

〈解説〉(1)「あいまいな，微妙な」　accurate「的確な」　explicit「明白な」　(2)「次々に」　(3)　後に続く文章がよい内容ではないことから判断する。　(4)「控えめな」　for the sake of～「～のために」　(5)　(X)　as with～「～と同様に」　disproportionate「不釣り合いな」　(Y)　so～that構文に注意する。ailment「病気」　at risk「危険な状態で」　(Z)　sewer system「下水道」　water supply「上水」　mandatory「強制的な」　contaminate「汚染する」　(6)　セクションの後半部分に書かれている。　(7)　セクションの最初の段落に書かれている。recede「退く」　subside「おさまる」　(8)　セクションの最初の部分に書かれている。

【6】I think the reason why Japanese children have a poor desire to learn is that they cannot have interest in the contents of lesson. If they aren't interested in lessons, a teacher must elaborate his lessons. Since the pattern practice is boring, take in a game etc. and let every student enable to work. Moreover, if the students have not mastered good learning habits, it is important to make it a rule to study every day, even in a few minutes. Probably, it is good to start with using morning time, or using the beginning of a lesson. A teacher has to consider the situation.

〈解説〉学習意欲を持たせること，学習習慣をつけること，いずれも簡単にはいかないが重要なことである。ささいなことから，短い時間から始めていくことが大切であろう。

2007年度　実施問題

【中高共通】

【1】(Listening Test)　Listen to the tape and answer the questions. You will hear the passage and each statement only once.

(☆☆☆◎◎◎)

【2】(Listening Test)　Listen to the tape and answer the questions. You will hear the passage, questions and answer options only once.

(☆☆☆◎◎◎)

【3】Choose the best item from (a) to (d) below to fill in the blank of each sentence.

(1)　We often hear it (　　　) that Japanese animation is becoming more and more popular abroad.

(a)　said　　(b)　saying　　(c)　says　　(d)　to be said

(2)　There were (　　　) in the movie theater.

(a)　left no vacant seats　　(b)　no seats vacant left

(c)　no vacant seats left　　(d)　seats left no vacant

(3)　It is (　　　) the fact that English is not the only important international language.

(a)　worth considering　　(b)　worth being considering

(c)　worth to be considered　　(d)　worth to consider

(4)　In Japan, (　　　) education is 9 years in total, and comprises 6 years of elementary school and 3 years of junior high school.

(a) compulsory　　(b)　dutiful　　(c)　formal　　(d)　responsible

(5)　Attending the international event has inspired Mr.Tanaka to spend almost three months' salary on language learning (　　　) improving his performance at work.

(a) as to (b) for the purpose of (c) in search of
(d) thanks to

(6) Too much expectation and urgency from instructors might cause learners to lose their ability to reach decisions ( ) their motivation to learn.
(a) as far as (b) as well as (c) much as
(d) not so much as

(7) Students who are ( ) creatively and comprehensively may be able to find appropriate solutions to any problem that arises in daily life.
(a) to use in thinking (b) used to be thinking
(c) used to thinking (d) using to think

(8) In busy, overpopulated classrooms, ( ) to use the newly developed instructive model as a guide to practical teaching action.
(a) it being difficulty (b) it can be difficult
(c) there can be difficulty (d) there must be difficult

(9) The students specializing in modern art began repeatedly visiting the recently built museum, which the faculty ( ) the esthetic sense of the young artists.
(a) hoped it would improve (b) hoped would improve
(c) would hope it improve (d) would hope to improve

(10) I'm ( ) to make my Japanese students adapt to my way of thinking, my educational efforts would have been a total failure.
(a) convinced of my trial (b) convincing that if I tried
(c) convinced that if I had tried
(d) convincing whether I would not have tried

(☆☆☆◎◎◎)

【4】Read the following passage and answer the questions (1) to (3).

"I feel calmed down when I do this." "I didn't quite understand but my brother told me to go with him. I said ok and came to see, and actually I feel pretty good." "I like the feeling of concentration while drawing calligraphy."

These are the comments made by the students at a calligraphy class, at Toyota Language Center, the Japan Society in New York. Perhaps it has not been (①) proven; however, Christopher Terry, one of the students said, "I have been doing this for the last three years and I have surprised myself. My blood pressure has come down."

Shodo is an art form using a brush and charcoal ink on paper, wood plaques and fabric. Although it (②) in the techniques used for letter writing, with its unique form of expression it has developed into an art genre.

Currently about 80 people are taking the calligraphy lessons, and sometimes it is amazing at the skills that they can develop after trying something only three or four times. <u>(A) Their skills maybe make Japanese people doubt that even Japanese elementary school children could achieve this much in such a short period</u>. In addition, they have fine posture keeping their back straight. As if everyone is a professional calligrapher, his or her attitude toward calligraphy is nothing (③) serious.

Masako Inkyo, the instructor, started calligraphy at the age of three. She is a well-known calligrapher, a member of the three largest *Shodo* professional associations in Japan, who has received many awards and holds the highest rank, based on work she has submitted. She says, "I don't tell them how to carry their posture, though I teach them how to hold a writing brush. In addition, they are different from Japanese who already have some idea at the beginning. They start from nothing. That's why they become so good quickly." Hearing her comment, I am even more surprised at the students' firm, fine posture without (④).

At this point, naturally, it is curious to find out why they became interested in this unique Japanese culture that is neither a comic book, nor a movie, nor Japanese animation. Robert Jacobs who has studied calligraphy over the last three years says, "It really relaxes me. It's a sort of therapy." Many students say, "Although I am concentrating, I don't feel tired. It's a nice feeling to move a brush. I feel tranquil and I like the concentration." One student says,

“That's why I don't even care about the person next to me. It is as though I enjoy the tension, concentration and serenity in my own space.” I also got the impression that there were many people whose work was entirely with computers, and the experience of a completely different sensation helped them to achieve an emotional and mental balance.

The ideas of these participants fit in with that of the calligrapher, Masako Inkyo. “I never teach how calligraphy should be but I would be happy if everyone could enjoy it and feel it in their heart.” They seem to understand what Inkyo says.

Of course there are some in the class who are in search of something other than mental satisfaction, some students' work is related to design. A student says, “The type of letters are completely different from English, and the shapes and movement are different. This helps me incorporate something new into my designs.”

One common theme from these comments is that calligraphy is understood like Zen and meditation, and that students are engaged in calligraphy with an artistic sensibility, <u>(B) as a means of self-expression</u>. More and more Americans enjoy Japanese language class at the Japan Society Language Center. The classroom is always full. Now their *Shodo* (calligraphy) class has become popular as well. However, in observing the class, I find that students seem to enjoy tension and concentration in the serene environment in their own way, and <u>(C) this makes me feel that calligraphy is not simply a fashion boom but a form of therapy that provides them with tranquility</u>. If so, the day may come when calligraphy fans are established through calligraphy in the way that the Zen boom established Zen fans.

Inkyo often receives orders of business cards or orders for the production of fashion-related items that are designed with calligraphy. It is natural for calligraphy to become a stylish design that looks like a unique pattern not found in English letters, and it might not be far off that the American “Way” of calligraphy may further become established in the U.S.

It seems that the aim of the American manner of calligraphy is to escape the urban noise and chaos, and refresh yourself.

(Source : *JAPAN CLOSE-UP, THE SHAPES OF JAPAN TO COME*)

(1) Choose the most suitable word from (a) to (e) below to fill in blank spaces (①) to (④).

① (a) artificially (b) coincidentally (c) historically
(d) medically (e) unexpectedly

② (a) originated (b) raised (c) stagnated
(d) synchronized (e) verified

③ (a) and (b) but (c) like (d) more (e) much

④ (a) compulsion (b) construction (c) instruction
(d) sustainment (e) vivification

(2) Translate the underlined parts (A), (B) and (C) into Japanese.

(3) Choose three statements from (a) to (g) below that correspond to the passage.

(a) According to Masako, starting from nothing doesn't hinder her students from becoming good at calligraphy quickly.

(b) Japanese comic books, movies and animation are no less popular than calligraphy among Masako's students.

(c) In Masako's class, calligraphy serves as a kind of therapy, but few students learn to feel relaxed and tranquil.

(d) Many people who use computers in their office achieve an emotional and mental balance in calligraphy class, because they don't have to concentrate in class.

(e) According to Masako, her students have to know how calligraphy should be in order to acquire calligraphic skills.

(f) Not all the students in Masako's class search after mental satisfaction. Some students think calligraphy gives them new ideas for their work.

(g) The writer thinks that calligraphy, in the same way as Zen did, may attract fans and that a new style of calligraphy unique to the U.S. might be established.

(☆☆☆◎◎◎)

【５】Read the following passage and answer the questions (1) to (6).

"With (1) faults, you don't have the luxury of tinkering under the hood to see what's what," writes USGS seismologist Susan Hough in her book *Earthshaking Science*. But some scientists want to sneak a look. Their idea: Drill the San Andreas. Find the biggest oil drilling rig in California and ram huge steel pipes into the depths of the fault and send a bunch of gadgets down there to sample the rock and record its twitching. The project is under way near Parkfield, a village in a dusty central California valley.

Parkfield's claim to fame is earthquakes. At the Parkfield Cafe there's a sign that says, "[　①　]." The quakes aren't actually very strong here. They tend to be magnitude 6. There has been a string of them. After the M6 in 1966, scientists realized that these quakes had occurred fairly regularly, roughly every 22 years, and so in the early 1980s the notion arose that there ought to be another Parkfield quake around 1988.

Scientists wired the fault every which way, hoping to detect signs of building strain, moving water, or some other quake precursor. But year after year, the quake refused to show. It became something of an (2) (　　　　) for everyone who argued that earthquakes follow patterns. Finally, on September 28, 2004, an M6 struck near Parkfield, although its epicenter was miles farther south than expected. A camera had been set up to catch the fault rupturing from north to south, but it broke from south to north.

"[　②　]" said UCLA's David Jackson, he of the chaos camp.

Most disappointing to scientists was the lack of any precursors. They pored over the data and could find no evidence of anything unusual on the fault prior to the September 28 rupture. Maybe there was a very tiny change in crustal strain a day before the quake --- but even that wasn't certain. The unsettling notion arose that the jig was up, that these things are just flat-out unpredictable, random, weird.

But science marches on --- and digs deeper. At Parkfield there are still seismometers and GPS stations everywhere, and now there's even that 185-foot oil-drilling rig, a monument to what you might call testosterone science. By late summer 2005 it had punctured the fault and reached its terminal depth of two miles.

"[③]," says Mark Zoback of Stanford University, part of the drilling team. Of (3) the chaotic versus linear debate, he says, "we're the guys who are trying to find out which side is right. Not to be sanctimonious, but (A) I think a lot of those positions are held more on belief than on data." His rig is the next best thing to sending a person down into the fault directly, although even the rig can't get instruments down to the six-mile depths where many large earthquakes start.

In Japan, government scientists say they have settled the question. Earthquakes are not random. They follow a pattern. They have detectable precursors. The government knows where Japan's big one will most likely strike. This is a country where the trains run on time, and earthquakes are supposed to do the same. "We believe that earthquake prediction is possible," says Koshun Yamaoka, a scientist at the Earthquake Research Institute of the University of Tokyo.

In fact, Japan has already named its next great earthquake: the Tokai earthquake. The government has identified and delineated by law the precise affected area --- a region along the Pacific coast about a hundred miles southwest of Tokyo. After a series of small quakes in the Tokai area in the 1970s, scientists predicted that a major quake might be imminent there. The Japanese government passed a law in 1978 mandating that preparations begin for the Tokai earthquake.

Scientists have estimated a death toll of between 7,900 and 9,200 for a quake striking without warning in the wee hours. Estimated property damage: up to 310 billion dollars. At the Tokai earthquake preparedness center in

Shizuoka, a map pinpoints 6,449 landslide locations. Another map shows where 58,402 houses could burn in quake-related fires. Its all remarkably enumerated. The only thing left is for the earthquake to happen.

There is, indeed, a plate boundary, called the Nankai Trough, that runs off the coast of the island of Honshu, where the Philippine plate is subducting beneath Japan. The boundary has generated massive earthquakes every 100 to 150 years. Two sections of it, side by side, broke in 1944 and 1946. But the section along Tokai hasn't generated a major quake since 1854, right about the time Commodore Perry sailed his warships into Tokyo Bay. The theory is that it's time for this part of the subduction zone to relieve its accumulated stress.

At the Earthquake Research Institute, Keiji Doi, who is in charge of public outreach, lays out the entire scenario. The land near Shizuoka is sinking toward the underwater trough at about five millimeters a year, indicating that strain is building up. "The earthquake occurrence is imminent, we believe," Doi says.

Up to this point, the Tokai tale is more a forecast than a prediction. But a precise prediction of time and place would be far more valuable for emergency planners. <u>(B) Thus has arisen the idea of "pre-slip," a notion that skeptics say is part science and part wishful thinking</u>.

Naoyuki Kato, another scientist at the Earthquake Research Institute, says his laboratory experiments show that before a rock fracture gives way, it inevitably slips a little. He believes that what happens in a lab at small scale will also happen on a fault hundreds of miles long and running deep into the crust, just before the next big one.

The government has an action plan built around pre-slip. [　　　　　　　　(4)　　　　　　　　] Police, soldiers, and firefighters will race to the border of the vulnerable area. The prime minister will make a speech and say that an earthquake is imminent. Posters outlining this plan show a cartoon prime minister sitting at a desk with hands folded, looking very worried, but.very much in charge.

Yet none of the experts on the Tokai earthquake describe this scenario with much conviction. <u>(C) Press them, and they will admit their uncertainty</u>. Yamaoka and Kato, for example, are both bullish on pre-slip, yet they also say it may be too small to be detected.

(NOTE) USGS : The U.S.Geological Survey

(Source : *NATIONAL GEOGRAPHIC, APRIL 2006*)

(1) Choose the best phrase from (a) to (e) below that explains the contextual meaning of the underlined word (1).

(a) cracks in the earth's crust resulting from the displacement of one side with respect to the other

(b) sudden shakings of the earth's surface,which may be violent enough to cause great damage

(e) rigid layers of the earth's crust that is believed to drift slowly

(d) wrong actions attributable to bad judgement or ignorance or inattention

(e) the part of earth's surface consisting of humus and disintegrated rock

(2) Choose the most suitable sentence from (a) to (e) below to fill in each of the blank spaces [①]~[③].

(a) A century later,we have a highly successful theory, called plate techtonics

(b) If you feel a shake or a quake get under your table and eat your steak

(c) In a sense we're testing the predictability of earthquakes

(d) We missed Parkfield by over ten years --- and that was an earthquake in a barrel

(e) Some of the simplest questions about earthquakes remain hard to answer

(3) Choose the most suitable word from (a) to (e) below to fill in the blank <u>(2) (　　　　)</u>.

(a) alteration (b) approximation (c) embarrassment

(d) evidence (e) expectation

(4)　Describe what the underlined part (3) is referring to in Japanese.

(5)　Translate the underlined parts (A), (B) and (C) into Japanese.

(6)　Arrange the following three sentences so they make sense in part (4).

(a)　If one or two meters show anomalies, scientists will confer and schoolkids will go home.

(b)　Strain meters are embedded in the ground all over the Tokai area.

(c)　Three anomalies will put the country on high alert.

(☆☆☆☆◎◎◎)

【6】Write two or more paragraphs entitled "**When to start English education in Japan**" You are expected to write about 100 words in English.

(☆☆☆◎◎◎)

解答・解説

【中高共通】

【1】(1)　F　　(2)　T　　(3)　F　　(4)　T

〈解説〉設問や選択肢が与えられていないので，細部にわたって聞き取ることが重要になってくる。キーワードに注意しながら，イメージを描けるようにするのがポイント。

【2】(1)　d　　(2)　b　　(3)　d　　(4)　b

〈解説〉要点をメモして，短時間に整理する技術が必要。正確に聞き取り，選択肢の違いに気づくようにする。

【3】(1)　a　　(2)　c　　(3)　a　　(4)　a　　(5)　b　　(6)　b　　(7)　c　　(8)　b　　(9)　b　　(10)　c

〈解説〉(1) 知覚動詞は，補語として原形不定詞・現在分詞・過去分詞をとる。目的語がものである場合は過去分詞がくることが多い。このitはthat以下の形式目的語。 (2) 過去分詞の形容詞的用法。修飾語句が長いときは，名詞の後に置いて修飾する。 (3) It is worth ～ing「～するだけの価値がある」 (4)「義務」という意味の単語を入れる。dutiful「従順な」 formal「形式的な」 responsible「責任のある」 (5)「仕事で能力を高める目的で，言語学習に約3ヶ月分の給料を費やす」 as to「～に関しては」 in search of「～を求めて」 thanks to「～のおかげで」 (6)「教師があまりに多く期待したりせかしたりすると，学習者は，学ぶ動機づけと同様，決定に達する能力を失うかもしれない。」という意味になる。as far as「～に関する限り」 much as「～だけれども」 not so much as「～すらしない」 (7) be used to ～ing「～に慣れている」 (8) it ～ to の形式主語構文。 (9) 関係代名詞の非制限用法。the facultyは挿入句で，先行詞はmuseumである。 (10) convince は他動詞なので，人が主語の時は過去分詞にして使う。後ろに仮定法過去完了の文が続いていることから時制が決まる。

【4】(1) ① d ② a ③ b ④ c (2) (A) 彼らの技術を見れば，日本人は，おそらく日本の小学生でもこれほど短期間で上達することはないと思うだろう。 (B) 自己表現の手段として (C) これを見ると，書道は単なる一時的な流行ではなく，彼らに平静をもたらすある種の心理療法なのだと私は感じる。 (3) a, f, g

〈解説〉(1) ①「3年間書道をしてきて，血圧が低下した」とあるので，「医学的に証明されているわけではない」となる。 ②「もともと手紙を書くために使われた技法だったが」という意味になる。 ③ nothing but「～以外の何物でもない」 ④ 前に，「学生にはどのような姿勢で臨むかは教えない」と書かれているので，そういった「指導」なしに学生が素晴らしい姿勢で臨んでいることに驚いている。 (2) (A) 無生物主語構文なので，人を主語に立てて堅苦しい訳にならないように工夫する。this much 「ここまでは」　(B)　as 「～として」　means 「手段」　(C)　無生物主語構文と，not～but… 「～ではなく…」をきちんと訳すこと。provide A with B 「AにBを与える」 tranquility 「平静」　(3)　aは，「マサコによると，何もない状態から始めることで，学生は書道が早く上達する。」第4段落の最後の部分に書かれている。fは，第7段落に書かれている。すべての学生たちが，書道に精神的な満足感を探しているわけではない。gは第8段落に述べられている。

【5】(1)　a　(2)　①　b　②　d　③　c　(3)　c　(4)　地震が不規則か規則的かという論争。　(5)　(A)　どちらの立場をとるかは，多くの場合，データが根拠となっているというよりも，信じたいという気持ちに基づいているように思う。　(B)　したがって「プレスリップ(前兆滑り)」という考え方が生まれたのであるが，疑い深い人はそれを科学と願望が入り交じった概念だと言っている。　(C)　彼らを追求すれば，地震予知の不確実さを認めるだろう。　(6)　b → a → c

〈解説〉(1)　faultの意味の中で，「断層」の意味に当てはまる表現を選ぶ。cracks「地割れ」　crust「地殻」　displacement「ずれ」

(2)　①　At the Parkfield Cafe がヒントになっている。　②　パークフィールドで振動が規則的に起こっているとわかり，いろいろ調査していたものの，失敗に終わったことからわかる。　③　前の文に，地震計を至る所に設置したり，断層に穴をあけたりしているという文がある。　(3)　地震を予知できるような目に見える証拠が年々見られなくなっていたので，地震には傾向があると論じていた人々は「困惑する」ことになった。　(4)　chaotic versus linearは「無秩序状態に対する対順序正しい状態」という意味なので，この場合は，地震が不規則か規則的かということになる。　(5)　(A)　on data とon beliefを比較している。belief「信じること」　(B)　倒置が行われていることに注意する。skeptic 「懐疑論者」　(C)　命令文＋andで「～しなさい，そうすれば…」の意味。press 「圧迫する」　uncertainty 「不確実さ」

(6)　計測器が東海地域のいたるところの地面に埋められる。そのうちの1，2個が異常を示したら，学童は帰宅させる。3個が異常を示したら，国が警戒態勢を引く。このような順になる。

【6】Generally, it is said that language education is good to begin at an early stage. It may be good for children to learn English at the time which does not still have a prejudice. Although I agree with the opinion that it is better to begin English education from an elementary school, it is based on the contents of lessons. They must be what children can enjoy. I would like children to understand that English is a means of talking with the foreigner instead of the purpose to study. I also would like them to study Japanese. If they don't have skills in Japanese, it would be difficult to communicate in English.

〈解説〉言語の早期教育が奨励されているが，早いからいいというわけではない。早期教育の問題点と思われる点も盛り込むことが大切である。

2006年度　実施問題

【中高共通】

【１】(Listening Test)　Listen to the tape and answer the questions. You will hear the passage and each statement only once.

(☆☆☆☆◎◎◎◎◎)

【２】(Listening Test)　Listen to the tape and answer the questions. You will hear the passage, questions and answer options only once.

(☆☆☆☆◎◎◎◎◎)

【３】Read the passage and answer questions (1) to (5).

Call it the dance of the jet set[1], the diplomat's tango: A man from the Middle East, say, falls into conversation with an American, becomes animated, takes a step forward. The American makes a slight postural adjustment, shifts his feet, edges backward. A little more talk and the Arab advances; a little more talk and the American (　①　). "By the end of the cocktail party, "says Middle East expert Peter Bechtold, of the State Department's Foreign Service Institute, "(X) you have an American in each corner of the room, because that's as far as they can back up."

What do you do when an amiable chat leaves one person feeling vaguely bullied, the other unaccountably chilled? Things would be simpler if these jet-setters were speaking different languages－they'd just get themselves a translator. But the problem's a little (　②　), because they're using different languages of space.

Everyone who's ever felt cramped in a crowd knows that the skin is not the body's only boundary. We each wear a zone of privacy like a hoop skirt[2], inviting others in or keeping them out with body language－by how closely we approach, the angle at which we face them, the speed with which we break a gaze. It's a subtle code, but one we use and interpret easily,indeed automatically, having absorbed the vocabulary from infancy.

At least, we *assume* we're reading it right. But from culture to culture, from group to group within a single country, even between the sexes, the language of space has distinctive accents, confusing umlauts[3]. That leaves a lot of room for misinterpretation, and the stakes have gotten higher as business has become increasingly international and populations multicultural. So a new breed of consultants has appeared in the last few years, interpreting for globe-trotters of all nationalities the meaning and use of personal space. [A]

For instance, says international business consultant Sondra Snowdon, Saudi Arabians like to conduct business discussions from within spitting distance－literally. They bathe in each other's breath as part of building the relationship. "Americans back up," says Snowdon, "but they're harming their chances of winning the contracts." In seminars, Snowdon discusses the close quarters common in Middle Eastern conversations, and has her students practice talking with each other at very chummy distances.

Still, her clients had better (③) careful where they take their shrunken "space bubble," because cultures are idiosyncratic in their spatial needs. (Y) Japanese subways bring people about as close together as humanly possible, for instance, yet even a handshake can be offensively physical in a Japanese office. And, says researcher and writer Mildred Reed Hall, Americans can even make their business counterparts in Japan (④) with the kind of direct eye contact that's normal here. "Not only (⑤) most Japanese businessmen not look at you, they keep their eyes down," Hall says. "We look at people for hours, and they feel like they're under a searchlight. " [B]

The study of personal space got under way in the early 1950s, when anthropologist Edward Hall described a sort of cultural continuum of personal space. (Hall has frequently collaborated with his wife, Mildred.) According to Hall, on the "high-contact" side of the continuum－in Mediterranean and South American societies, for instance－social conversations include much eye contact, touching, and smiling, typically while standing at a distance of about a foot. On the other end of the scale, say in Northern European cultures, a lingering gaze may feel invasive, manipulative, or disrespectful; a social chat takes place at a remove of about two and a half (⑥).

In the middle-of-the-road United States, people usually stand about 18 inches apart for this sort of conversation- unless we want to win foreign friends and influence people, in which case, research shows, we'd better adjust our posture. In one study, when British graduate students were trained to adopt Arab patterns of behavior (facing their partners straight on, with lots of eye contact and smiling), Middle Eastern exchange students found them more likable and trustworthy than typical British students. [C]

Don't snuggle up too fast, though. Men in that study were more irritated by their partners when they were forced to talk at close range. Spatially speaking, it seems men and women are subtly foreign to each other. No matter whether a society operates at arm's length or cheek-to-jowl[4], the women look at each other more and stand a bit closer than do the men.

It just goes to show that you can't take things for granted even within the borders of a single country. (partly omitted)

Nor are things easier within the United States. Researchers have found, for instance, that middle-class, Caucasian school-teachers often jump to mistaken conclusions when dealing with a child from a different background: If a girl from an Asian family averts her eyes out of respect for her teacher's authority, the teacher may well go on alert, convinced that the child is trying to hide some misbehavior. Ethnically diverse workplaces can be similarly booby-trapped. [D]

Such glitches[5] are all the more likely because spatial behavior is automatic－it snaps into focus only when someone doesn't play by the rules. Say an American businessman is alone in a roomy elevator when another man enters. The newcomer fails to perform the national ritual of taking a corner and staring into space; instead, he stands a few inches away, smiling, which is simple politeness in some cultures. "You start to search for a reasonable explanation," says psychologist Eric Knowles, at the University of Arkansas. "In many cases you come up with one without even being aware of it. You say, 'Is this guy a picpocket? Is he psychotic?' If no explanation seems to fit, you just think, 'This guy's weird, I better get out of here.'"

(NOTES)

1 jet set: Wealthy people who travel around the world from one fashionable place to another.

2 hoop skirt: A long, full skirt supported by a series of connected hoops, or rings (popular in the late 1850s).

3 umlaut: Change in a vowel sound, often indicated by the symbol(¨).

4 cheek-to-jowl: Cheek-to-cheek (very close).

5 glitches: Minor problems or malfunctions.

(Source : Peter S.Gardner, *New Directions, Second Edition*)

(1) To fill in the blanks (①), (②) and (④), choose the most suitable word for each from (a) to (e) below, and write the letter of the answer you have chosen.

① (a) assembles (b) manipulates (c) retreats
(d) speculates (e) undergoes

② (a) easier (b) less important (c) more interesting
(d) more pleasant (e) tougher

④ (a) disappointed (b) dishonest (c) embarrassing
(d) satisfied (e) uncomfortable

(2) To fill in the blanks (③), (⑤) and (⑥), write a suitable word.

(3) According to the passage, choose two true statements from the statements below.

(a) We each use a different language of space, inviting others in or keeping them out with body language.

(b) We have absorbed subtle codes in the language of space since we were little children.

(c) Misinterpretation of space is more likely because of global business and growth of population.

(d) Saudi Arabians like to take a bath together to build their relationship.

(e) In Middle Eastern society, personal space is much closer than in South American society.

(f) Some students from Asian families avoid direct eye contact with teachers to hide their misbehavior,

(g) When an American businessman stands in an elevator with a stranger, he is likely to gaze at the stranger.

(4) Put the following passage into the most appropriate place. Choose from [A] to [D]

In contrast, the misuse of space can call whole personalities into suspicion: When researchers seated pairs of women for conversation, those forced to talk at an uncomfortably large distance were more likely to describe their partners as cold and rejecting.

(5) Translate the underlined (X) and (Y) into Japanese.

(☆☆☆◎◎◎◎◎)

【４】Read the passage and answer questions (1) to (10).

Review of studies involving different methods and various populations reflects <u>(1) consistency in the patterns of the family contexts</u> that bring about or stand in the way of the development of empathy. Children who were physically abused by their parents show notably less empathy than children of nonabusive parents. This consistent finding strongly suggests a causal link between physical abuse and the absence of empathy. This failure to develop empathy is hardly a surprise, yet it is a vivid reminder of the array of damaging effects of human cruelty— from individual to family to society as a whole.

How do children acquire prosocial norms and how early are these acquired? They arise in the context of secure attachment to a nurturing adult model who provides responsive caregiving by either (2) a cohesive family or a reliable extended social support network. The social norms that are established in early childhood are taking turns, sharing with others, cooperating, especially in learning and problem solving, and helping others, in response to visible distress. These norms, though established on a simple basis in the first few years of life, open the way to much more complex and beneficial human relationships that have significance throughout the life span. These norms are readily practiced because they tend to earn respect, provide gratification, and amplify the effectiveness of anything the individual could do alone. (3) To minimize interindividual and intergroup hostility in childhood, educational programs need to take account of the importance and usefulness of factors that influence the development of attachment and prosocial behavior.

The pioneers of research on prosocial behavior, Marian Radke-Yarrow and Carolyn Zahn-Waxler, in a valuable overview of research on this topic, defined prosocial behavior as helping rather than hurting or neglecting, respecting as opposed to denigrating, and being psychologically supportive and protective rather than dominating or (4) exploitative. Such tendencies appear surprisingly early in life. Newborns, who make distress cries in response to the cries of other infants, are showing signs of empathy even at this very early stage of life. Children in their second and third years show emotional distress and take (5) (________) actions when in the presence of suffering and distress of others. (partly omitted)

How important is the family in promoting or retarding these tendencies? Unfortunately, less research attention has been devoted to the development of prosocial than to the development of antisocial behaviors. In addition, research that does deal with prosocial behaviors has too rarely taken a developmental approach. Nevertheless, useful information is available.

Therg is evidence that family settings in which the requirements and expectations incorporate prosocial behavior do in fact shape such behavior. For example, children who are responsible for tasks helpful to family maintenance, especially caring for younger siblings, are generally more (6) altruistic than children who do not have such tasks. A pattern of parental responsiveness, high expectations, firmness, and warm emotion tends to foster a sense of social responsibility in children. Such children are inclined to behave prosocially in relation to the needs of others. Both direct family observations and experimental studies have examined the effects of a model on later prosocial or antisocial behavior. In the experimental studies, an adult model, behaving as a parent often does, demonstrates a prosocial act such as sharing toys, coins, or candy that have been won in a game. The sharing is with someone else who is said to be in need though not present in the experimental situation. The adult plays the game and models the sharing before leaving the child to play. Similar designs are used in studies of (7) (______) where the procedures involve a game with rules in which an adult model either cheats or adheres to the rules. Although the contact is brief－and therefore a much less powerful influence than a parent's enduring relationship would be－the model's action is nevertheless salient because it occurs in a controlled experimental setting. The results are clear. Children exposed to such models, when compared with similar children in control groups, tend to show the behavior manifested by the models－whether it is honesty, generosity, helping, or rescuing behavior. (8) There is also evidence from naturalistic studies of toddlers' prosocial actions that delayed imitation by children of their mothers' ways of comforting and helping occurs spontaneously in children's efforts to help others. Indeed, the imitations often involve exact reproductions of the mother's behavior. Given the child's pervasive exposure to the parents, the potential for observational learning in this sphere as in others is very great.

Many laboratory and clinical studies of social learning indicate that certain factors enhance the impact of a model for the child: the adult's power, the adult's perceived competence, and the adult's long-term nurturance of the child. All of this puts securely attached children in a strong position to adopt salient patterns of behavior through observational learning from their parents and other family members. The combination of early attachment plus abundant modeling over the years of growth and development leads to prosocial behavior that becomes firmly established. Prosocial behavior is particularly significant because of its powerful adaptive qualities－it is likely to open up new opportunities for the growing child, strengthen additional human relationships on the basis of mutual respect, and thereby contribute to the building of a sense of personal worth.

Young children's caring and prosocial responses have also been studied in relation to their mothers' mental health. Their responses were observed in both experimental and naturalistic settings. Results showed that attachment alone, children's problems alone, and maternal diagnoses alone were not strong predictors of deficits in caring behavior. The highest frequencies of caring were from children with the more severely depressed mothers. Girls were significantly more caring than boys. These surprising findings underscore the importance of studying interacting influences on the underlying processes in the development of children's caring responses.

(Source : David A. Hamburg and Beatrix A. Hamburg, *Learning to Live Together*)

(1) In the first paragraph, the writer refers to an example of (1) consistency in the patterns of the family contexts. Explain the example in Japanese.

(2) Fill in the blank below with a word used in the second paragraph, in order to explain the underlined part (2).

In a cohesive family, all the members have strong and close (　　) among themselves as a whole unit of people.

(3) Translate the underlined sentence (3) into Japanese.

(4) The word (4) 'exploitative' means (a), (b), (c), or (d). Choose one.

(a) being extremely obedient under overwhelming power

(b) trying to exclude privileged people from a certain area

(c) treating people unfairly to gain advantages

(d) saying things to make someone seem less important

(5) From (a) to (d) below, choose the most appropriate word to fill space (5).

(a) aggressive (b) negative (c) passive (d) positive

(6) Extract a phrase from the fifth paragraph that most approximates the underlined word (6) 'altruistic'.

(7) From (a) to (d) below, choose the most appropriate word to fill space (7).

(a) generosity (b) helping (c) honesty (d) sharing

(8) Translate the underlined sentence (8) into Japanese.

(9) According to the sixth and seventh paragraphs, which statement below is true? Choose one from (a) to (d) below.

(a) Despite studies about the relation between mothers' mental health and children's caring behavior, we cannot point out just one single factor that will lead to the lack of caring.

(b) According to laboratory and clinical research, there are some notable factors that function negatively in children's acquisition of patterns of prosocial behavior.

(c) Prosocial behavior bears powerful adaptive qualities only when acquired through observational learning supported by adults' modeling.

(d) If their mothers are mentally healthy, children show caring and prosocial responses more frequently than those whose mothers are suffering from mental diseases.

(10) From (a) to (d), choose the best definition for "prosocial behavior" mentioned in the passage.

(a) behavior of youngsters that is usually shown just before going into societies as adults

(b) behavior that should be desirably enhanced to support and contribute to societies

(c) behavior of children that is socially admitted as effective and influential
(d) behavior that denigrates societies to interindividual and intergroup hostility

(☆☆☆☆☆◎◎◎◎◎)

【5】Read the passage and answer the question.

To Cultivate "Rich Humanity"

The ideal for the future of school education is described in the first report of the Central Council for Education issued in 1996 titled "The Model for Japanese Education from the perspective of the 21st Century." The report states that "children in the future need the basic abilities and skills by which <u>they can discover problems on their own, learn, think of their own free will, take an initiative in decision making, act upon their own free will, and solve problems, regardless of how society might change.</u>" Also important is "Rich Humanity," which contains a sense of self-discipline, an ability to collaborate with others, sympathy for others and the emotional sensitivity to be inspired or to be moved. It goes without saying that health and physical strength are essential. We have named these qualities "Zest for Living."

(Source : *White Paper, Ministry of Education, Culture, Sports, Science and Technology, 2002*)

(Question)

What activities should we develop and give in class in order to realize what is stated in the underlined part? Answer in English. You are expected to write about 100 words.

(☆☆☆☆◎◎◎◎◎)

解答・解説

【中高共通】

【1】略

【2】略

〈解説〉リスニングテストでは2種類の出題が予想される。まとまった英文(passage)とそれに関する発言(statement)を聞き解答するものと，まとまった英文(passage)とそれに関する質疑応答(questions and answer)を聞き解答するものである。どちらも放送は1回しか(only once)読まれないので，集中して聞くことが求められる。日ごろからテレビやラジオなどの英語番組を利用して，リスニングに慣れたり，英検(準2級・2級レベル)のリスニングテストCDなどを利用して，実力試しをしておきたい。

【3】(1)　①　c　②　e　④　e　(2)　③　be　⑤　do　⑥　feet　(3)　a, b　(4)　C　(5)　X　後ずさりできるのはそこまでだから，アメリカ人は部屋の隅にいることになる。　Y　例えば，日本の地下鉄車内では，人ができるだけぴったりくっついて乗っているが，会社の中では，握手が不快な体への接触になり得ることさえある。

〈解説〉(1)　①　直前の文で，アラブ人は前に出てくると書かれている。アメリカ人はその反対だから，cを選ぶ。　②　直前の文で，simplerが使われているので。「でも問題はちょっと手ごわいです」の意味になる。　④　直後の文で，日本人は相手を見ないだけではなく，目をそらしていると書かれている。このことから，アメリカ人は視線を合わせることで日本の交渉相手を不愉快にさせると考える。

(2)　③　had betterとcarefulをつなぐのはbe動詞の原形。　⑤　Not onlyが文頭に出ているので，その直後は倒置の文が来る。lookと一般動詞を使い，全体が現在時制なので，doを入れる。　⑥　この文脈で，地中海周辺や南アメリカでは約1フィートの距離を置くと述べられているので，北ヨーロッパでは，2.5フィートと考える。　(3)　(a)　第二～三段落と一致。　(b)　第三段落と一致。　(c)　第四段落と不一致(人口の増加ではなくて多文化共存が原因)。　(d)　第五段落と不一致(風呂に入るのではなく，息がかかるくらい近くで話すことが述べられている)。　(e)　第五段落と不一致(南アメリカ社会の記述はない)。

(f)　第十段落と不一致(視線を合わせないのは，先生への尊敬の気持ちから)。　(g)　第十一段落と不一致(アメリカ人は知らない人をじろじろ見たりはしない)。　(4)　それとは対照的に(In contrast)とつながるのは，直前の文脈で，アラブ式の行動様式を取り入れた英国の学生が，中東の学生から受け入れられた例が述べられているC。

(5)　X　back up「後退する」，That's as far as ～「それが～できる範囲だ」　Y　bring～together「～をくっつける」，humanly possible「人間の能力で，人ができる限り」

【4】(1)　両親から肉体的虐待を受けた子供は，虐待を受けていない子供よりも他人の気持ちを理解できないということ。　(2)　relationships

(3)　幼年期の個人・グループ間の対立を最小限に抑えるために，教育プログラムは愛情と向社会的行動の発達に影響を与えるような要素の重要性と有益性を考慮に入れる必要がある。　(4)　c　　(5)　d

(6)　in relation to the needs of others　　(7)　c　　(8)　子供が他の子供を助けようとするとき，自分の母親の慰め方や助け方のまねが，後になって自然に現れてくるという証拠も，幼児の向社会的行動の自然主義的研究から明らかである。　(9)　a　　(10)　b

〈解説〉(1)　直後の文(Children who were physically～nonabusive parents.)の内容をまとめる。　(2)　結束のある家族では，全員が一つのユニットとして，強くて密着した関係(relationships)を持っている。

(3)　take account of～「～を考慮に入れる」，prosocial「向社会的な，社会支持の」　(4)　exploitative「搾取する，人を食い物にする」

(5)　他の赤ん坊の泣き声に答えて泣く赤ん坊は，共感(empathy)を示している，と直前の文にあることから，同じような状況で積極的な(positive)行動をとると考える。　(6)　in relation to the needs of others「他の人が必要とするものに応じて」をaltruistic「愛他的な」に近い表現と考える。　(7)　直後の文で，手本となる大人が，あるゲームでルールを守るか守らないかということが述べられているので，cを選ぶ。
(8)　that以下はevidenceに対して同格。that以下の主語はdelayed imitation, 動詞はoccurs。spontaneously「自発的に，自然に」
(9)　a　第七段落の第一，二文と一致。　b　第六段落と不一致(子供が向社会的な行動を身につけるときに否定的な機能をする要素がある，という記述はない)。　c　第六段落と不一致(向社会的行動が強力な適応性を持つのは，大人の手本を観察してそれらが得られたときだけと言う記述はない)。　d　第七段落と不一致(非常にうつの状態にある母親に，優しさの度合いが最も高い子供がいる例が，第七段落に述べられている)。　(10)　全体の文脈で，prosocialはantisocial「反社会的な」に対する語として使われているので，bを選ぶ。

【5】(解答例)　The most important thing to do in class is that students should be given more time to think on their own and act according to what they think themselves. Classes usually tend to be like a one-way street. Teachers speak and students just listen. Teachers are required to call on their students in class more frequently and let them express themselves. In English class, for example, an activity like ‘three-minute speech'may be very effective. In front of the class, students speak in English about themselves. This kind of activity will be really helpful to students in the future. (99語)
〈解説〉先生が話し生徒が聞くという，「一方通行」にならないように，生徒が自分で考え行動する時間を，授業中にもっと与えられるべきだと主張する。例えば，英語の授業では，「3分スピーチ」などの活動をやらせてみる。(このような自由英作文問題は，必ず具体的な例を入れて話を展開すること)

2005年度　実施問題

【中高共通】

【1】Read the passage and answer questions (1) to (4).

We define a collectivistic culture as one in which the collectivity's goals are valued over those of the individual. In contrast, an individualistic culture is one in which the individual's goals are valued over those of the collectivity. Individualism-collectivism is perhaps the most important dimension of cultural differences in behavior across the cultures of the world (Oetzel & Bolton-Oetzel, 1997). HarryTriandis, a psychologist at the University of Illinois, has written extensively about the individualistic-collectivistic classification of cultures (Hui & Triandis, 1986; Triandis, 1986, 1990, 1994, & 1995).

Japanese culture is an example of a collectivistic culture (Hofstede, 1990). Harmony (wa) is very important to the Japanese. The [A] nature of Japanese culture is evident when observing a typical business office in Tokyo. More than a dozen employees are packed into an office that in the United States might house two or three individuals. The Japanese workers sit at small desks, facing each other, clustered in the middle of the room. Their boss sits among them. Individual privacy is completely (①); instead, much informal conversation occurs among the office workers as they help each other with various work-related tasks.

When the 5:00 P.M. bell rings, signaling the end of the workday, no one gets up to leave. Neckties are loosened and jackets are shed, and the office situation becomes more relaxed. But the employees keep right on working. Finally, hours later, at 10:30 or 11:00 P.M., the office workers go home and the office is dark. The employees will be back at their small desks the next morning at 8:00 A.M. Perhaps one night per week, these office workers go out together for dinner. Most individuals drink sake or beer until they are drunk. After several drinks, the workers may play a joke on their boss or argue violently with him/her (the following day, all that transpired will be forgotten). The drinking session has a strong bonding effect, and the office workers regard themselves as something like a family. All decisions are made with the group in mind, rather than what is best for one of the workers. Thus is collectivistic (②) developed in Japan.

Long-term relationships based on trust are very important in a collectivistic culture. For example, many Japanese companies provide their workers with lifetime employment. Maintaining positive long-term relationships is stressed. An individual should not (③) another person in public, as doing so would disrupt personal network relationships. Individuals are more likely to say what the other person wants to hear, rather than conveying information in a more direct manner that might solve a problem. Employees are particularly reluctant to tell their boss that the boss's pet idea is not working.

Face, a public self-image that an individual wants to present in a particular social context, is a major consideration in dealing with others. Every effort is made so that someone does not lose face in front of others. The Japanese pay much attention to group memberships and to other individuals in their personal networks. Fitting in with others, creating and maintaining obligations, conformity, and being relationship-oriented are highly prized. Individual achievement, personal recognition, and thinking mainly for oneself are strongly (④). A popular Japanese saying is: "The nail that protrudes gets hammered down."

—— part omitted ——

Individualistic-collectivistic cultures strongly influence communication behavior. Reciprocally, human communication is a means through which individualism and collectivism are taught to individuals and maintained as a culture's orientation.

Nigerian students at a U.S. university have a background rich in [B] values versus the [C] orientation of their classmates. Ibo villages in eastern Nigeria collect funds to send their most academically talented young people to overseas universities. When such an individual comes back to Nigeria, he/she is expected to return to his/her home village and to begin making sizeable contributions toward the university education of other talented youth. One Ibo village might boast that it has supported an MIT graduate and a Berkeley Ph.D. in astrophysics, for example. One can imagine that the Ibo students feel they are achieving their education not just for themselves, but for their people.

Another example of [D] culture involved a young woman from the United States, Kristen, who had been working in a Japanese company for two weeks when her boss's mother died. On the morning of the funeral, Kristen arrived in the office wearing a colorful dress, but she sensed from her coworkers that something was wrong. The others were all dressed in dark clothes. A close friend suggested that Kristen might go home for lunch, which was an unusual suggestion. Kristen took the hint, returning from lunch in a black dress. When she entered the office, all thirty colleagues gave her a standing ovation! The unpredictable stranger in their work unit had behaved in a culturally appropriate way. They felt (⑤) for their collectivity, which would otherwise have been embarrassed by her appearance at the funeral.

These examples illustrate (1) the differences between communication behavior in an individualistic and a collectivistic culture and (2) the special problems of communication between individuals who do not share similar backgrounds. The nature of the self is different in an individualistic versus a collectivistic culture. Culture shapes one's self, and thus one's communication, perceptions, and other behavior. In an individualistic culture, the individual perceives himself/herself as independent. Being overly interdependent on others is considered weak or unassertive. In a collectivistic culture, the individual mainly thinks of himself/herself as connected to others. To be independent in one's thinking or actions would be considered selfish, rude, and in poor taste. An individual who is not a good team player is punished for breaking the norm on collectivism. <u>Interaction between individuals with these different perceptions of self can easily result in misinterpreting the other's behavior.</u>

(Source: Everett M. Rogers/Thomas M. Steinfatt, Intercultural Communication)

(1) To fill in the blanks (①) to (⑤), choose the most suitable word for each from (a) to (d) below, and write the letter of the answer you have chosen.

① (a) deserved (b) lacking (c) protected (d) outstanding

② (a) solidarity (b) opposition (c) independence (d) isolation

③ (a) contradict (b) watch (c) compromise (d) discuss

④ (a) believed (b) enhanced (c) discouraged (d) promoted

⑤ (a) worried (b) uneasy (c) relaxed (d) relieved

(2) According to the passage, write either 'true (T)' or 'false (F)' in the space provided, for each statement below.

(a) In Japanese companies, employees are not willing to argue against the boss's idea.

(b) The Japanese pay much attention to group memberships and individual achievement.

(c) Nigerian students from Ibo villages are expected to educate young people in the United States.

(d) Kristen's colleagues were embarrassed by her colorful appearance at the funeral.

(3) To fill in the blanks [A] to [D] with 'collectivistic' or 'individualistic', choose the most suitable set from (a) to (d).

(a) A : individualistic B : individualistic C : collectivistic D : individualistic

(b) A : collectivistic B : individualistic C : individualistic D : collectivistic

(c)　A : collectivistic　　B : collectivistic　　C : individualistic
　　D : collectivistic

(d)　A : collectivistic　　B : collectivistic　　C : individualistic
　　D : individualistic

(4)　Put the underlined sentence into Japanese.

(☆☆☆☆◎◎◎◎)

【2】Read the passage and answer questions (1) to (8).

Future historians will doubtless view this unfolding century as (1) pivotal: Perhaps no previous generation has shaped the choices available to its children and grandchildren as much as we will during the decades ahead. (A) Whether our offspring inherit a world of prosperity and possibility or their options are limited by our current environmental misadventures depends directly on the decisions we make as citizens, business people, and politicians.

The good news is that humanity is better equipped than ever to create a sustainable civilization, an Eden reborn. The idea of sustainable development－meeting the needs of the current generation without jeopardizing the prospects of the next－has moved out of the classroom and into the real world, to pilot projects and niche markets that are generating encouraging results.

While (①) is by no means ensured, a solid foundation is being laid on several fronts. One of the easiest hurdles we face may be meeting the energy needs of the next century, because today's oil and coal fields could be replaced by solar generators and wind turbines located everywhere from mountain passes to rooftops. At the same time, hydrogen can be derived from water using solar－and wind－generated electricity. Sent along pipelines, (2) the pollution－free fuel that is now used to power many space vehicles will eventually power cars, homes, and factories.

But even in the information age, we still live in a materials-driven world, and restoring (②) will mean finding new ways of providing the tons of metals, wood, cement, and plastics we depend on. Instead of clearing forests for wood and paper and ripping open the earth to extract metal, why not follow nature's model of recirculating materials? If we generated only useful byproducts, and not waste, our environmental footprint could be substantially reduced. Many forward-thinking cities already set ambitious goals for waste reduction: Nearly half the municipalities in New Zealand, for example, are aiming to become "zero waste" cities by 2020, with virtually no materials going to landfills.

Reducing our consumption of materials requires (③), starting with smart product design. By 2015, for instance, the European Union will require that 95 percent of the materials in all new cars be remanufactured and 85 percent be recycled. That promises a new generation of cars that, instead of being junked, can be easily dismantled at the end of their useful lives and transformed into new vehicles and other products. The Xerox Corp. already designs its copiers to be remanufactured: Instead of heading to the landfill, the used machines are returned to the company, where up to 90 percent of their parts are (3) into something new.

Some pioneering companies have even changed (④); they locate their factories near each other, for instance, so the effluent from one factory can be used as the raw material for another. The city of Kalundborg, Denmark, has established a network of 12 symbiotic industries. Natural gas that was previously flared off by Denmark's largest refinery is being used as feedstock in a plasterboard factory; fly ash from a power plant goes to a cement manufacturer; and nitrogen-rich sludge from a pharmaceutical plant is used as fertilizer on nearby farms.

Even (⑤)－to sell as many goods as possible－can be reassessed in the name of reducing materials consumption. Why not sell people the services they need－transportation, for example－rather than more materials-intensive goods? Car-sharing companies in Europe, and increasingly in the United States, allow drivers to eliminate a second car in favor of essentially renting a communal vehicle. People get the transportation they need, they save money, and they avoid (4) <u>clogging roads and parking areas with cars that would otherwise largely sit idle.</u> These imaginative solutions could help us achieve the 90 percent reduction in materials that some scientists say is necessary in wealthy countries to bring our appetites in line with a healthy environment. And these remedies can do so without measurably lowering our quality of life.

Among the most difficult challenges in the next century will be feeding more than 8 billion people in a world short of water. (B) <u>Biotechnology could play a big role in making crops less demanding of water and less vulnerable to pests,</u> but other technologies can be used now, from superefficient drip irrigation systems to ancient farming methods that increase a soil's capacity to retain water. Still, we also may need to shift our diets. More than a third of the world's grain goes to feed animals that in turn produce meat, eggs, and dairy products. This gives humans a protein-and-fat-rich diet, but (5) <u>the conversion process</u> is inefficient. If the world's affluent were to consume less meat－living a little lower on the food chain－it would be easier to provide a healthy diet for all.

The biggest challenge of all, however, we may confront within ourselves. The dramatic economic advances of the past century were driven in part by a culture of materialism, and accelerated growth seems to be a universally accepted goal. Today, new homes in America are 38 percent larger than they were in 1975－despite a decline in household size. And in 2001, the number of cars in the United States surpassed the number of licensed drivers. The planet cannot long support a species whose appetites cannot be satisfied. At the same time, as a nation, we are fatter, more indebted, and more stressed than ever. These trends suggest that our quality of life is declining even as our wealth increases. Consumption, it seems, is undoing us.

(Source: THE FUTURE of Earth : U.S.News & World Report, Special Edition)

(1) Choose the best phrase from the below (a) to (d) that explains the contextual meaning of the underlined word (1).

(a) unstable because a variety of environmental problems came up all at once

(b) fruitful because great environmental inventions have been brought about

(c) important in that decisions made in this century have great effects on the future

(d) desperate in that people have no ways to overcome environmental issues

(2) Write down a word from the passage to which the underlined words (2) refer.

(3) From (a) to (d) below, choose the word for the blank space (3).

(a) restored (b) reassembled (c) retreated (d) reduced

(4) Choose a word from (a) to (d) below to describe the underlined situation (4).

(a) congestion (b) contamination (c) digestion (d) confusion

(5) In Japanese, describe what "the conversion process", indicated by (5), is.

(6) Choose the best phrase from the below (a) to (e) for each blank (①) to (⑤).

(a) a fundamental purpose of business

(b) a mix of common sense and ingenuity

(c) a socially just and environmentally benign future

(d) our balance with nature

(e) the manufacturing process itself

(7) Put the underlined (A) and (B) into Japanese.

(8) The passage above, with the final paragraph omitted, is to conclude with the sentence below. To complete the sentence, pick up one word from the ninth paragraph for the blank.

"Success, once measured in terms of higher salaries and more goods, would be judged by a new standard: the highest quality of life delivered with the lowest level of ( )."

(☆☆☆☆☆◎◎◎◎◎)

【3】Read the passage and answer the questions.

Improvement of English classes

In order to be able to "make use of English", it is necessary not only to have a knowledge of grammar and vocabulary but also the ability to use English for the purpose of actual communication. Thus, in English classes, instruction mainly based on grammar and translation or teacher-centered classes are not recommended. Through the repetition of activities making use of English as a (①) of communication, the learning of vocabulary and grammar should be enhanced, and communication abilities in "listening," "speaking," "reading," and "writing" should be (②). Such techniques for instruction are necessary.

<u>To carry out such instruction effectively, it is important for teachers to establish many situations where students can communicate with each other in English and routinely to conduct classes principally in English.</u> Through such opportunities, learners can experience the fulfillment of expressing themselves and understanding others, and feel the joy of learning English. Furthermore, it is also important to (③) creative teaching methods so that learners can become interested in the importance and necessity of acquiring English, which can broaden the student's world and possibilities.

Additionally, making use of assistant language teachers (ALTs) and the system of special part-time instructors, small-group teaching and the streaming of students according to (④) will be positively adopted. Measures such as the promotion of (⑤) English education and the dissemination of excellent classroom practices are required.

(Source: Action Plan to Cultivate "Japanese with English Abilities"
Ministry of Education, Sports, Science and Technology)

(1) To fill in the blanks (①) to (⑤), choose the most suitable word for each from below and write the letter of the answer you have chosen. (You can use each word only once.)

(a) devise (b) discharge (c) efficiency (d) fostered

(e) innovative　(f) intangible　(g) means　(h) proficiency
(i) sequence　(j) shrunk

(2) In order to establish the situations mentioned in the underlined part, what qualities or what abilities do you think are required of JTLs (Japanese Teachers of Language), and what would you do to acquire them? Answer in English. You are expected to write about 100 words.

(☆☆☆☆◎◎◎◎◎)

解答・解説

【中高共通】

【1】(1) ① (b)　② (a)　③ (a)　④ (c)　⑤ (d)
(2) (a) T　(b) F　(c) F　(d) F　(3) (c)　(4) 自己に対する認識を違っている人間同士の交流は，相手の行動への誤解を生みやすい。

〈解説〉(1) ① 前の3つの英文の内容：「日本の職場は1つのオフィスの中で何人もの従業員が働いている」から判断し，「個人のプライバシーは完全に欠けている」という意味の英文を完全させる。 ② 第3段落の内容から「このようにして，日本では集団の結束が発達した」という意味の英文を完成させる。 ③ 第4段落の内容から「個人は人前で別に人間に逆らうべきではない」という意味の英文になるような答を選ぶ。 ④ 第5段落の内容から「個人の業績，や自分のことを中心に考えることは強く敬遠される」という意味の英文になるような答を選ぶ。 ⑤ 第7段落の内容から「お葬式にふさわしい服装をしてきたので，自分たちの集団性が維持されたためにほっとした」という意味の英文を完成させる。 (2) (a)「日本の企業では，従業員は上司の考えに反論したがらない」第4段落の内容から，正しい。(b)「日本人は集団の一員であることと個人の業績に多くの注意を払う」

第5段落に，個人の業績は重視しないとあるので間違い。 (c)「ナイジェリアの学生はアメリカの若者を教育することを期待されている」第6段落の内容から，ナイジェリアの学生が教育するのは自国の若者である。 (d)「クリスティンの同僚は葬式での彼女の派手な容姿にはずかしい思いをした。」第7段落より，クリスティンは葬式には派手な服装で行かなかったので間違い。 (3) A「日本文化の性格」から判断 B，C「ナイジェリア人の学生」と「彼女のアメリカ人の級友」の国民性から判断 D 集団性を重視する日本文化の例をあげている (4) 'with these different perceptions of self'がindividualsを修飾している。 'result in'＝「結果として～となる」

【2】(1) (c) (2) solar-and wind-generated electricity (3) (a) (4) (a) (5) 世界の穀物の三分の一が動物のえさとなり，その動物が人間の食べる肉，卵，酪農製品を産み出すという過程。

(6) ① (c) ② (d) ③ (b) ④ (e) ⑤ (a) (7) (A) 我々の子孫が繁栄と可能性のある世界を受け継ぐか，現在の環境破壊によって彼らの選択が狭められるかは市民，会社員そして政治家としてのそれぞれの立場での私たちの決断に直接かかっている。 (B) バイオテクノロジーは，いままでより水を必要としなくて，害虫に強い穀物の生産に重要な役割を果たすであろう。 (8) consumption

〈解説〉(1) 下線部(1)の後の文の内容：「自分たちの子孫にとって重要な選択をできる世代は今までになかった」から判断する。'pivotal'＝中枢の，重要な (2) 下線部(2)の意味：「無公害燃料」とは何かを考える。 (3) 第5段落の内容：「消費を削減するためには車やコピー機などの製品の部品や材料の再利用をする」から判断する。'restore'＝修復する，復元する (4) 下線部(4)は「道路や駐車場を車で動きがとれなくする」という意味。 (5) 'conversion process'「(食物を)転換・転化していく過程」とは第8段落の第4文を指している。

(6) ① 第3段落の第1文が「社会的に公平で環境に優しい未来を確実に保証する一方で…」となるような答を選ぶ。 ② 第4段落の第2文の意味から「自然との調和を修復するということは原料を供給する新しい手段をさがすことである」という意味の英文になるような答を選ぶ。　③　第5段落の内容から「原料の消費を削減することは常識と創意工夫の両方を必要とする」という意味の英文を完成させる。
④　第6段落の内容から「さきがけとなる企業は生産工程そのものを改革している」という文になるように答を選ぶ。　⑤　-to sell as many goods as possible-：「できるだけ多くの品物を売ること」が(　　)の内容を説明している。　(7)　(A)　主語が'Whether…misadventures'までであることを掴む。'whether A or B'「AするかBか」'misadventure'＝不運，災難'depend on'＝(事が)～次第である，～による　(B)　'play a big role in…'＝「…に重要な役割を果たす」'less…pests'までが前の'crops'を修飾している'vulnerable to…'「…に対して弱い，攻撃を受けやすい」
(8)　最終段落の内容から「成功は，かつて高い給料や生産量で計られてきたが，最も低い消費によってもたらされる最も高い質を持った生活という新しい基準によって判断されるだろう」という意味の英文を完成させる。

【3】(1)　①　(g)　②　(d)　③　(a)　④　(h)　⑤　(e)

(2)　JTLs are required to be equipped with sufficient abilities in communicating in English to be able to teach classes mainly in English as well as to have qualities such as creativity, cooperativeness and enthusiasm to devise and implement communication activities with ALTs.

In order to acquire those qualities and abilities, JTLs should study and practice English by themselves on a daily basis by making use of mass-media or chances to communicate with native speakers of English. Also, they should positively attend seminars and training for English teachers to learn not only new theories and methods but also to experience language-use activities themselves.

〈解説〉(1)　①「コミュニケーションの手段としての英語を活用できる活動」という意味の英文にする。　②「「聞くこと」「話すこと」「読むこと」「書くこと」におけるコミュニケーション能力を育成する」という意味の英文になるような答を選ぶ。　③「創造的な指導法を工夫することが重要である」という意味の英文を完成させる。　④「能力に応じたクラス編成」という文になるように答を選ぶ。　⑤「革新的な英語教育の促進」という文になるように答を選ぶ。

(2)「そのような指導を効果的に行なうためには，教師は生徒がお互いに英語でコミュニケーションをとれるような状況をたくさん設定し，日常的に授業はおもに英語で行なうことが大切である」という下線部の意味を取る。

英語教師に必要とされる資質と能力としては，英語のコミュニケーション能力，活動を工夫する独創性，外国人講師との協調性，生徒を粘り強く指導していく情熱と寛容の精神などがあげられる。

そのためには，英語のコミュニケーション能力を高めるために日常的に英語の学習に取り組む，英語能力を測る試験を受けてみる，教員対象の研修に進んで参加し自らコミュニケーション活動を体験したり，よりよい教授法を学んだりする，ALTや地域に住む外国人との交流を積極的に頻繁に行なうなどが考えられる。

2004年度　実施問題

【中高共通】

【１】(Listening Test)　Listen to the tape and answer the questions.

(☆☆☆◎◎◎◎◎)

【２】(Listening Test)　Listen to the tape and answer the questions.

(☆☆☆☆◎◎◎◎◎)

【３】Read the passage and answer the questions (1) to (4).

Foreigners go through many levels in their experience of Japanese society. The new arrival explores the physical level － sitting on the floor, taking off shoes, and so on. From there he goes into deeper levels of human relationships, social rules, and finally philosophy and psychic motivation. This is difficult, but foreigners like me, who have invested years of our lives in this culture, must constantly expand our understanding. More important, we must decide whether we can personally accept certain aspects of this culture.

I felt this tension in myself recently when I had to help at the funeral of a distant in－law. In this kind of situation, my husband's two elder sisters seem to wish to educate me in social rules. The real meaning of the event (paying respects to the deceased) was swallowed up in many complicated social observances, and expression of my real feelings was not permitted. I had to (　①　) to the group activity or else.

A

I also often find that my accomplishments don't matter to my in－laws, compared to how I keep my house or how I behave in front of guests (easy ways of evaluating whether I fit into the "group" of Japanese housewives). It's one of my greatest disappointments living here that any contribution I wish to make on my own terms counts for nothing if I don't first get a perfect score on their terms. That's why, when people used to ask me how I liked living in Japan, I usually answered, "It feels like every day is an examination."

<u>It is a pervasive stereotype of Japan that the people identify themselves in terms of membership in a group</u>. People strive to carry out social responsibilities with an almost religious fervor to avoid the fate of nakama－hazure (ostracism). Individuals seem to exist for the group rather than the group existing for them.

B

Although for some people in Japan, this may seem outmoded and ridiculous, it is still true in society as a whole. Yet, paradoxically, the power of the group is actually the greatest threat to society. People think they are protecting the group, when really all they're doing is preventing healthy growth and development. A group can't create － it can only maintain. (　②　) is the province of the exploring individual mind.

As the new millennium gets under way, Japan has to decide what to do about this issue of group versus individual. For instance, much lip service is paid in education to "individuality". But this is mostly limited to primary school, where there are "opinion presentations" and even a "children's Diet session". These things disappear at the junior high and high school levels, where "individualism" becomes a faraway dream compared to the harsh realities of finding a job or getting married. This is a pity, because today's children, who are actually inventing themselves using their access to a great variety of lifestyles and ways of thinking through the media, really need to be seen as individuals. Because of their youth, this urge takes highly visible and dramatic forms, and the adults see these actions as endangering their chances.

Instead of encouraging individuality, the adults are afraid of it, and try to (③) it by force, resulting in even more rebellion and, increasingly, violence.

C

What children need are models of free, proud, creative individuality. But how can adults be models for their children if they don't know what individuality is themselves? What children need is acceptance of their own individuality. But how can adults accept in their children what they can't accept in themselves? It seems to me that Japanese society is constructed upside down. Young children are free to be individuals, but this gradually decreases until, as adults, people are unable to express themselves, fearing to lose their livelihood or social position. Surely the opposite makes more sense? Surely individuality, like responsibility (which, by the way, in English means the ability to respond to our world, not the threat of blame), should (④) as one grows older until one is an autonomous member of society with plenty of experience and creativity, and the courage to contribute them?

All the time I've lived in Japan, I've enjoyed what the Japanese call "kawatta" (weirdness). Japanese people who are strongly individualistic are fascinating to me; they almost have the air of having escaped from a prison. As a mother of teenagers, I'm also enjoying the many "kawatta" things my kids and their friends do. At the same time, I'm making sure that as they encounter the difficulties of life, they have (⑤) principles to guide them. These are the essential complement to individual freedom: kindness and respect for other human beings, whoever they may be, respect for life, and emotional intelligence. They can be understood, taught and learned by anyone.

D

Instead of being afraid of being shut out of some group or other, our children need to be taught that they belong to the ultimate group of living beings on this planet, and they can never be shut out of this as long as they follow the universal principles of life. And they can make important contributions to this group from their precious individuality.

Let's have the courage to value each other as human beings, remembering John Steinbeck's words: "And this I believe: that the free, exploring mind of the individual human is the most valuable thing in the world."

(Source: Rebecca Otowa The Value of A person,
The English Teachers' Magazine February 2001)

(1) To fill in the blanks (①) to (⑤), choose the most suitable word for each from (a) to (d) below, and write the letter of the answer you have chosen.

① (a) belong (b) conform (c) object (d) recommend

② (a) Accomplishment (b) Contribution (c) Creation (d) Maintenance

③ (a) encourage (b) permit (c) punish (d) suppress

④ (a) complete (b) continue (c) decrease (d) increase

⑤ (a) common (b) firm (c) no (d) vague

(2) According to the passage, write either 'true (T)' or 'false (F)' for each statement below.

(a) "Individuality" in education is always respected from primary school to high school in Japan.

(b) The author adapted easily to Japanese society and culture thanks to her husband's two elder sisters.

(c) The author thinks Japanese people still tend to think more of the group rather than individuals.

(d) Though young children are free to be individuals, they become less free as they grow up in Japan.

(3) Put the following paragraph into the passage. Choose the right place from [A] to [D].

This phenomenon isn't limited to Japan; in fact I recognize many parallels with my own childhood experiences in the sixties in the United States. Even so, Americans grow up with at least the ideal of freedom and equality for all, whereas this ideal is still very new in Japan and probably has not yet taken root in the national psyche. Is this why children's needs seem to be going unmet?

(4) Put the underlined sentence into Japanese.

(☆☆☆☆◎◎◎◎)

【4】Read the passage and answer the questions (1) to (5).

(A) The question of what to do with the 11,000 tons of garbage produced each day in New York City has again surfaced, this time with Mayor Michael Bloomberg's budget, which proposes to halt the recycling of metal, glass, and plastic to save money. Unfortunately, this would mean more garbage to dispose of when the goal should be less.

The city's garbage problem has three faces. It is an economic problem, an environmental challenge, and a potential public relations nightmare. When the Fresh Kills landfill, the local destination for New York's garbage, was permanently closed in March 2001, the city found itself hauling garbage to distant landfill sites in New Jersey, Pennsylvania, and Virginia — some of them 300 miles away.

Assuming a load of 20 tons of garbage for each of the tractor trailers used for the long-distance hauling, some 550 rigs are needed to move garbage from New York City each day. These tractor trailers form a convoy nearly nine miles long, impeding traffic, polluting the air, and raising carbon emissions. This daily convoy led Deputy Mayor Joseph J. Lhota, who supervised the Fresh Kills shutdown, to say that getting rid of the city's trash is now “like a military－style operation on a daily basis”

Instead of rapidly reducing the amount of garbage generated as Fresh Kills was filling, the decision was made simply to haul it all elsewhere. Fiscally strapped local communities in other states are willing to take New York's garbage － if they are paid enough. Some see it as a (B) bonanza. For the state governments, however, that are saddled with increased road maintenance costs, the arrangement is not so attractive. They also have to contend with the traffic congestion, noise, increased air pollution, and complaints from nearby communities.

Virginia Governor Jim Gilmore wrote to Mayor Rudy Giuliani in 2001 complaining about the use of Virginia as a dumping ground. “I understand the problem New York faces," he noted. “But the home state of Washington, Jefferson and Madison has no intention of becoming New York’s dumping ground”

The new governor of Virginia, Mark Warner, proposed in early April 2002 a tax of $5 per ton on all solid waste deposited in Virginia. (①)

In Pennsylvania, the General Assembly is considering legislation that would restrict garbage imports from other states. As landfills in (C) adjacent states begin to fill up, there will be progressively fewer sites to take New York's garbage, pushing disposal costs ever higher.

Landfilling garbage uses land. For every 40,000 tons of garbage added to a landfill, at least one acre of land is lost to future use. (②)

Mayor Bloomberg's office has proposed incineration as the solution to the garbage mess. (③) Like hauling the garbage to distant sites, incineration treats the symptoms, not the causes of New York's mountain of garbage.

The amount of garbage produced in the city is a manifestation of a more fundamental problem － the evolution of a global throwaway economy, Throwaway products, facilitated by the appeal to convenience and the artificially low cost of energy, account for much of the garbage we produce.

(④) We have substituted facial tissues for handkerchiefs, disposable paper towels for hand towels, disposable table napkins for cloth napkins, and throwaway beverage containers for refillable ones. In perhaps the ultimate insult, the shopping bags that are used to carry home throwaway products are themselves designed to be discarded, becoming part of the garbage flow. The question at the supermarket checkout counter, "Paper or plastic?" should be replaced with. "Do you have your canvas shopping bag with you?"

The challenge we now face is to replace the throwaway economy with a reduce/ reuse/ recycle economy. The earth can no longer tolerate the pollution, the energy use, the disruption from mining, and the deforestation that the throwaway economy requires. For cities like New York, the challenge is not so much what to do with the garbage as it is how to avoid producing it in the first place.

New York recycles only 18 percent of its municipal waste. Los Angeles recycles 44 percent and Chicago 47 percent. Seattle and Minneapolis are both near 60 percent recycling rates. But even they are not close to exploiting the full potential of garbage recycling.

There are many ways of shrinking the daily mountain of garbage. One is simply to ban the use of one－way beverage containers, something that Denmark and Finland have done. Denmark, for example, banned one－way soft drink containers in 1977 and beer containers in 1981. If Mayor Bloomberg wants a closer example of this approach, he need only go to Prince Edward Island in Canada, which has adopted a similar ban on one－way containers.

There are other gains from reusing beverage containers. Since refillable containers are simply back－hauled to the original soft drink or brewery bottling sites by the same trucks that deliver the beverages, they reduce not only garbage but also traffic congestion, energy use, and air pollution.

(　⑤　) For example, Germany now gets 72 percent of its paper from recycled fiber. With glass, aluminum, and plastic, potential recycling rates are even higher.

The nutrients in garbage can also be recycled by composting organic materials, including yard waste, table waste, and produce waste from supermarkets. Each year, the world mines 139 million tons of phosphate rock and 20 million tons of potash to obtain the phosphorus and potassium needed to replace the nutrients that crops remove from the soil. (D) Urban composting that would return nutrients to the land could greatly reduce this expenditure on nutrients and the disruption caused by their mining.

Yet another garbage－reducing step in this fiscally stressed situation would be to impose a tax on all throwaway products, in effect a landfill tax, so that those who use throwaway products would directly bear the cost of disposing of them. This would increase revenues while reducing garbage disposal expenditures, helping to reduce the city's fiscal deficit.

There are munerous (E) win－win－win solutions that are both economically attractive and environmentally desirable, and that will help avoid the unfolding public relations debacle created by the image of New York as garbage capital of the world. A response to this situation that treats the causes rather than the symptoms of garbage generation could work wonders for the city.

(Source: Lester R. Brown The Earth Policy Reader)

(1) Put the underlined (A) and (D) into Japanese.

(2) From (a) to (e) below, choose the word with the closest meaning to the underlined word (B).

(a) bankruptcy (b) convenience (c) disposal (d) fortune (e) standard

(3) Write down two examples contained in the passage to which the underlined words (C) refer.

(4) Choose a sentence from (a) to (e) below for each of the blank spaces (①) to (⑤), and write the letter of the answer you have chosen.

(a) A large surrounding area is also lost, as the landfill with its potentially toxic wastes most be isolated from residential areas.

(b) But burning 11,000 tons of garbage each day will only add to air pollution, making already unhealthy city air even worse.

(c) It is easy to forget how many throwaway products there are until we actually begin making a list.

(d) This is expected to generate an annual cash flow of $76 million for the Virginia treasury, but it will not help New York with its economic woes.

(e) We have the technologies to recycle virtually all the components of garbage.

(5) Explain the meaning of the underlined words (E) in Japanese.

(☆☆☆☆◎◎◎◎)

【5】Read the passage and answer the questions.

Developing a strategic plan to cultivate
"Japanese With English Abilities"
－Plan to improve English and Japanese abilities－

July 12, 2002

1. Objectives

With the progress of globalization in the economy and in society, it is essential that our children (①) communication skills in English, which has become a common international language, in order for living in the 21 st century. This has become an extremely important issue both in terms of the future of our chidren and the further development of Japan as a nation.

At present, though, the English－speaking abilities of a large percentage of the population are inadequate, and this imposes restrictions on exchanges with foreigners and creates occasions when the ideas and opinions of Japanese people are not appropriately evaluated. However, it is not possible to (②) that Japanese people have sufficient ability to (③) their opinions based on a firm grasp of their own language.

Accordingly, we have formulated a strategy to (④) "Japanese with English abilities" in a concrete action plan with the aim of drastically improving the English education of Japanese people. In addition, we (⑤) to make improvements to Japanese－language education.

(1) To fill in the blanks (①) to(⑤), choose the most suitable word for each from below and write the letter of the answer you have chosen. (You can use each word only once.)

(a) acquire (b) aim (c) cultivate (d) express
(e) require (f) satisfy (g) state (h) utilize

(2) Write your own idea in English about a plan to improve the English education of Japanese people. Write about 100 words.

(☆☆☆◎◎◎◎)

解答・解説

【中高共通】

【1】省略

【2】省略

〈解説〉1. 2. は，リスニングに関する問題である。放送を通じて，先ず英文が二度流され，続いて質問が出される。事前に配布の解答用紙に四選択肢が示されていることであるから，目を通しておくことによって，質問のおおよその予測ができる。放送される英文については，一度目は何について述べていて，話題の中心は何かに注意して聞くようにする。二度目は，特に話題の中心について確認するようにすることである。

【3】(1) ① (b) ② (d) ③ (d) ④ (d) ⑤ (b)
(2) (a) F (b) F (c) T (d) T (3) C (4) 人々は集団の中で仲間として認識しているというは，日本人全体に見られる

固定観念である。

〈解説〉(1)　①「グループの活動か何かに従う」の意である。　②「維持することが個人の心を探る領域である」の意である。　③「大人は個性を力で押さえようとする」の意である。　④「個性は年齢を重ねるにつれて深まっていくべきである」の意である。　⑤「日本人には子供たちを導く確固たる方針がある」の意である。　(2)　(a)　本文のThese things disappear at junior and high school level.の箇所から判断する。(b)　本文のThe real meaning of the event was swallowed up in many complicated social occasions.の箇所から判断する。　(c)　本文のpeople are unable to express themselves, fearing to lose their livelihood or social position.の箇所から判断する。　(d)　(1)の④の箇所に関連することから判断する。　(3)　示されている文章の「自由とすべてのものが平等であるとすることを維持することの困難さは，60年代の子供時代にアメリカ味わったことだが，少なくともその理想をもって大きくなった。しかし，新しい思想であり，日本人の心にこれは根づいていない」とする内容から判断する。　(4)　上の文章の流れから，内容を伝えるようにすることである。

【4】(1)　(A)　ニューヨーク市で毎日出される，11,000のごみをどう処理するかという問題は，こんどはマイケル・ブルームバーグ市の予算として浮上している。費用節約のために，金属，ガラスやプラスチックの再生利用の中止の提案が行われている。　(D)　栄養素を土に戻し田園での堆肥化することは，栄養素や採掘によって生ずる混乱解決への費用の大きな削減になるであろう。　(2)　(c)　　(3)　1．ヴァージニア州知事の州をごみ捨て場とすることへの不満。　2．ペンシルヴィニア州議会が他州からのごみ輸入を規制する法令を検討中であること。　(4)　①　b　　②　a　　③　d　　④　e　　⑤　c

(5)　リサイクルによる方法，ごみになるものへの禁止法令，ごみを堆肥して利用する方法。

〈解説〉(1)　下線部は冒頭であったり，文中であったりするが，その前後関係の文脈とともに，主述の関係，時制，仮定法等の関係から判断し，内容を伝えるようにすることである。　(2)　Source of sudden great wealth or luckで「人によってはこれを突然の思わぬ幸運とみているものもいる」の意である。　(3)　Virginia Governor Jim Gilmore ～.の箇所から判断する。もう一つは，In Pennsylvania, ～.の箇所から判断する。
(4)　①「ヴァージナア州知事の一屯当たりに5ポンドの税の提案」の内容から判断するようにする。　②　前文の「少なくとも1エーカーの土地を失うことになる」の内容から判断するようにする。　③「ブルームバーグ市長のごみの焼却提案をした」こととの関連で判断するようにする。　④　前の文の「リサイクルで，いろいろな物ができる」ことの内容から判断するようにする。　⑤　前後の生産物とごみの状況やデータ関連の記述から判断するようにする。　(5)　下から五段落から各段落で述べていることの中心の話題を把握して述べるようにする。

【5】(1)　①　(a)　②　(g)　③　(d)　④　(c)　⑤　(b)

(2)　There are some ways to improve the English education of Japanese people. The thing is how often students or learners of English are given chances to listen to and speak English.

It depends on the skills of teachers to teach them orally in each lesson of English based on the methodological language theory as well as practicability for the use of English.

So English teachers should be so traind that they can teach communicative English for every student to achieve his or her purpose.

One more important thing is that each prefecture must prepare much more appropriate examinations like the system of TOEFL or TOEIC for communication, but never the ones like filling in blanks or funny grammar questions only for grammar's sake or just for checking knowledge like university English examinations.

〈解説〉(1)　①「言語技能を身に付ける」の意である。　②「～を述べることはできない」の意である。　③「意見を述べる」の意である。④「英語力を身に付けて日本人を育成する」の意である。　⑤「日本人の英語教育の改善を目指している」の意である。　(2)「改善の方法は幾つかあると思われるが，生徒あるいは学習者がどれくらい英語を聞いたり，話したりする機会を持てるかである。そのためには，英語の先生になる人材をその方向で訓練することである。また，採用に当たり関係者は，現在の試験問題のように大学入試の典型例に見られるような判じものの内容の読解や，文法のための文法を問う方法は廃止し，語学本来の目的沿った方向に向かうことが極めて大切である。」という趣旨のことを述べるようにする。

2003年度　実施問題

【 1 】(Listening Test)

Listen to the tape and answer the questions.

(☆☆☆◎◎◎)

【 2 】(Listening Test)

Choose the correct answer from the four alternatives below.

(1) (a) To tell everything they are thinking in order to get the better of the person they are talking to.
(b) To show displeasure or disagreement with someone else directly.
(c) To keep interaction going smoothly to avoid a confrontation.
(d) To express their ideas and feelings verbally in an argument.

(2) (a) It brings about a noisy fight and they become closer friends.
(b) It creates an open confrontation and damages the relationship between them.
(c) It creates a silence in which both sides become stubborn and do not communicate.
(d) It brings new ideas and closer friendship between them if both sides are reasonable.

(3) (a) They should show they are willing to accept new ideas and reach a compromise.
(b) They should agree with everthing mentioned.
(c) They should have a heated discussion to solve problems.
(d) They should be silent in order to avoid misunderstanding and a lasting grudge.

(4) (a) It is very important to win an argument not only in America but also in Japan.

(b) There are differences between Americans and Japanese when they show displeasure or disagreement.

(c) When Japanese people are angered or displeased by someone, they should state their opinions more like Americans.

(d) Japanese people don't show displeasure or disagreement directly because they don't hold differing opinions.

(☆☆☆◎◎◎)

【３】 Red the passage and answer questions (1) to (4).

Many people firmly believe that once they learn to speak a language they will be able to communicate perfectly with speakers of that language. My position is that they are both wrong and right. Let me explain what I mean.

On the surface level, I feel it is simplistic to assume that speaking a language "correctly," with flawless grammar and an elaborate vocabulary, will enable people to communicate successfully. In fact, preoccupation with completeness and grammatical correctness can be a dead giveaway. Native speakers will immediately sense that something is unnatural. It is (①) if the form, tone, and facial expressions that accompany the speech are not "natural" from their point of view.

Let me illustrate this from my experience in learning French. I began to study French in school when I was seven years old and later took additional calsses in French, never progressing beyond the "French Ⅱ" level. I had never lived in France nor had friends with whom I spoke French until I went to France at the age of twenty-four.

I lived in France for three years, working as a junior officer in an international organization. I entered my third year in France before I could converse adequately in French about limited topics. However, since I had started studying French when I was a child, my accent had always been fairly natural. One day a young friend of my landlady's daughter listened to my French for a few minutes, then exclaimed in surprise, "My God, a little

Japanese girl who speaks French with an accent of the sixteenth century!"

The young Frenchman astutely made the point that I have been trying to make: Only non-native speakers speak "correctly," using complete sentences with complete subject-verb agreement, pronouncing each word accurately.

Listen to the speech around you. Especially among young people, knowing what to leave out, what to say in slang, and what to break down is crucial in order to sound "(②)." It is also far more difficult to do this than to learn to speak in a grammatically "correct" way.

I therefore tell my students to free themselves from their preoccupation with using correct grammar and a sophisticated vocabulary. Instead, I tell them to concentrate on getting their intentions through accurately. Their sentences do not have to be elaborate or even complete; in fact, short strings of words are usually better. But they should make sense to the listener. This is where the issue of culture comes in.

As repeatedly emphasized in the chapters above, the first step in communicating successfully in another language is understanding the unspoken assumptions, unconscious conventions, and deep cultural values underlying that language. It thus turns out to be true on a deeper level that successful communication requires a language be used "correctly," in other words, in culturally appropriate ways.

For example, the speech and actions of Americans are governed by values central to their culture, in particular equality, independence, and individualism. Japanese speakers in turn base their behavior and speech on their own values, including respect for those in superior positions, mutual dependence, and group harmony. One system is not superior to the other, only different. It means, however, that one cannot carry over the value system of one's own culture when dealing with those who speak a different language.

Just as it is inappropriate to praise your daughter or husband when speaking in Japanese, criticizing or degrading your wife or son out of modesty will be totally misunderstood when speaking in English. In France, one of the first phrases that a child learns to say is "It's not my fault!" She will face many (③) situations as she realizes that in Japanese, the preferred mode is to begin every other sentence with "I'm sorry, but..." .

Of course by the time a speaker masters all the cultral nuances of a language, acquires idiomatic expressions, figures out what words to leave out and where to use slang, he will already be a native or near-native speaker. In the process of reaching that stage, I feel that it is more fruitful to concentrate one's energies on understanding the cultural nuances underlying a language and on acquiring the patterns that put these nuances into practice.

It is important to begin by freeing one's mind from the shackles of the linguistic conventions of one particular language and culture and to maintain an open mind. One added dividend of becoming self-conscious about the communication patterns of your own language is that you learn to organize your thoughts and communicate more successfully in your native language. Being able to listen carefully and express yourself clearly should (④) in useful when dealing with any language.

(Source; Mary Muro *Intercultural Miscommunication*)

(1) To fill in the blanks (①) to (④), choose the most suitable word for each from (a) to (c) below, and write the letter of the answer you have chosen.

① (a) worse (b) animat (c) better

② (a) puzzled (b) correct (c) natural

③ (a) bumpy (b) trifle (c) comfortable

④ (a) have (b) put (c) come

(2) According to the passage, write either 'true (T)' or 'false (F)' in the space provided, for each statement below.

(a) You should always use your own cultural perspective when speaking a foreign language.

(b) The author speaks French fluently because she studied it in France when she was a child.

(c) Being aware of cultral differences is very helpful in communicating more successfully in a foreign language.

(d) The speech and actions of Americans are based on respect for those in superior positions, mutual dependence and group harmony.

(3) Choose the most suitable sentence from (a) to (d) which describes the main point of the passage. Write the letter of the answer you have chosen.

The passage above says that

(a) we need to carry over the value system of our own culture when dealing with those who speak a different language.

(b) we need to make sure everything we say is complete and grammatically correct.

(c) successful communication requires language be used correctly and in a culturally appropriate way.

(d) speaking a language with no grammatical mistakes corresponds to understanding the cultural nuances underlying the language.

(4) Choose the most suitable title of the passage above from (a) to (d), and write the leteer of the answer you have chosen.

(a) GRAMMAR AND VOCABULARY

(b) SPEAKING WELL AND COMMUNICATING WELL

(c) CORRECT SPEECH EQUALS NATURAL SPEECH

(d) HOW TO LEARN FRENCH

(☆☆☆◎◎◎)

【4】Read the passage and answer the question (1) to (5).

(A) <u>Genetic studies show that dogs evolved from wolves and remain as similar to the creatures from which they came as humans with different physical charactertics are to each other</u>, which is to say not much different at all. "Even in the most changeable mitochondrial DNA markers [DNA handed down on the mother's side], dogs and wolves differ by not much more than one percent," says Robert Wayne, a geneticist at the University of California at Los Angeles.

Wolf-like species go back one to ten million years, says Wayne, whose genetic work suggests dogs of some sort began breaking away about 100,000 years ago. Wolf and early human fossils have been found close together from as far back as 4000,000 years ago, but dog and human fossils date back only about 14,000 years, all of which puts wolves and/or dogs in the company of man or his (B) <u>progenitors</u> before the development of farming and permanent human settlements, at a time when both species survived on what they could scratch out hunting or scavenging.

Why would these (C) <u>competitors</u> cooperate? The answer probably lies in the similar social structure and size of wolf packs and early human clans, the compatibility of their hunting objectives and range, and the willingness of humans to accept into camp the most suppliant wolves, the young or less threatening ones.

Speculators suspect, as Kipling did, that certain wolves or protodogs worked their way close to the fire ring after smelling something good to eat, then into early human gatherings by proving helpful or unthreatening. As packs of 25 or 30 wolves and clans of like-numbered nomadic humans roamed the landscape in tandem, hunting big game, the animals hung around campsites scavenging leftovers, and the humans might have keyed off the wolves, with their superior scenting ability and speed, to locate and track prospective kills. At night wolves with their keen senses could warn humans of danger approaching.

(　①　) In many instances food would have been plentiful, predators few, and the boundaries between humans and wildlife porous.

(D)<u>Through those pores and into our hearts slipped smaller or less threatening wolves, which from living in packs where alpha bosses reigned would know the tricks of subservience and could adapt to humans in charge</u>. Puppies in particular would be hard to resist, as they are today. Thus was a union born and a process of domestication begun.

Over the millennia admission of certain wolves and protodogs into human camps and exclusion of larger, more threatening ones led to development of people-friendly breeds distinguishable from wolves by size, shape, coat, ears, and markings. (　②　) They would assist in the hunt, clean up camp by eating garbage, warn of danger, keep humans warm, and serve as food. Native Americans among others ate puppies, and in some societies it remains accepted practice.

By the fourth millennium B.C. Egyptian rock and pottery deawings show hounds hunting with men, driving game into nets. (　③　) Feral dogs roamed city streets, stealing food from people returning from market.

Thousands of years later dogs still can be trouble. From 1979 to 1998 more than 300 people in the United States were killed in dog attacks. Most were children. In 1994, the last year data were compiled, an estimated 4.7 million Americans were bitten, 6,000 of them hospitalized. Despite their penchant for misbehavior, and sometimes because of it, dogs keep turning up at all the important junctures in human history.

In ancient Greece, 350 years before Christ, Aristotle described three types of domesticared dogs, including speedy Laconians used by the rich to chase and kill rabbits and deer. Three hundred years later Roman warriors trained large dogs for battle. (　④　)

Dogs won few friends in the Dark Ages, when they scavenged corpses of plague victims, but they were much in favor by the second millennium, chasing rabbits and stags for British royalty. In 17th-century England dogs still worked, pulling carts, sleds, and plows, herding livestock or working as turnspits, powering wheels that turned beef and venison roasts over open fires. But working dogs were not much loved and were usually hanged or drowned when they got old.

"Unnecessary" dogs meanwhile gained status among royalty. King James I was said to love his dogs more than his subjects; Charles Ⅱ was famous for playing with his dog at Council table, and his brother James had dogs at sea in

1682 when his ship was caught in a storm. As sailors drowned, he allegedly cried out, "Save the dogs and Colonel Churchill!"

By the late 19th century the passion for breeding led to creation of private registries to protect prized bloodlines. The Kennel Club was formed in England in 1873, and 11 years later the American Kennel Club (AKC) was founded across the Atlantic. Today the AKC registers 150 breeds, the Kennel Club lists 196, and the Europe-based Federation Cynologique Internationale recognizes many more. Dog shows sprouted in the mid-1800s when unnecessary dogs began to vastly outnumber working ones, as they do to this day, unless you count companionship as a job.

(E) Which many do. In a recent survey of U.S. dog owners 94 percent listed companionship as a key benefit while only 6 percent hunted with dogs and only 4 percent used them in farming.

People find ways to keep dogs even under the toughest conditions. In New York City almost 100,000 are registered, and officials believe unregistered dogs outnumber those three to one, putting the total at roughly 400,000. Caring for a dog in a city where apartments are tiny, streets and sidewalks are packed, and indoor and outdoor space is scarce is a challenge, but New Yorkers rise to it.

(Source: National Geographic January 2002, Karen E. Lange: *Wolf to Woof*)

(1) Put the underlined (A) and (D) into Japanese.

(2) From (a) to (e) below, choose the word with the closest meaning to the underlined word (B).

(a) ancestors　(b) adversaries　(c) colleagues

(d) offsprings　(e) subordinates

(3) Write down two words contained in the passage to which the underlined word (C) refers.

(4) Choose the sentences from (a) to (d) below for each of the blank spaces (①) to (④).

(a) Dogs were generally smaller than wolves, their snouts proportionally reduced.

(b) The brutes could knock an armed man from his horse and dismember him.

(c) Times might not have been as hard back then as is commonly thought.

(d) Then, as now, the relationship was not without drawbacks.

(5) Explain the meaning of the underlined sentence (E) in Japanese.

(☆☆☆◎◎◎)

【5】Read the passage and answer the questions.

According to the International Mathematics and Science Study of the International Association for the Evaluation of Educational Achievement (IEA), the academic ability of Japanese children has maintained the top level in all three surveys conducted since 1964, and is on the whole strong internationally. However, problems have been pointed out, such as the fact that the ratio of Japanese children who (①) mathematics and science, as well as the ratio of Japanese children who wish to enter mathematics and science related careers, are at the lowest level interntionally.

Under the new Courses of Study, based on these circumstances of children's learning, at elementary and lower secondary schools, education content is reduced by about 30% for each academic year. However, most of this is transferred to later academic years or school levels and taught systematically along with the material traditionally taught at these levels in order to make the material easier to understand for children. Put another way, the change is not so much one of reducing (②), but rather one of spending ample (③) in order to firmly instill the material.

In addition, the range of elective courses at lower secondary schools has been (④), enabling students to study in line with their interests and inclinations. At upper secondary schools, the number of compulsory course credits has been reduced, offering students a wide range of elective courses that they can select in accordance with their interests, career inclination, and level of proficiency, and which enables each of them to amply develop their abilities. Thus, student scan study subjects in more depth—as deeply as their level of motivation takes them. The standard of educational content at the upper secondary school graduate level is as before, and there will be no lowering of academic ability due to the new Courses of Study.

(⑤), recently, the gist and aims of the new Courses of Study have not been thoroughly understood, and some aspects have been misunderstood. For example, it has been said, Instead of 3.14, 3 will be used for, and The number of English words learned at lower secondary schools will be 100, but these are misconceptions. It is necessary to have a full understanding of the new Courses of Study.

(Source: White Paper: Japanese Government Policies In Education, Science, Sports and Culture 2000 Ministry of Education, Culture, Sports, Science and Technology)

(1) To fill in the blanks (①) to (⑤), choose the most suitable word for each from below and write the letter of the answer you have chosen. (You can use each word only once.)

(a) interest　(b) dislike　(c) relations　(d) reinforcement
(e) quantity　(f) ability　(g) Besides　(h) time
(i) like　(j) However　(k) expanded　(l) support
(n) reduced

(2) Write your own idea in English about the sentence underlined above. Write about 100 words.

(☆☆☆◎◎◎)

解答・解説

【1】省略

【2】省略

【3】(1) ① (a) ② (c) ③ (a) ④ (c)

(2) (a) F (b) T (c) T (d) F (3) (c) (4) (b)

〈解説〉(1) ①「話し言葉を言う場合の語形，調子や顔の表情が，母国語話者から見て自然でなければ，なお具合が悪い」に留意する。②「特に若者の間で，何を省くか，仲間でどのような言い方をするか，またどんなことをかみくだいて言うかなどが，自然な言い方の条件である」に留意する。 ③「日本語で経験するように，いろいろの難しい場面に出会う」に留意する。 ④「人の言っていることをよく聞いて，的確に表現することがどんな言語の場合にも役に立ちます」で，come in useful＝be useful some time or otherに留意する。 (2) 本文の(a) one system is not superior to the other, only different.の内容に留意する。(b) 本文のSince I had started studying French when I was a child, my accent had always been fairly natural.に留意する。 (d) 本文の下から二段目の最後の文に留意する。 (3) It thus turns out to be true on a deeper level that successful communication requires a language be used "correctly," in other words, in culturally appropriate way.の文に留意する。(4) 本文のテーマは，「上手に話し，上手に意思の疎通を図ること」であることに留意する。

【4】(1) (A) 遺伝子の研究によって，犬は狼から進化したものであり，身体の特徴が異なる人間がお互いに似ているように，犬は進化の元の狼に似ているところが残っているということが分かっている。

(D) 小型であるか横暴さの少ない狼が，このすき間を通して私たちの心に侵入してきて，第一ボスが実験を握っている群れに住んで，従属の要領を知り，指揮を取っている人間に適応することになるだろう。

(2)　(a)　(3)　wolves and humans　(4)　①　d　②　c　③　b　④　a　(5)　不要な犬と人間のための働き手としての犬とどちらが役にたつか。

〈解説〉(1)　(A)～as humans with different physical characteristics are similar to each otherとして内容を取るようにする。　(B)　関係代名詞whichの非制限用法で，先行詞のsmaller or less threatening wolvesとの関係で，Through those pores, smaller or less theratening wolves slipped into our heartsが倒置されていることに留意する。　(2)　～before the development of farming and permanent human settlersから判断するようにする。

(3)　設問の次の文から，人間と狼の関係をつかむようにする。

(4)　それぞれについて，まず選択肢を事前に読んでおいて，問われている設問の前の段落との関係の中で補うようにする。　(5)　～when unnecessary dogs began to vastly ouynumber working dogs,の文を中心にして，Which manyの受けるものを決める。do「役に立つ」の意である。

【5】(1)　①　(i)　②　(e)　③　(h)　④　(k)　⑤　(j)

(2)　The present Courses of Study provide the basic framework for curricula: the aim of each subject and aims and contents of teaching at each grade of each school level.

It shows four guidelines of education, two of which I think are the basis of the present Course of Study and keep the academic ability of students. One is to enhance children's ability to think and learn for themselves and the other one is to develop a comfortable educational environment which successfully equips students with essetial knowledge and skills as well as develops students' individual personalities.

So each school is responsible for making educational curriculum so that students are encouraged to study by themselves by the good teaching in each classroom

〈解説〉今回の教育課程では，特に，「自ら学び，自ら考える力を育成すること」並びに「ゆとりある教育活動を展開する中で，基礎・基本の確実な定着を図り，個性を生かす教育を充実すること」の下に，教育活動を展開し，これまで詰め込みがちだった教育を，子供たちに考えさせる教育へと転換し，生徒一人一人の主体的な学習を進めるものであることを，述べるようにすることである。

●書籍内容の訂正等について

弊社では教員採用試験対策シリーズ（参考書，過去問，全国まるごと過去問題集），公務員試験対策シリーズ，公立幼稚園・保育士試験対策シリーズ，会社別就職試験対策シリーズについて，正誤表をホームページ（https://www.kyodo-s.jp）に掲載いたします。内容に訂正等，疑問点がございましたら，まずホームページをご確認ください。もし，正誤表に掲載されていない訂正等，疑問点がございましたら，下記項目をご記入の上，以下の送付先までお送りいただくようお願いいたします。

① **書籍名，都道府県（学校）名，年度**
（例：教員採用試験過去問シリーズ　小学校教諭 過去問　2025 年度版）
② **ページ数**（書籍に記載されているページ数をご記入ください。）
③ **訂正等，疑問点**（内容は具体的にご記入ください。）
（例:問題文では“ア～オの中から選べ”とあるが,選択肢はエまでしかない）

〔ご注意〕
○ 電話での質問や相談等につきましては，受付けておりません。ご注意ください。
○ 正誤表の更新は適宜行います。
○ いただいた疑問点につきましては，当社編集制作部で検討の上，正誤表への反映を決定させていただきます（個別回答は，原則行いませんのであしからずご了承ください）。

●情報提供のお願い

協同教育研究会では，これから教員採用試験を受験される方々に，より正確な問題を，より多くご提供できるよう情報の収集を行っております。つきましては，教員採用試験に関する次の項目の情報を，以下の送付先までお送りいただけますと幸いでございます。お送りいただきました方には謝礼を差し上げます。
（情報量があまりに少ない場合は，謝礼をご用意できかねる場合があります）。

◆あなたの受験された面接試験，論作文試験の実施方法や質問内容
◆教員採用試験の受験体験記

送付先		
	○電子メール：edit@kyodo-s.jp ○FAX：03-3233-1233（協同出版株式会社　編集制作部 行） ○郵送：〒101-0054　東京都千代田区神田錦町2-5 協同出版株式会社　編集制作部 行 ○HP:https://kyodo-s.jp/provision（右記のQRコードからもアクセスできます）	

※謝礼をお送りする関係から，いずれの方法でお送りいただく際にも，「お名前」「ご住所」は，必ず明記いただきますよう，よろしくお願い申し上げます。

教員採用試験「過去問」シリーズ
石川県の
英語科 過去問

編　集　　© 協同教育研究会
発　行　　令和6年1月25日
発行者　　小貫　輝雄
発行所　　協同出版株式会社
〒101-0054　東京都千代田区神田錦町2 - 5
電話　03－3295－1341
振替　東京00190－4－94061
印刷所　　協同出版・POD工場

落丁・乱丁はお取り替えいたします。